DATE DUE

NEW	DEC 17 1988
JUN 24 1984	DEC 14 '88 Ret'd
BOOKS	NOV 27 1990
9 - NOV 1984	NOV 21 '90 Ret'd
PAID NOV 20 '84	
1 8 DEC 1984	RET'D NOV 27 '01
	JAN 8 - 2002
RET'D DEC 03 '84	RET'D DEC ⊳ 6 '02
DEC 3 '84 RET'D.	
FAC. MAY 31 '88	
FEB 12 '88 Ret'd	
OCT 28 1988	
NOV 14 1988	
NOV 30 1988	
UPI SPO-125	PRINTED IN U.S.A.

SENECA'S DRAMA

NORMAN T. PRATT

SENECA'S DRAMA

THE UNIVERSITY OF

NORTH CAROLINA PRESS

CHAPEL HILL AND LONDON

© 1983 The University of North Carolina Press

All rights reserved

Manufactured in the United States of America

Library of Congress Cataloging in Publication Data

Pratt, Norman T. (Norman Twombly), 1911–
  Seneca's drama.

  Includes bibliographical references and index.
  1. Seneca, Lucius Annaeus—Dramatic works. I. Title.
PA6685.P7 1983   872'.01   82-23791
ISBN 0-8078-1555-1

TO BARBIE

CONTENTS

PREFACE

Seneca's Drama is meant to fill a gap in the growing literature on these plays. There is no single book in any language that treats and inter-relates the three major ingredients of the drama: Neo-Stoicism, de-clamatory rhetoric, and Seneca's society.

Since Seneca was a turning point in the development of Western tragic drama and his influence was strong in England and Europe dur-ing the sixteenth and seventeenth centuries, understanding of him is essential to many students of drama. Therefore the study is written not for specialists and not just for classicists but for anyone interested enough to want coverage of the evidence and the more important points of scholarship. As a result, classical readers will not find as much literary analysis of the Latin as they might like.

Neo-Stoicism and its role in the drama receive the major attention because Seneca's brand of Stoicism is not well understood and, in my opinion, is the most substantive single ingredient, often in technical ways that have escaped notice. At the same time, the relationship between the rhetoric of the day and the drama has been explored more fully than ever before. Also, the story of Seneca's public career is included because it and its connection with the drama are often dis-torted and because it is a very engrossing subject. Above all else, the study stresses the functional interaction of the factors that shaped the nature of this drama.

My obligations to persons and institutions are many. Colleagues and students at Indiana University have been parties to the development of my ideas. Colleagues S. C. Fredericks and Cecil W. Wooten have made comments on parts of the material; Edwin S. Ramage has read the whole text and suggested numerous improvements. The American School of Classical Studies at Athens twice provided a congenial place to work. In 1962–63 the Bollingen Foundation granted a fellowship for work on Seneca. Indiana University has been exceedingly generous with its program of sabbatical leaves and other assistance. Particularly humane is its fund for supporting the research of emeritus faculty.

Longboat Key, Florida   Norman T. Pratt
1 August 1982

SENECA'S DRAMA

1. ORIENTATION

Criticism still has some distance to go in understanding the nature of Senecan drama and consequently the nature of its impact upon later drama. A very profitable approach to these matters can be shown by differentiating the basic themes in a Greek tragedy and a Shakespearean play. So we can get our bearings by seeing what Seneca departed from and where he led.[1]

Oedipus the King and *King Lear* are highly comparable. Both are filled with the theme of seeing and not-seeing expressed in language and action throughout. Beneath this parallelism, however, the vision resulting in each case is quite different in orientation and nature, and the differences are significant in relation to fundamental changes that took place in Seneca.

When Oedipus sees the truth, what does Sophocles lead us to see? In Knox's analysis, the final vision is of a paradox. "The *Oedipus Tyrannus* of Sophocles combines two apparently irreconcilable themes, the greatness of the gods and the greatness of man, and the combination of these themes is inevitably tragic, for the greatness of the gods is most clearly and powerfully demonstrated by man's defeat. . . . Sophocles' tragedy presents us with a terrible affirmation of man's subordinate position in the universe, and at the same time with a heroic vision of man's victory in defeat."[2] The two sides of the paradox are starkly laid against each other, incapable of any real resolution.

Such logical conflict is disturbing enough under any circumstances, but the paradox has unique force in this drama because the relationship between divine power and human power is shocking. In one terrible sense, this relationship is compatible, for it is finally revealed that the gods and Oedipus are not in conflict at all. Rather, they are working "together" for the revelation of the same truth. The superiority of the gods is demonstrated by having the hero's status crushed under the weight of pollution brought down upon himself by his own supreme effort.

In another way, the relationship between divine and human greatness is discordant and rasping. The sense of irrationality is greatly intensified by the very rationality of Oedipus' search for the polluted one: investigating, remembering, tracking, cross-questioning, applying all his energetic intelligence.[3] Sophocles' art engrosses us in the unfolding of evidence and the exercise of logic. And what does this searching intelligence finally reveal? The ignorance of man and the unfathomable order of the gods.

The hostility of the world where Oedipus' experience takes place may be accounted for partially in terms of ritual. Some years ago it was the fashion to emphasize the ritual origin of Greek tragedy and to analyze its form and meaning in ritualistic terms. To be sure, one of the few things that we can come close to knowing about the origin is that a major source was choral song performed in worship of Dionysus, a divinity of fertility or, more accurately, liquid nature: "not only the liquid fire in the grape, but the sap thrusting in a young tree, the blood pounding in the veins of a young animal, all the mysterious and uncontrollable tides that ebb and flow in the life of nature."[4]

It has been proposed that the origin of Greek tragedy had no connection with Dionysus but came about through the creative acts of Thespis and Aeschylus.[5] However, as important as these creative acts were, there are too many bits and pieces of data associating tragedy and Dionysus[6] to explain away, no matter how difficult it may be to put the evidence together intelligibly.[7] For one thing right on the surface, Athens was a strongly traditional society, and the mere fact that drama was performed at Dionysiac festivals points to a more than artificial connection.

There is much that we do not know about this matter. The skein of available evidence is scanty and tangled. Yet it seems clear enough from data concerning such fertility rites and from the evidence of the plays themselves that Greek tragedy received from ritual—like Dionysiac ritual—a conception of nature: nature as a complex of forces bringing health or disease to plants and animals. The purpose of such ritual was to effect a harmony between the powers of nature and individual living things or social organisms: to avert destructive impurities, to achieve life-nourishing purity.

The view that these dramas are founded on and conditioned by ritual has contributed considerable illumination, as well as much distortion when carried to extremes. For example, Francis Fergusson's analysis of *Oedipus* is built on the following ideas:

> The Cambridge School of Classical Anthropologists has shown
> in great detail that the form of Greek tragedy follows the form of a
> very ancient ritual, that of the *Eniautos-Daimon*, or seasonal god.
>   It is this tragic rhythm of action which is the substance or
> spiritual content of the play, and the clue to its extraordinarily
> comprehensive form.[8]

It is unjust to be captious about this approach, for it has succeeded in revealing fresh implications and in reminding us that we are dealing not merely with literary masterpieces but with dramas rooted in communal ritual. However, to use a well-worn example, serious distortion results from viewing Oedipus as a ritual scapegoat through whom the impurities of the city are exorcised. It is a major aspect of the drama that impurity and abnormality in the family of Laius have brought upon Thebes a taint that must be removed. This aspect must be recognized if we are to understand the role of Apollo the purifier. However, at the end of the tragedy we are left not with a purified Thebes but with a suffering tragic hero and the mystery of his experience. There is a great difference in level of maturity between the plays themselves and the ritualistic concepts by which these anthropologists and their followers analyze the texts. The fifth-century dramatist shows himself far more sophisticated than such analysis represents him to be. In the case of *Oedipus*, ritual archetype is transformed to tragic view.

Even so, the conditions ensuring health in nature and society, namely, the purity of the family and the sanctity of blood relationship, have been violated. Apollo by his nature must reveal the corruption, and in one dimension the self-blinding is a sacrifice performed by the king as both the source of the taint and the responsible agent of the community. These features carry the imprint of a ritual view of man's environment. That is, the world is potentially ever a hostile place where the uneasy relationship between man and nature may develop impurity, and the only recourse is some kind of sacrificial purification.

Such is the character of the unstable world revealed to us by Sophocles in the intensity of Oedipus' suffering. It is a radically dualistic world. It contains the good king Oedipus seeking rational answers. But it is also a mad world of accident and coincidence: where a Corinthian shepherd takes an infant from a Theban shepherd; where Oedipus consults the oracle because of an insult by some drunken Corinthian; where the paths of father and son meet at a crossroad; where the lone survivor of Laius' band is the same Theban shepherd; where the son arrives in Thebes at a time of great crisis; where the queen is the marriage-prize for the one who solves the crisis; where the same two old shepherds survive, the only two men who can connect the foundling with the house of Laius and with Corinth. These coincidences are the marks of an arbitrary world where crucial things just happen. Oedipus is trying to make sense in a world that does not make sense. He is in a divinely ordered system where his rational purpose is disastrously turned against him by the force of capricious circumstance. The divine order brings disorder to human experience.

If in this fashion we can say that *Oedipus* transmits the picture of disorder in nature, Shakespearean criticism is in substantial agreement that *King Lear* expresses the theme of nature in disorder. The terms "disorder in nature" for Sophocles and "nature in disorder" for Shakespeare are only superficial catch phrases, but they show a contrast between two types of tragedy, radically different in their conceptions of evil. In *Oedipus* nature itself wounds human life. Suffering is built constituently into the makeup of how things are, above and beyond man's influence upon what happens. The unique power of this Greek tragedy lies in its intense and bare concentration upon the imperfection of the world, or rather its imperfectibility. In *Lear* nature itself is not defective, but only part of it, the human dimension. Nature is flawed through man who has the "ability to achieve salvation" and the "liability to damnation," in Heilman's language.[9] Shakespeare's world is *theoretically* perfectible, and suffering is caused by a falling-off from what might have been. No such formulation of Oedipus' case is possible.

Lear does not have the concentrated power achieved by Sophocles— this was gone forever with the end of Greek tragedy—but it is unmatched in poetic richness and range of insight. These qualities emerge from a mighty moral struggle between two sets of characters ranged about Lear and Gloucester, in fact, two groups of six each: the essentially evil Goneril, Regan, Burgundy, Cornwall, Oswald, and Edmund; and the essentially good Cordelia, France, Albany, Kent, the Fool, and Edgar.[10] The two groups live by different sets of values belonging to two kinds of nature. It is a commonplace of Shakespearean interpretation to recognize that "nature" is the dominant idea and metaphor of the drama.[11]

Critics analyze the moral struggle in various terms. One scholar finds the key in the interlocking of two doctrines current in Elizabethan times, those associated with Hooker and with Hobbes.[12] In the former, the traditional view of sixteenth-century Christianity, nature is benign, "an ordered and beautiful arrangement, to which we must adjust ourselves." In Hobbes, man is bedeviled, torn in the conflict between the irreconcilable forces of reason and passion. Characteristically, the views of both Hooker and Hobbes can be squared with both Christianity and Stoicism, for these two traditions were strongly fused in Elizabethan religious and philosophical thought. This scholar goes on to show the dramatic consequences of these ideas; for example, "Cordelia embodies the [ordered and beautiful] Nature which Edmund denies to exist, and which Lear—although he believes in it—cannot recognize when it is before him."[13]

Another critic, regarding *Lear* as a Stoic play, finds a similar opposition between the ordered harmony of Stoicism and Edmund's egocentric, Epicurean view of nature:

> The divergent points of view toward nature and the gods are sharply drawn, with the proponents of "Nature" and of Stoicism radically differing. On the one hand, blind nature, controlled only by fortune and chance; on the other, a nature governed by gods who represent a law of retributive justice.
>
> In the end, it is a true Stoic world, and justice has been dispensed.[14]

Other interpretations are less philosophical but show the dramatic and poetic workings of the same kind of conflict. Heilman's *This Great Stage* is a landmark in analyzing the terms and figurative patterns used to express both destructive force and spiritual illumination. In various forms, "nature" is a giant metaphor for both moral order and the falling-away from moral order. Others find that the drama is centered around the religious theme of the acquisition of spiritual vision: the storm buffeting Lear conveys at once the blackness of passion that has come upon the king and the flashes of the vision emerging in him.[15] According to another interpretation, Shakespeare has used the setting of Lear's pre-Christian world to examine the moral and religious ideas under attack from the rationalism of his day and to show, without the authority of revealed religion, that the values of patience, fortitude, love, and charity can emerge from within man himself. The poet "shows us his pagan characters groping their way towards a recognition of the values traditional in his society."[16]

Particularly impressive is the analysis by Campbell. *Lear* is a morality play taken outside the strictly Christian tradition and transformed into the magnificent tragedy of "a completely unstoical man," who finally achieves spiritual vision compounded of "Stoic insight and Christian humility." What is more, Lear's illumination comes about through a sequence of experiences recognized as the path to wisdom in the Stoic thought of Cicero, Seneca, Plutarch, Epictetus, and Marcus Aurelius. This moral philosophy was a major influence upon thought in the England of Shakespeare's time. Therefore Stoic ideas loom large in what Lear comes to understand: the values of resignation to the will above man, humility in human relationships, and willing obedience to destiny. The thought of *King Lear* is thus a product of grafting Renaissance Stoicism upon traditional Christian piety.

Such an interpretation works well in giving account of the play dramatically. As Campbell goes on to show, the king initially breaks the cardinal Stoic principles of right behavior. The kingship is important to him for its trappings. He must have his proper retinue. In rejecting Cordelia and banishing Kent, he violates all reason and is addicted to anger—temporary insanity in Stoic terms. Self-knowledge and self-control are quite beyond him.

The search for sanity and truth begins. Lear is helped along the way by his companions Kent and the Fool, both of whom Campbell connects with the Cynic-Stoic tradition brought to the Elizabethans by Roman satire. By their blunt and searching comments, the plain-speaking Kent and the wise Fool stimulate the king to strip off superficiality and to see more deeply into the fundamental human needs of protection and compassion.

However, Stoicism is not adequate to answer the questions raised by the dramatist. The tragedy does not end in a mere victory over passion nor, certainly, in conventional tranquillity and unperturbability. Perhaps Shakespeare instinctively saw the psychological naiveté of Stoicism. For him, passion is overcome not by reason but by the greater and purer passion of "utter devotion to the eternal blessings of the spirit," as Campbell puts it.[17] The suffering of Lear in the storm has Stoic meaning: after being subjected to the storm of unreason within himself and the storm of discord in the elements of nature, he is chastened and led to recognize the humanity shared with his fellows. But the experience is purgatorial also in a Christian sense and reaches the level of salvation: having passed through the storm, he is ready to receive Cordelia's love fully and to return it fully. The final result is not the negative indifference of Stoicism but the active healing force of unselfish love. In the final scene where Lear enters with Cordelia dead in his arms, the agony of loss yields to the ecstasy of redemption, and Lear's heart bursts in the joy of it.

For the contrast between *Lear* and *Oedipus*, we must note one common feature of all these Shakespearean interpretations: the keen sense of loss and waste left to us at the end is linked with the notion that a moral and religious order has emerged from all the destruction. At least in *Lear*, if not more generally in Shakespeare, our feeling of the tragic comes essentially from the paradox of a moral order containing elements so destructive that order can be restored only at the price of prodigious suffering and ravage. If we recognize that Christian ideas stand conspicuously behind the pagan scene of *Lear*, the explanation of the paradox is not far to seek. It fits rather comfortably into the frame of traditional Christian beliefs in the dualism of God and the Fiend, uncontrolled human choices of good and evil, the purgatorial effect of suffering, and the saving power of love.

The point about *Lear* to be stressed is that it ends, as the most powerful tragedies do, in affirmation, in this case the affirmation of a continuing, self-asserting moral order. No matter how desperately high the price, the forces of disorder have been purged away. This kind of statement cannot be made about *Oedipus*. For Sophocles, the divine order involves moral values, to be sure, but it is not identical with them and is fundamentally an order of nature rather than morality. We cannot find a meaningful, decisive relationship between moral values or the lack of them and the downfall of Oedipus. For that matter, "downfall of Oedipus" is not accurate, for Sophocles does not affirm a moral order but the qualities of a great human spirit who, in the face of utter disorder, remains on his feet and goes on.

As we move from the themes of *Oedipus* to the themes of *Lear*, we encounter significant changes in the conceptions of order and disorder and in the treatment of moral matter, changes that make great differences between Greek and later tragedy. That this reorientation began in Senecan drama will be a major topic in the following chapters. For the sake of introductory statement here, a few general points will be outlined briefly.

Seneca's *Agamemnon* treats the familiar subject of Agamemnon's return and death, but the prevailing tone is the insecurity of emotional turmoil shared by every speaking character and group. To show the obliteration of any hope of security, the dramatist fuses the abstract idea security-insecurity, expressed in a massive system of language throughout the play, with the personification Fortune and the metaphor "sea storm." The shifting movement connected with Fortune is conveyed by language of wavelike motion. This language blends with the figure "sea storm," which is developed in close relationship with Fortune. In the very first choral passage, Seneca writes that Fortune allows kingship no peace but buffets it with repeated storms. Agamemnon is puffed up by the windblast of Fortune. Clytemnestra tosses in tides of conflicting emotions. And so forth. Thus the metaphor "sea storm" becomes a major device expressing the emotional and intellectual chaos of the play, much in the manner of Lear on the stormy heath.[18]

This parallel is mentioned not to show a specific connection between Seneca and Shakespeare (such source hunting has not been profitable) but to indicate that the great change from the orientation of *Oedipus* to the orientation of *Lear* had already largely taken place in Seneca. In Seneca we have one of the basic revolutions of dramatic thought in the tradition of Western tragedy, although obviously such change does not operate mechanically in the intricate works of later drama, and of course Senecan influence varies greatly in kind and degree.

To go from Sophocles to Seneca is to move from one conception of the human condition to a radically different conception. The catastrophe in *Oedipus* involves a confrontation of two statuses, human and divine. It does not come from moral conflict. The conflict cannot be reconciled, the dualism cannot be removed in terms of moral state. Seneca writes a different, introspective kind of drama, a unique product of three major elements: the hypertensive mode of rhetoric as a form of expression, feeling, and thought; the Stoic, and specifically Neo-Stoic, conception of a rational moral order threatened by the human passions; and the personal experience of a statesman whose ideals were tortured by the moral savagery of his Rome. The order of Nature *versus* the chaos of men's actions:

> O Nature, whence all gods proceed;
>   And Thou, King of Olympian light,
> Whose hand makes stars and planets speed
>   Round the high axis of the night:
> If thou canst guide with ceaseless care
>   The heavenly bodies in their train,
> To make the woods in winter bare

And in the springtime green again,
Until the summer's Lion burns
  To bring the ripening seed to birth
And every force of nature turns
  To gentleness upon the earth—
Why, if such power is in thy hand
  To balance by an ordered plan
The mass of things, why dost thou stand
  So far from the affairs of man?
Thou dost not care to help the good
  Nor punish men of evil mind.
Man lives by chance, to Fate subdued,
  And evil thrives, for Fate is blind.
Vile lust has banished purity,
  Vice sits enthroned in royal state;
Mobs give to knaves authority
  And serve them even while they hate.
Poor is the prize sour virtue gains,
  Want lies in wait for honesty,
Sin reigns supreme. What good remains
  In shame, what worth in dignity?[19]

2. INTRODUCTION TO THE DRAMA

Present-day criticism of Senecan drama began in the 1920s. In 1922 Münscher's survey of work on the tragedies during 1915–21 mentioned an item that he considered a curious reversion to earlier doubt about ascribing the plays to Seneca the Stoic.[1] Herrmann's substantial book in 1924 was essentially in the vein of older scholarship but anticipated later concentration on the dramatic psychology.[2] In 1927–28 Regenbogen's very influential monograph on the philosophical and cultural orientation of the drama first appeared.[3] The same period saw the publication of two indispensable aids, an *index verborum* of the plays and a study of their rhetoric.[4]

Earlier scholarship, from the fourteenth century to the twentieth, gradually made its way through a number of problems.[5] The manuscripts vary in the *praenomen* given for the "Annaeus Seneca" or "Seneca" named as author. It was not clear that the dramatic poet and the philosopher were one and the same. One family of manuscripts includes a tenth play, the *Octavia*, which seemed not to be the work of our Seneca because he appears as a character in it. Doubts were raised by verbal echoes among the plays (suggesting imitation), variations between plays in the treatment of plot material, the incomplete state of the *Phoenissae*, the excessive length of the *Hercules Oetaeus*, and other eccentricities. By the early 1900s, most of these basic matters were settled, and it was possible to study the nine tragedies as the work of the younger Lucius Annaeus Seneca, the Stoic. Today, however, doubt about the authenticity of the *Oetaeus* has still not disappeared, and the authorship of the *Octavia* remains moot. Our reasons for considering the *Oetaeus* genuine and the *Octavia* not will be given later.

Other general questions have become embedded in the standard repertory of Senecan scholarship. Although such a statement may seem presumptuous, it is true that several of these issues are either insoluble or no longer very valuable. These matters include the chronology of the plays, the question whether they were written to be staged or to be read, and their relationship to Greek tragedy and earlier Roman drama.

Attempts to fix the dates of the plays have favored two periods, the years of exile on Corsica (A.D. 41–49) and the long period of Seneca's association with Nero (A.D. 49–62). Certainly both periods were long enough for the composition, especially since Seneca apparently wrote rapidly, but they are so long that assigning the plays to either of them is not very useful for interpretation.

A more exact chronology simply cannot be supported with acceptable evidence. The classic example is Herrmann's preference for 49–62 and his conclusion that the sequence of the titles in manuscript tradition A is the chronological order (excluding the *Octavia*): *Hercules Furens*, *Thyestes*, *Phoenissae*, *Phaedra*, *Oedipus*, *Troades*, *Medea*, *Agamemnon*, *Hercules Oetaeus*.[6] His supporting data are of the following kinds. The *Furens* dates from the beginning of the principate. The character Hercules represents Nero (who actually encouraged this identification). Lines 215–22, describing how the infant Hercules throttled the serpents, praise Nero, who, according to Tacitus (*Ann.* 11.11.6), was said to have been guarded by snakes at his cradle. Amphitryon defending the reputation of the hero against Lycus' charge of immorality is really Seneca defending Nero's love of music and women. Words of warning and praise given to Hercules-Nero reflect the initial Senecan program of moderate government. Hercules' pacification of the world represents Rome's internal peace. Such data indicate to Herrmann the probability of an early date for this play.

As he continues to develop the chronology, assumption is piled on assumption. The *Oedipus* is placed in the middle of the sequence for reasons sifted from the work of other scholars. Lines 113–23, in which the chorus celebrates the victories of the followers of Bacchus over the Arabs and Parthians, are taken to refer to the Parthian war under Nero and the capture of the Parthian capital Artaxarta. He also mentions, but does not accept, the identification of Oedipus and Nero—a kind of scholarly game in which Nero is identified with this dramatic character or that and is being adulated or (secretly) castigated according to the subjective interpretation of selected passages.

The *Agamemnon* is placed late for similar reasons: praise of Apollo (Nero) and Juno (Octavia?) suggests that the play is to be dated at a time when Nero was famous as a lyre player and had not yet cast off Octavia. The chronology constructed from such alleged historical references is then "corroborated" by an analysis of variations in plot material and verbal echoes between "earlier" and "later" plays, moving from the *Furens* to each of the eight following plays, then from the *Thyestes* to each of the following seven, and so forth. All this is a display of amazing virtuosity in deciding which expression is the echo of which.

Herrmann's theory has been sketched, not to pillory it, but to illustrate the ingenuity plied in thousands of pages to date the plays through historical allusions and other internal elements. One scholar of good critical standards is inclined to accept 45–46 as the earliest possible date for the *Medea* and 54 as the latest possible date of the *Furens*, though he admits that "in general the tragedies may have belonged to any stage of Seneca's literary career."[7] This conjecture for the *Medea* depends upon a choral passage that develops the rhetorical and Stoic commonplace that the limits of nature controlling the Golden Age were broken by man's first sea voyage; the Argo has expanded the range of man's fears and opened the world to exploration (301–79, especially 364–79). There is speculation that Seneca here refers to Claudius' expedition to Britain because of passages like "cities have placed their walls in new lands" and the concluding idea that the semilegendary land of Thule, traditionally located six days' sail north of Britain (perhaps Iceland or Norway), will no longer be the outermost limit. This is the famous passage on which Ferdinand Columbus commented in the margin of his copy, "This prophecy was fulfilled by my father Admiral Christopher Columbus in 1492."

In the case of the *Furens*, the date is calculated by the theory that the figure Hercules in the *Apocolocyntosis*, written after Claudius' death on 13 October 54, is a parody of Seneca's own hero in the tragedy.[8] The theory can be supported with a kind of evidence because in the satire (*Apocol.* 7.1) Hercules is expressly given the role of tragic actor, but it is not at all certain that Seneca would have had to write the drama first. Nevertheless, these small data for the *Medea* and the *Furens* are the best that have been found. At least they are superior to a more recent interpretation: Medea's wild words in the prologue about using the sun-chariot to melt the Isthmus of Corinth allude to Nero's project of cutting the Corinthian canal and to the great fire in Rome![9]

Seneca's dramatic activity in the early 50s may be shown more objectively by Cichorius' skillful interpretation of a passage in Quintilian (8.3.31). Quintilian remembers a discussion between Seneca and Pomponius Secundus about the acceptability of a certain phrase in tragic diction, a discussion conducted in "prefaces" (*praefationibus*). If Quintilian was born about A.D. 35, the incident remembered from his youth (*iuvenis admodum*) happened in the early 50s. Seneca did not return from exile until 49 and Pomponius was away in Germany during 50 and 51, so the discussion could not have taken place until shortly after 51. Further, Cichorius believes that the prefaces were introductory remarks before *recitatio* and assumes that if Seneca was then giving readings of his plays, he was then also writing them.[10] This evidence is not completely tight but is strong.

Chronology and the study of dramatic technique are of course often linked. For example, Hansen studies the use of introspective scenes of passion and finds that they increase in importance according to the sequence of titles in manuscript tradition E: *Furens, Troades, Phoenissae, Medea, Phaedra, Oedipus, Agamemnon, Thyestes, Oetaeus*.[11] His contribution to the understanding of speeches of passion in Seneca is considerable, but his theory that there is a discernible progression from a "pathos-style" used for the development of plot to a "passion-style" of self-contained scenes is not convincing as a demonstration of chronology. In fact, one would expect that dramatic technique would develop in the opposite direction. There are, as we shall see, variations of intensity in the plays, but they depend upon the plot material, and the rhetorical mode is so strong and pervasive that a development of dramatic art is simply not visible. As for the sequence of titles in tradition E, it should not be used as an indication of chronology because the order, unlike that of family A, shows a mechanical associative grouping: the two Hercules plays frame the listing (the *Oetaeus* concludes the myth); two titles by chorus follow; then two plays named for the heroine; finally, three titled after the principal male characters.

A piece of potential external evidence is given by Tacitus (*Ann.* 14.52.3), who reports under the year 62 the growing breach between Nero and Seneca and the accusation that the adviser wrote poetry more diligently and competitively after Nero became addicted to it. "Poetry" (*carmina*) could refer to the drama, of course, but we have no way of knowing that it does. If some of the drama was composed at this time along with the prose writings of the same period,[12] Seneca was very busy indeed.

The problem of dating the plays could occupy us much longer because the literature about it is huge, but the result is that no acceptable chronology has been established and is not likely to be unless new evidence appears. Standards of valid philological evidence have often been abused in treating the problem. Composition of some of the tragedies in the early 50s is a reasonable theory.

For what kind of audience were the plays written? External evidence is either lacking or ambiguous. We have no evidence that these plays were produced. There are many indications both that dramas were then staged in the theater and that they were presented through reading to nontheatrical audiences. For example, among the contemporaries and near-contemporaries of Seneca was Pomponius Secundus, like Seneca a prominent statesman as well as a dramatic poet. His verses were ridiculed by an unruly audience in the theater (Tac. *Ann.* 11.13.1). Curiatius Maternus first became well known when he attacked Vatinius in dramatic readings (*recitatione tragoediarum*) in the reign of Nero; he later gave readings from his *Cato*, which he was preparing for publication in order to turn his attention to a *Thyestes* (Tac. *Dial.* 11, 2–3). Any fading of live theater at the time of Seneca was compensated by the popularity of *recitatio*.

The debate, then, is not about the state of the theater but whether internal characteristics suit composition for performance in the theater. Perhaps the best way through the thick welter of arguments and counterarguments is to examine a notable example of each main viewpoint.

In a long chapter,[13] Herrmann tries to demonstrate that Seneca wrote for the stage. Here is a summary of his points, with some evaluation added. He dismisses as insoluble the question whether the plays were actually staged and concentrates on whether they were written for live performance. He examines the reasons why most scholars think that they were composed to be read, either in public recitation or in private reading. Some of these he correctly finds dubious or inconclusive: Seneca's character and antagonism toward public shows, the decline of live theater, the argument that the loss of political freedom was inimical to political opinions alleged to lurk in the texts, the cost of theatrical performance, and the dramatist's inattention to the continuity and clarity required for performance in the theater. Herrmann rejects the conflicting arguments against performance, namely, that the plays are uninteresting for public audiences and that Seneca would not have catered to public taste for the sensational by writing so realistically.

Another set of arguments against composition for performance has been drawn from violations by Seneca of dramatic principles and conventions laid down in Horace's *Ars Poetica*: prohibition of prodigies and murders on stage, the rule of five acts, the appearance of divinities only when absolutely necessary, restriction to three speaking characters, and a functional role for the chorus. As to the three dramatic unities, which do not appear in the *Ars*, Herrmann cites scholars who find that the unities of place and time are not always observed and use these "violations" as evidence that the plays are "tragédies de lecture." Objection has also been made to the use of two choruses in two of the plays and to the complexity of the choral passages for staging.

Herrmann generally explains such departures in Seneca as dictated by legitimate purposes such as his conception of scene. He also points out that the observance and nonobservance of dramatic conventions have been used on both sides of this question and are therefore indecisive. In addition, one may ask, is there any necessary connection between Horace's poetic version of late-Greek literary theory and what Seneca chose to do as a dramatist? Actually, we shall find that irrelevant criteria have constantly been applied in the criticism of Senecan drama and that the problems with which this criticism has been—and to a considerable extent still is—obsessed will largely disappear when the mutual reinforcement of declamatory rhetoric and Neo-Stoicism is understood.

Other arguments are discounted by Herrmann less convincingly. One is the popularity of public readings. Another is based on the information in Quintilian given above, that Pomponius and Seneca discussed proper language for tragedy in "prefaces" that may have been introductory remarks before *recitatio*. A third matter has exercised more discussion and more disagreement than any other single issue. Certain scenes and techniques are problematic for staging: the shooting of an arrow at one son in the *Furens* (991–95), the incantation scene in which Medea slashes her arm to draw blood (*Med.* 807–11), Jocasta's stabbing herself in the womb (*Oedip.* 1038–39), the piecing together of Hippolytus' shattered body by Theseus in the *Phaedra* (1247–72), the movement of the table in the banquet scene of the *Thyestes* (989), the appearance of phantoms, and the realistic facial expressions and violent gestures to be performed by actors who would be wearing masks and boots.

Herrmann tries to depreciate such evidence by giving parallels to some of these items in Greek tragedy and by emphasizing the technical sophistication of the Roman theater. On his behalf it may be added that drama has usually found ways to present or suggest what it wants to show on the stage.

Having rejected the views against composition for performance, Herrmann turns to what he considers counterevidence in the texts. The plays contain Roman elements designed, he argues, to please a public audience. The moderate conventional ideas expressed are an adaptation to public taste of the more sophisticated philosophical and religious views that would have appealed only to an elite. Scenes of Hades, necromancy, incantation, ghosts, and Furies were written for the superstitious and traditionalist public. Monologues are used heavily as asides to create the verisimilitude necessary in the theater. Simple pronouns referring to various characters would be clarified by gestures in live performance. Seneca does not always indicate the entries and exits of his characters; this procedure would cause confusion in recitation-drama but not in seen drama. The texts are full of details about the actions and gestures of the characters, by which the dramatist could "direct" an acted version. Similarly, indications about stage equipment, sound effects, and light effects are provided in the text. Finally, Herrmann argues, the dramas are full of spectacle and showmanship understandable only if they were written for theatrical audiences. For these reasons, unlike other scholars who consider some of the plays playable and others not, he concludes that all of these homogeneous dramas were written to be performed on the stage.

This use of internal evidence has not won acceptance for a number of reasons. In general, the fact that the plays show theatrical features proves only that they were written in a theatrical tradition, an obvious truism, not that they were written to be performed. However, such scenic devices do have a significance that seems obvious but has often been disregarded: they show that Seneca was indeed consciously writing drama, not rhetorical or philosophical skits. Rhetoric and philosophy are the main ingredients, but they must be analyzed as the ingredients of his *drama*. Another inference, opposite to Herrmann's reasoning, is that Seneca wrote much more scenic detail into his texts than the Greek dramatists ever did because he was creating greater visibility in drama that would be heard, not seen. In doing so, he may well have been thinking specifically in terms of the Roman theater. At least Herrmann gives in his concluding section a credible account of how the plays would have been staged in the theater of the day.

The best treatment of the tragedy as recitation-drama was given more recently by Zwierlein.[14] He starts with the untheatrical features already met in the discussion of Herrmann. Only a few of the more telling points will be mentioned here. The scenic difficulties in the last act of *Phaedra* lead Zwierlein to make a significant observation for the Senecan conception of scene in general, that the final horrors of Phaedra's suicide and the assembling of Hippolytus' body are not conceived for the stage but are designed to draw all possible aspects of emotion from the situation, to move the hearer inwardly rather than through the eyes. When Agamemnon has Calchas summoned in the *Troades* (351–53) and starts speaking to him two lines later, Seneca is composing for the hearer whose experience is imaginative and is not attached to the realities of time and place. In the *Phoenissae* (427–43), the attendant in the city describes Jocasta's rush to the battlefield, where she then immediately appeals to her sons, that is, the attendant's words convey the hearer's imagination from one scene to another. For parallels to such a mental shift of scene, Zwierlein has to leave dramatic literature and go to such semidramatic authors as Plato and Theocritus. Evidence is given also for lack of clarity in the framing of scenes, unmotivated actions of characters, dumb-show description of action, long asides interrupting dialogue, untheatrical entrance monologues, and separation of the chorus from the action.

More original and weighty is his analysis of structural features that are unnatural for the theater but completely accountable in declamation-drama. The Senecan play is broken up into scenes that are only loosely related, if at all. Of the *Troades*, Zwierlein observes that the purpose of the dramatist "is not to create a continuous action, but to juxtapose different self-contained pictures."[15] In the *Oedipus*, the state of the hero does not develop; he knows himself guilty from the beginning of the action. The scene of the lovesick Phaedra (360–403) comes after the nurse, in conversation with her desperate mistress, has proposed making trial of Hippolytus, but what follows in the action is another graphic portrayal of Phaedra's anguish. Although this scene interrupts the sequence of the action, it is important for its psychological interest. The disconnected scenes of the incomplete *Phoenissae* are not unlike the other dramas and show Seneca writing for the auditor.

There are many "rhetorically effective scenes and themes which are projected out of the action"[16]: the magic scene in the *Medea* (670–739), descriptive digressions like the messenger's description of Pelops' palace and its surroundings in the *Thyestes* (641–82, over forty lines), or Creon's account of the sacred grove in the *Oedipus* (530–47). Even at peaks of action, similes are extended to epic length, as when Atreus in the *Thyestes* (497–503), seeing the returning Thyestes and his sons for the first time, takes seven lines to compare himself to a hound on the scent. The prevalence of monologues greatly abbreviates the action in favor of the set piece.

So with excellent evidence Zwierlein makes his point convincingly, that the most prominent structural characteristics of the drama move the focus away from characters living the action continuously to a spasmodic series of more or less connected elements. It can be said with considerable truth that the action is developed only as much as it needs to be in order to provide the occasions and the motives for the big effects. The result is a series of static moments that can be exploited by the speaker and appreciated by the hearer for their force and inventiveness.

Zwierlein goes on to examine the case for nontheatrical drama in classical antiquity and specifically the question whether Seneca's nontheatrical form was his innovation or came from a historical development.[17] By the end of the fifth century, the Greek plays were circulated as books and so became a kind of *Lesedrama*, but the poet did not write to suit the requirements of a reading public. Zwierlein takes the passage in Aristotle (*Rh.* 3.12.2) to mean that Chaeremon (a fourth-century dramatist) wrote for the stage but in a style more suited to reading than to performance. He concludes, somewhat rashly because the evidence is slight, that at the time of Aristotle the ground was prepared for *Lesedrama* both in theory and practice. He also accepts the hypothesis that the next stage in the historical development was the use of tragic myth and form by the Cynics and other philosophers to present their philosophies to a wider public in *Lesedrama*. Tradition has it, for example, that Diogenes of Sinope, the famous Diogenes, wrote a *Thyestes* justifying the eating of human flesh and an *Oedipus* portraying incest as natural on his principle that everything found in nature is acceptable. The mimes of Theocritus and Herodas show that the Greeks came to regard dramatic forms, originally for scenic presentation, as literary forms that could set aside the rules of the stage. Thus Zwierlein concludes that the Hellenistic period knew true *Lesedrama*.[18] He is uncertain whether such drama was written for private reading or for recitation[19] but feels that recitation cannot be excluded and that even stage-drama could have been recited, as well as drama not intended for the stage.

Turning to Roman nontheatrical drama, Zwierlein treats the institution of the literary *recitatio* by Asinius Pollio, its growing popularity for the presentation of literary works (including drama), and the coexistence of stage-drama and recitation-drama. He considers Seneca the heir of Hellenistic nontheatrical drama and one of a number of Latin poets who wrote for recitation as a form of publication. Therefore his drama is not *Lesedrama*, although plays were read privately after their recitation, but truly recitation-drama. Paradoxically, the great Senecan influence upon theatrical drama came from a poet who wrote his works for recitation.[20]

This view of the antecedents of Senecan drama is tempting because it would explain precisely why the Roman wrote philosophically oriented recitation-drama. But it must remain only an attractive hypothesis. In particular, the evidence about Cynic drama, on which the whole theory hinges, is very cloudy. There is doubt about such crucial points as the ascription of titles to authors, the meaning of the term "tragedy" in this context, and the reliability of the evidence from late authors.[21] Also, unfortunately for the theory, Seneca in his prose writings shows no sign of familiarity with Diogenes or Crates as writers of drama, although he respectfully mentions both of them as philosophers.[22] On the other hand, Seneca's writings sometimes do have depth of source that does not appear on the surface. In any event, Zwierlein's view of Senecan recitation-drama is very persuasive, and it may be hoped that no more scholarly time will be spent on this outmoded topic of the Senecan audience—no doubt a futile hope!

The possible connection between Hellenistic drama and Seneca has brought us into the most important of the heavily debated issues, the question of sources. The major effort of research has of course been to put the nine tragedies into the tradition of Greek tragedy. Thus a standard handbook statement reads:

> *Hercules* [*Furens*], based generally on the *Hercules Furens* of Euripides; *Troades*, with a dual source in Euripides' *Troades* and *Hecuba*; *Phoenissae*, reminiscent at first of Sophocles' *OC*, but bringing in Jocasta . . . ; *Medea*, mainly drawn from Euripides, but other sources may here and there be latent; *Phaedra*, the Euripidean myth, but with a repentant Phaedra; *Oedipus*, with a considerable Sophoclean basis; *Agamemnon*, in which a debt to Aeschylus is rather to be assumed than easily traced; *Thyestes*, a horrific treatment of the gruesome myth, without extant source; *Hercules Oetaeus*, of dubious authenticity, with little in it, apart from subject, to suggest the *Trachiniae*.[23]

The a priori reasons for expecting Greek influence are strong: the persistence of genres in Greek and Latin literature; the dominating prestige of the tradition of Greek tragedy, the continual imitation of it, and its continuing life in education; the well-known popularity of Euripides, the revival of his plays, and the influence of his rhetoric and psychological power, especially the conception of human life as the battleground of conflicting emotions and the demonic nature of love, overspreading Hellenistic and Latin literature. For our purpose, not the least important fact is the great prominence of Euripides in the rhetorical tradition, which leads Quintilian (10.1.67) to call him the best tragedian for orators. However, it would be a miracle if, for the eight Latin plays that have Greek counterparts more or less, we had preserved either wholly or partly those particular Greek tragedies that were their sources. The large Greek and Roman productivity in the genre makes the very idea extremely improbable.

A comparison of pairs of Greek and Senecan plays where, according to our handbook, the Greek is "generally" or "mainly" the source shows that the differences are more obtrusive and significant than the similarities. Euripides' and Seneca's *Furens* line up part by part as follows:

EURIPIDES

SENECA

Amphitryon explains the background of Theban history, the absence of Heracles on his last Labor to fetch Cerberus from Hades, and Lycus' threat to murder Heracles' family. He urges Megara to cling to the hope that Heracles will return in time. The chorus of Theban elders briefly sing of their own feebleness and the beauty of Heracles' children.

Juno's monologue announces her withdrawal from the sky, where Jupiter's amours and other interlopers threaten her Olympian position. Her vicious plan, set out in great mythological detail, is to call down the forces of evil upon the presumptuous Hercules by making him overcome himself in maddened violence. The chorus, at the beginning of a new day, contrasts the peaceful pursuits of lowly people and the self-destructiveness of the ambitious and foolhardy, including Hercules.

In the first episode, Lycus taunts his victims, who respond spiritedly and prepare to die. The chorus eulogizes the heroic deeds of Heracles and helplessly bursts into tears when the victims come forth to die.

After Amphitryon has rehearsed the Labors and other exploits of his son and has prayed for his return to punish the evil usurper, Megara calls upon Hercules to break the bounds of nature that keep him in Hades. Lycus defends his murderous seizure of power and offers dynastic marriage to Megara, who refuses contemptuously and threatens to kill Lycus if he forces her. Lycus exits, and the approach of Hercules is heard. The chorus hopes that Hercules will overcome the laws of Hades with his heroic strength just as Orpheus did with his music.

In the second episode, Megara and Amphitryon say their farewells, she to her three sons and he to life. Heracles appears, is told of the crisis in a scene of high emotion, and leads his family within to prepare for action. Youth is so beautiful, the chorus sings, that good men should be rewarded by having it twice, but even so the old singer will always praise the triumphs of Heracles.

Hercules, entering with Theseus, shows the beast Cerberus as evidence of his success in Hades, where he might have remained as king if he had wished. He challenges Juno to require another exploit and, learning about the situation, leaves immediately to kill Lycus. In the meantime, Theseus is urged on by Amphitryon's questions to give a long account of the system of Hades and of Hercules' bold and violent behavior there. He announces the approach of the victorious hero. The chorus again speaks of Hercules' bold invasion of Hades, describes the host of dead moving toward the underworld while the living precipitate themselves toward death, and calls for a celebration of the Herculean peace now won.

Lycus confronts Amphitryon, who maneuvers him inside the palace to encounter Heracles. The chorus joyously hears the cries of Lycus from within and formally sings of the just retribution supported by divine justice.

Hercules gloats over the death of Lycus and his supporters, and calls upon the gods to attend the celebration. Amphitryon urges him to purify his hands of blood and to pray to Jupiter for peace and rest, but Hercules replies that the blood of the evil king is an offering acceptable to the gods and that he joins Jupiter in praying for peace in the universe, claiming for himself combat with any new monster. Then, in an extended passage showing Seneca's dramatic intensity in all its power, Hercules goes mad, in hallucination seeing all nature convulsed and wildly aspiring to reach the sky as a Labor truly worthy of him. Under the delusion that his own sons are Lycus' and that Megara is Juno, he kills them all and falls senseless. The chorus asks all nature to mourn and prays that sleep will dispel his delusions and restore him to piety and virtue.

In the fourth episode (or second prologue), Lyssa, the spirit of mad-

In another graphic, psychologically effective scene, Hercules recovers and

ness, and Iris appear. Iris explains that they have come to carry out Hera's rage against Heracles as a demonstration of divine power and forces the reluctant Lyssa to cast her spell. The chorus agonizes and imagines the scene of violence in the palace.

learns the truth in a series of reactions to the recognition of the dead, the silence of Amphitryon and Theseus, his father's revulsion from his bloody hands, and the recognition of the bloody weapons that only he can wield. He rages against himself, calling upon all nature to react in horror against him, one whose heart is too savage. Amphitryon tries to persuade him that his acts were error, not crime, but he threatens suicide. He is finally dissuaded when his father threatens to take his own life. In filial obedience, Hercules decides that his next Labor is to live.

The messenger reports the catastrophe. Heracles is shown tied with rope to prevent more violence. Amphitryon tells him what has happened. Theseus enters, having heard that Lycus has seized the throne. Heracles wants to die, but Theseus' sympathy and counsel restore his courage and his confidence that the anthropomorphic behavior of Hera does not represent true divinity. He leaves with Theseus for Athens, where he will be purified and recognized as a hero.

Even this summary shows the Senecan characteristics that have stirred the issues of scholarship being treated here. For example, summarizing Seneca is more intricate than summarizing Euripides. The essential reason for this is that the course of the Euripidean play unfolds as continuous dramatic action, whereas the Latin proceeds jerkily from one effect to another within a bare framework of action: Juno's spectacular monologue, Amphitryon's account of the Labors, Theseus' disquisition on Hades, the mad scene, the recovery scene. Each act has a notable verbal peak that highlights the speaker and attracts the attention of the hearer, whether the declamatory feature advances the action or does not, as is the case with Amphitryon's and Theseus' discourses.

However, the difference is not simply that Seneca reorganizes the traditional material for striking effects. His whole conception of the hero and the theme is non-Euripidean. The Greek Heracles is a heroic figure whose life is blasted by the intervention of a vindictive divine force, and he becomes even more deeply a hero by understanding the nature of the force that has crushed him and by resolving to endure the pain. He has stood up to the unaccountable blows that are part of the human condition. Seneca's Hercules has fallen into the cult of belief in superhuman physical strength and has become a savage who considers himself strong enough to break the laws of nature and force his way to divinity. Juno's threat to turn Hercules against himself is a metaphor for the moral war within the great but arrogant hero. He has lost piety and virtue. He regains them when he rejects his arrogance by subjecting himself to the will of his father. The conception is a simple, moralistic one, but it is Senecan, not Euripidean, and dramatic because the whole play revolves around it.

Attempts to make the Euripidean *Furens* strictly the source of the Senecan have not been successful.[24] There is no convincing evidence of imitation to be found in the text. The only clear relationship is that Seneca essentially follows the same scheme of events, which means only that Euripides' structure of the plot had become traditional. We have no way of knowing from what source Seneca derived the traditional plot or even from what kind of source.

The case of the two *Medeas* is much the same. The two Medea-Creon scenes are roughly comparable but contain minor differences like the difference in the purpose of the two women: the Euripidean Medea wants to stay in Corinth, the Senecan wants her children to stay. Similarly, the Medea-Jason scenes are an essential confrontation and follow the same general lines, except that the Senecan Jason is less egocentric than the Euripidean, being concerned about the children and the impasse between fidelity to Medea and his own survival. The messenger scenes report the same catastrophe at the palace, of course, but the Senecan is only twelve lines long because the effect of Medea's magic has been so fully and specifically anticipated in the ostentatious third episode containing the nurse's description of Medea's magical preparations and the mistress's wild incantations. The exodes present the killing of the children. Otherwise there is no clear Euripidean imprint in the Senecan version. Such rough correspondences are the only indication that Euripides was a Senecan source. They are completely inadequate evidence and at the most show only what is obvious, that the Greek play became the classic version of this dramatic myth.

It is even questionable whether Seneca was significantly interested in fifth-century Greek tragedy as drama. His prose writings do not show it.[25] They contain one reference to the topic of the rising of the Nile in

Aeschylus, Sophocles, and Euripides (*Q.N.* 4.2.17) and two quotations of Euripides, one a six-word aphorism to the effect that "truth speaks simply" (*Ep.* 49.12), given without identifying the source, and the other a longer passage on wealth as a blessing, allegedly defended against the disapproval of the audience by Euripides in the theater (*Ep.* 115.14–15). The latter quotation caps a series of aphoristic excerpts from Greek tragedy concerning the power of wealth, which unmistakably has the ring of being derived from a handbook of quotations[26] under the entry "money, the power of."

So all of the few references to the Greek tragedians are either informational or moralistic. This argument is, of course, from silence—an almost total silence—but it does supplement the failure of source hunting in the dramatic material and indicate the futility of side-by-side comparison of particular Greek plays and particular Senecan plays as being derived from them. Comparative study of a Greek tragedy and a corresponding Senecan drama tells us a great deal about similarities and differences in the purposes of the two but practically nothing about sources.

Other sources of the Senecan *Medea* are also possible.[27] Greek and Latin versions of the story, both dramatic and nondramatic, abounded, and the many different theories about the Senecan sources are a tangle of quasi-evidence and speculation with no clear solution. Perhaps the prevailing view is that Seneca mixed Euripides as his primary source with elements from Ovid, whose drama *Medea* has survived in just two verses but has been variously reconstituted from Ovid's treatment of the story in *Heroides* 12 and the seventh book of the *Metamorphoses*. Certain Senecan details have been attributed to Apollonius' *Argonautica*. The earlier Latin plays of Ennius and Accius have figured in the controversy. Seneca's contemporary Curiatius Maternus, mentioned above, wrote a *Medea* apparently for *recitatio*. The list could be greatly extended.

The superficiality of the relationship between Seneca and Euripides increases the importance of possible links with other Latin drama. Unfortunately, this matter is equally opaque. Certainly Seneca knew Ovid's poetry well: after Virgil, Ovid is cited most frequently in the prose writings.[28] However, we know nothing about the Ovidian *Medea*. It is not acceptable to try to reconstruct Ovid's dramatic version from his accounts appearing in other, nondramatic genres. It is woefully weak to draw a significant parallel between Medea's words in Seneca (*incerta vaecors mente vaesana feror / partes in omnes*, 123–24) and the second Ovidian fragment (*feror huc illuc ut plena deo*)[29] since both wordings are commonplace poetic and rhetorical language to express distraction.

The fragments of Ennius and Accius are no more helpful. The plays of Ennius and probably Accius belong to a different category than the plays of Seneca because these dramatists wrote free translations or adaptations of Greek plays. The surviving pieces of the Ennian *Medea* show an adaptation of the Euripidean play to Latin and the Roman audience, a far cry from Seneca's composition of his play in the Euripidean tradition. If Seneca had written as Ennius did, the question of sources would never have arisen. For these reasons, it is quite irrelevant to note parallels between Ennius and Seneca or Accius and Seneca, parallels that result merely from the common subject matter. Probably the most important contribution of the earlier Latin dramatists to Seneca was their development of a tragic diction and style appropriate in Roman eyes for Latin versions of the serious, highly esteemed Greek plays. The resulting mode is heavy, grandiose, intense, and packed with rhetorical devices. Seneca seems to have been mindful of the styles of Ennius and Accius. At least he comments (*Ep.* 58.5) that many words used by them have become obsolete.

The source hunting ends in frustration. One scholar finds that the differences between Euripides and Seneca can be explained in the case of *Medea* as coming from Ovid and can be attributed to a "nameless poet" for the *Furens*.[30] According to another, it is an open question whether Hercules' recognition that only he could have used his weapons to slay the children, a detail not found in Euripides, was derived "from a republican drama."[31] Another, analyzing Seneca's concentration of the plot material in the *Troades*, recognizes the truth that "numerous comparisons with Euripides do not decide the question of Seneca's sources."[32] Still another, writing about the *Phaedra*, decries preoccupation with the question of sources and inattention to Seneca's own characteristics of thought and meaning.[33] The writer of the best comprehensive article on Senecan drama concludes that Seneca has "borrowed his general plots from the Greeks, and he has borrowed (or presumed his hearer's knowledge of) many scenes and several speeches. . . . But on the whole the relation is not particularly close."[34]

There is simply no way to decide which of the many theories for the individual plays is valid. The conjectures are so complex that they give the picture of dramas composed by consulting a catalogue of items from this source or that, that is, of dramas composed as no drama is composed.[35] One solution is to conclude that his sources are concealed in the mass of literary and philosophical writing during the more than four hundred years between Euripides and Seneca, and will never be known. Another answer, to which one is driven by the sheer failure of the source hunting, is to surmise that Seneca's originality is much greater than the nature of his drama, written in a traditional genre, has allowed us to recognize.

Of the two problematic plays, the *Oetaeus* and the *Octavia*, the former is here considered Senecan. There are reasons to have doubted its authenticity. Almost half again longer than the next longest play, the *Furens*, its last three acts seem interminable: the second episode in which Deianira decides upon suicide, the third episode portraying Hercules' anguish, and the exode culminating in the appearance of the deified hero. It contains many echoes of the other plays. Despite a growing tendency to accept the play as Senecan, peculiarities of language and style still leave substantial doubt in some minds.[36]

On the other hand, the unusual length results from the full development of two contrasting patterns of *furor* that concern the Neo-Stoic dramatist intensely: the anguish of Deianira, which causes her death, and the agony of Hercules, which is surmounted in apotheosis.[37] The individual parts of the play are written expansively and perhaps never received a final pruning, but the whole structure is quite normal for Seneca. Verbal echoes are characteristic of all the plays, apparently because Seneca composed by themes and by language expressive of the themes. As for so-called eccentricities of language, the notable ones are few[38] and admissible in a graphic and original style. Certainly they are far less important than the fact that the figurative language of the *Oetaeus* not only matches the language of the other plays but also most fully expresses the figurative patterns characteristic of Senecan drama. Because of the double theme, the heavily figured style reaches its peak in this play. For example, the Stoic notion of fire as both destructive and creative is flamboyantly exploited in portraying the destructive passions of Deianira and Hercules and the creative process of the hero's deification.[39] We shall see later that the two Hercules plays taken together express Neo-Stoicism powerfully. The *Oetaeus* should be recognized as the culmination of Neo-Stoic thought in Senecan drama, no matter how long it is.

The *Octavia* will not be included in our material because it seems not to be Seneca's. Despite continuing attempts to prove that it is,[40] too many arguments contravene. The appearance of Seneca as dramatis persona, trying unsuccessfully to control Nero's passion for Poppaea and his murderous hatred of Octavia, can be explained as a feature of clandestine drama written by Seneca for the anti-Neronian "underground," although it was unheard of in antiquity for a poet to introduce himself in serious drama.[41] The evidence that the details of Nero's death in A.D. 68, three years after Seneca's death, are used in the text (619–31, 752) is not conclusive. However, other arguments cannot be turned aside. The author of *Octavia* does not command a languge as varied as Seneca's, his metrics are more limited, the imagery is spare, and in general the drama lacks the force and intensity achieved by Seneca.[42]

The best evidence, then, indicates that the nine tragedies, including the incomplete *Phoenissae*, were composed by Seneca for *recitatio* and that any sources used specifically are unknown. Now to be considered are the formal ingredients of language, meter, and imagery, a mixture of rhetoric and poetry that is at once powerful and bombastic. Here our knowledge is much firmer, and the factors involved much closer to the unique qualities of the drama.

The world of rhetoric and declamation was the environment of the young Seneca. His own teachers of rhetoric included Mamercus Scaurus, L. Junius Gallio (brother Novatus' father by adoption), Musa, Julius Bassus (Sen. *Contr.* 10. pref. 2–12), and the only one mentioned by Seneca himself, Fabianus Papirius, the rhetorician and philosopher. The result of all this exposure, actively supported by the elder Seneca, was an effective style of oratory and written prose that carried Seneca high in public life, made him popular with his contemporaries and the young, and was controversial in the eyes of traditionalists. One of these, the rhetorician, advocate, and educator Quintilian, was an influential critic of Seneca's declamatory style.[43] Quintilian is careful to admit that Seneca was intelligent, zealous, and fluent as an orator, but, following the honored tradition of Cicero and the periodic style, he rejects the new style represented by Seneca as an unfortunately popular corruption of good standards, lacking dignity and straining after novelty and epigrammatic brevity.

Seneca's prose style is essentially the declamatory style. A great authority on ancient artistic prose describes the declamatory tone as "always passionate." The vehemence, the intensity, comes from an abundance of figures of speech and thought, moral epigrams (*sententiae*), and pointed brevity, relieved only by other mannerisms such as the analytical or descriptive digression.[44] Seneca's own ideal was a moderate version of the new style, a combination of intensity and fluency. In a letter (*Ep.* 100) to Lucilius, who has criticized the weakness of Fabianus' style, he praises his teacher's simple fluency while admitting a lack of forcefulness.

The ostentation of his prose has often been criticized, now as well as in his own time, but the criticism is the inevitable result of departure from a great tradition. The style was natural for him, creative in its innovation, and effective for his purposes.[45] It was natural because of his training in the rhetoric of the day, including the ideas and writing of his father, whose Latin was somewhere between Ciceronian tradition and the new style and in turn influenced the son's style.[46] Also, the style was a new literary dialect with the vitality of a vocabulary expanded to include semipoetic words and words in common use. Finally, it was an effective instrument for the semipopular exhortation of Neo-Stoicism, done so distinctively that the fusion of rhetoric and philosophy has correctly been recognized as a unique Senecan achievement.[47] For this reason, it is impossible to distinguish sharply between the rhetoric and the philosophy in all of Seneca's writings, including the drama.

The poetic style of the drama is even more monotonous than the prose because it is less varied. In an essay or a letter, Seneca exhorts or consoles or counsels or confesses in a wide range of mood all the way from light witticism to heavy despair. The dramatic style is unrelievedly intense because, one imagines, it was poetry and therefore serious, and because it was poetry written in a philosophical dramatic tradition—probing relationships between gods and men and the wellsprings of human action.

The style has been called baroque because of the excessive rhetorical ornamentation.[48] This criticism is valid, but the term is misleading because it suggests disorder and Seneca's style is very tightly organized. Also, the rhetoric is not merely ornamental but the very essence of the language. The standard work on the subject[49] demonstrates an absorption of the rhetorical mode in Seneca's mind so complete that it constitutes his linguistic psychology, not merely the achievement of effects but a way of thought. For example, Canter's summary tables show: what he calls "tropes" (metaphor, synecdoche, metonomy, periphrasis, irony, hyperbole) average one occurrence every 2 to 4 verses; figures of thought (interrogation, apostrophe and exclamation, climax, antithesis) appear once every 14 to 30 lines; figures of expression (anaphora, paronomasia, chiasmus, asyndeton, polysyndeton, word order) average once every 4 to 6 verses.[50]

Perhaps the best illustration of the verbal complexity natural to the rhetorical mind is the use of word order for strong effects.[51] It includes groups of two words (not in grammatical agreement) of related meaning, juxtaposed so as to emphasize relationships like cause and effect (e.g., *praeceps citato*); three-word groups in which agreeing noun and adjective are separated by another word that completes their meaning (*viribus vinci suis*); four-word groups in the order abab (*sublime classes sidus Argolicas*) or the order abba (*suasque Perseus aureus stellas*); five-word groups combining the features of three-word groups and four-word abab (*binos propinqua tinguit Aethiopas face*) or abba (*meumque victrix teneat Alcmene locum*). The effect of these collocations is to produce a sustained tight texture of language.

When these figures of speech and thought are massed together line after line, the result is a mannered style both condensed and florid. The rhetorical style is a successful instrument for the kind of tragic drama Seneca chose to write, a drama of heightened sensibilities, sharply focused passions, aphoristic moralism, and philosophical chiaroscuro. In both the language and the thought, tension is never relaxed.

Another rhetorical convention is used so excessively that it is a major blemish. Description[52] had long been a popular device with certain rhetoricians and poets, such as Ovid, but in Seneca it becomes an almost invariable habit. Whether a long description of the deaths of Astyanax and Polyxena (*Troad.* 1068–1164), a dreadful account of the murder of Agamemnon (*Agam.* 897–905), an enumeration of the traditional victims of punishment in Hades (*Phaedr.* 1229–37), or the hundreds of epithets applied to any kind of noun, ornamentation is the rule rather than the exception. The use of an unmodified word is a missed opportunity for a graphic or clever or learned attribute. As a result, Seneca's texts are loaded with miscellaneous learning, most of it conventional. "He employs over seven hundred proper names or adjectives of peoples, countries, towns, mountains, rivers, islands, etc. with geographical, mythological, or historical application."[53] This abuse of technique is the bad side of a poetic style that is truly rhetorical, that is, aimed exclusively at the effects of words.

Seneca was more creative as a writer of prose than of poetry, but his control of the poetic ingredients is impressive. The meters of his dramatic poetry are unexceptional but sound.[54] The iambic trimeters of the dialogue parts are carefully written. The choral meters tend to be monotonous because of his preference for anapests, but he uses also asclepiads, glyconics, sapphics, and mixed meters.[55] They are not fully dramatic in the sense that the choral meters of Greek tragedy are dramatic because they usually lack the strophic correspondence of the stasima that the Greek chorus chanted and danced.[56] Rather, the Senecan choral meters belong to the tradition of Latin lyric poetry. Seneca does not mention Catullus and merely quotes Horace three times (*Ep.* 86.13, 119.13, 120.20), always from the *Satires*, but his lyric meters appear to be influenced by Horace, and it is significant that themes and language from Horatian lyric reappear thickly in Senecan dramatic odes as well as elsewhere in his writings.[57]

The imagery is strong, massive, and gross. It is drawn from many sources of reference. For example, Canter finds that the metaphors are derived largely from many aspects of the human sphere but also from the world of nature.[58] On the surface, the imagery looks like an indiscriminate mass, but analysis shows that it is systematic and also truly dramatic because it supports and communicates the themes of the drama.[59] Significantly, the figurative language is substantially the same in all the plays. Derived only secondarily from conceptions of the themes in individual plays, it comes primarily from the comprehensive interpretation that all the dramatic material demonstrates one central theme, the mortal combat between passion and reason, irrationality and rationality.

Most of the imagery appears in systems of vocabulary pairing positive and negative implications. The systems vary somewhat in kind. There are conceptual images or abstract ideas expressing the dichotomies control-unrestraint, security-insecurity, bright-dark, clean-foul. "Fire" and "sea storm" are the two major metaphors. "Fire" is used positively to refer to the processes and conditions of nature and to the gods, that is, the notion of natural order, but most of the time negatively to describe the nature and action of destructive passion. "Sea storm" conveys both the violence of passion and refuge from it. Fortune is a mixed figure used as abstract idea, as personification, and in the metaphor of the wheel, primarily to reinforce the idea of insecurity.

The Stoicism of the imagery is obvious. Seneca uses dozens of words meaning "control," "check," "limit," and the like in opposition to those meaning "excessive," "raging," "unrestrained," and the like, a poetic polarization of the qualities of rationality and irrationality. Similarly, the Stoic definition of the results of reason and passion, that is, security and insecurity, is conveyed by opposing equally numerous terms of "peace," "serenity," or "hope" to terms of "doubt," "uncertainty," "flight," "anxiety," or "fear." The fact that the major metaphors involve water and fire is consistent with the central role of these elements in the Stoic view of the universe: "Water and fire rule the earth; they are its source and its destruction" (*Q.N.* 3.28.7). Particularly striking is the exact correspondence of the positive and negative uses of "fire" in the imagery with the traditional Stoic distinction between celestial creative fire and terrestrial destructive fire.[60] It is notable also that the states of unrestraint, insecurity, darkness, foulness, and their opposites are not confined to the human scene or the animate world but spread to the world of physical nature: constellations, islands, cities, rivers, and so forth.[61] The imagery describes the unified, sentient universe of the Stoics.

The quantity of the imagery is so excessive that it loses imaginative quality and becomes stereotyped. In the *Furens*, for example, one of the patterns appears on the average every second or third line.[62] It is obvious that the patterns constantly overlap. Rhetorical and philosophical purposes of the imagery are inseparable, for items in the patterns are used both descriptively for graphic effect and dramatically to depict irrationality as destructive, chaotic, dark, foul, and deathly, the negation of order, security, brightness, and life.

Within this framework, variations result from Seneca's interpretation of the kind and degree of irrationality to be found in the plot material. In the *Troades*, the figurative language is relatively restrained because the dramatist is treating not only the active fury of the victorious Greeks but also the passive condition of the Trojan victims.[63] The passions of Medea and Phaedra are so explosive that the full force of the imagery is released in these plays.[64] In the *Oedipus*, the king's irrationality consists in his fear of Fate. As a result, the images normally used for active force are minor, but images conveying insecurity saturate the text.[65]

The imagery is part of the dramatist's system of writing commentary on the action as it unfolds. It is only one aspect of a complete Senecan technique of writing rhetorical, philosophical recitation-drama. We have seen that Seneca follows the traditional dramatic format closely enough to make him vulnerable to criticism of his departures from it. His purposes required many modifications of tradition. For example, we shall see that his prologues and choral odes are written as functions of his own kind of drama. His exposition is untraditional because he exploits the preknowledge of the plot that he could presume in his hearers, unlike the Greek tragedians.[66] So his exposition is sparse and allusive. Also, by playing upon the preknowledge and creating anticipatory suspense, he invites his auditors to recognize the significance of what is happening and to anticipate the outcome. Some of this foreshadowing is ingenious. Medea does not decide to kill the children until lines 549–50, but in the prologue Seneca has her say that she has her revenge in hand, in words (*parta iam, parta ultio est: / peperi,* 25–26) that remind the informed hearer that she will decide to get revenge through the children whom she has borne.[67] The prologue of the *Furens* alludes to the fact that Hercules' might will be turned by madness into a tool of Juno's rage.[68] The divination scene in the *Oedipus* (291–402) is a clever allegory in which the physical and anatomical details of the sacrifice and divination are manipulated verbally to evoke the disastrous history of the family, including the self-blinding of Oedipus and the suicide of Jocasta within the play.[69] When analyzing Senecan dramatic technique, we repeatedly find the explanation in verbal effect.

The greatest need in the criticism of this drama is to understand its legitimacy as drama of a new kind in the ancient tradition. It cannot be explained as an inferior imitation of Greek tragedy because, though inferior, it is not imitative in the strict sense of the word and has its own nature and motivation.

3. PHILOSOPHY

The presence of Stoicism in the imagery shows how deeply the philosophy saturates the drama. Before this saturation is analyzed in some detail, the nature of Seneca's Neo-Stoicism must be considered carefully. Its development was more complex and its content, the major source of thematic material in the drama, more substantive than is commonly understood.

For the understanding of Seneca's growth and development, some biography will be necessary. A piece of it is inserted here.

> nomenque terris qui dedit Baetis suis
> Hesperia pulsans maria languenti vado (Sen. *Med.* 726–27)

The river Baetis (Guadalquivir), which "gave its name" to the province of Baetica in south-central Spain, was navigable for small boats northeast up to the town of Corduba (Cordoba). Here L. Annaeus Seneca was born about 4 B.C., the second of the three sons of L. Annaeus Seneca senior and Helvia. The father and apparently the mother both were born in Spain, presumably of immigrant families from Italy, although the time of immigration and other details are not known. Some evidence indicates that the *nomen* Annaeus was of Etruscan or Illyrian origin.[1] The mother's family, of unknown origin, seems to have been wealthy and socially prominent.

Corduba was an important center politically and commercially. It was founded in 152 B.C. by M. Claudius Marcellus after his campaigns and received the status of colony with Roman citizenship perhaps during the absentee governorship of Pompey in 54 B.C., but more probably later under Augustus. When at this time the two provinces of Spain were reorganized as three, Baetica was made a senatorial province and Corduba functioned as one of its four administrative centers.

The major reason for the prominence of the town was its location at the most northern point where the Baetis was navigable down to the sea, in an area productive in agriculture, sheep raising, and mining. Mineral deposits were very rich, so rich that Posidonius, quoted by Strabo,[2] perpetrated an old pun in saying that Pluto (=Plutus, god of riches) really inhabited the underground in this district of Turdetania. Strabo imagines that Homer located the Elysian Plain there because of Phoenician reports about the natural bountifulness of the region. In the Sierra Morena near Corduba, gold, silver, copper, and lead were mined. We learn, again from Strabo, that at this time the silver mines were operated under private ownership or lease, whereas the state controlled the gold. Precise information is lacking, but possibly Seneca's family was involved in these local enterprises quite successfully, for it had achieved the financial status required for equestrian rank.

Seneca has often been taken as a "typical" Spaniard. Michener finds that he has become a culture hero:

> Most Spanish intellectuals, especially those with a mordant cast of mind, consider themselves the children of Seneca; his ideas are as vital today as they were when he first propounded them, and I have known one politician, one novelist and one bullfighter [an interesting grouping!] who have assured me that the principles by which they live and practice their art derive from Seneca. His capacity to see the world cynically but with wit endears him to the Spaniard; his exaggerated sense of pundonor was one of the foundations of that philosophy; and his skillful use of words served as a proptotype for Spanish verbosity.[3]

More important for our purposes than this image making by hindsight are attempts to find Spanish characteristics in what Seneca thought and wrote. On gory details in his plays: "This has been taken by modern Spanish historians to be a markedly Spanish trait: and so it is."[4] On his Stoicism: the Spaniards "are born disciples of Seneca, natural stoics who bear and forbear."[5] Also, "Stoicism, the instinctive philosophy of the savage everywhere, is the fundamental philosophy and almost the religion of Spain. . . . [Seneca, Marcus Aurelius, and Lucan] have taken so important a share in moulding the later developments of Stoicism because that philosophy answered to an instinct they already felt in their veins." More generally: "It is naturalism, the passion of life, the stimulating appeal of aspiring and inexhaustible energy, in harmony with the movement of life itself, that has forever moved the Spanish soul. There is no more inspiring moralist, it has often been said, than the old Spaniard Seneca."[6]

The point raises many doubts and reservations. In what sense was the Senecan family Spanish? We get the impression that the family and their associates were a tight band of Romans who happened to be in Corduba. At what stage in the variegated history of Spain can we speak of "the Spanish temperament"? Are there national traits at all, or just tendencies? Are these constant enough to provide a basis of interpretation? How significant are they in the case of a boy who was taken as a young child from Corduba to Rome? Can Spanish and Roman characteristics be differentiated?

Yet the mysteries of psychological chemistry are involved, and we are told that traits and tendencies are formed early in the development of personality. At any rate, the student of Seneca is bound to feel the presence of an idiosyncrasy coming from some source, a mix of intensity and grandiosity that finds its closest parallel in the epic of Lucan, Seneca's nephew of precisely the same origin. It is not just flippant to say that in some respects Senecan drama shows what has been called the national Spanish trait of getting "pleasure from racing an engine with the exhaust open"![7] Obviously we cannot securely interpret Seneca in terms of so-called Spanish qualities, but it would be hyperskeptical not to keep them in the back of our minds as a potential cause contributing to the extreme tensions and reactions characteristic of him.

Corduba was also a cultural center of considerable note. The town must have enjoyed the excellence of the Spanish schools known from the good quality of the Latin used in local inscriptions, including poetic writing.[8] Cicero mentions that Q. Metellus Pius, proconsul in Spain from 79 to 72 B.C., gave audience to native Cordovan poets even though their Latin sounded "thick and foreign" (*Arch.* 26). The rhetorician Marullus, perhaps also from Corduba, taught the fellow townsmen[9] Seneca the elder and M. Porcius Latro in his school at Rome. Latro as a distinguished declaimer was heard by celebrities like Augustus, Agrippa, and Maecenas, and set poetic language going in Ovid's mind (Sen. *Contr.* 2.2.8). L. Junius Gallio, rhetorician and Roman senator, may also have been a Cordovan. The surrounding area of the province Baetica was the origin of the authors Pomponius Mela and Columella and later the emperors Trajan and Hadrian. It is an interesting footnote that Corduba herself continued to have eminent sons: Bishop Osio (Hosius), champion of the Nicene Creed against the Arian heresy in the fourth century; Averroës, the twelfth-century Islamic philosopher; and his contemporary, Moses Maimonides, doctor and philosopher of Judaism.[10]

The Beginnings

The eclecticism of philosophy in the first century appears clearly in two of the three philosophers who can be considered Seneca's teachers. Apparently the earliest was Sotion of Alexandria, whom Seneca heard as a "boy" (*puer, Ep.* 49.2), a term commonly used of males until the age of seventeen but not to be pressed exactly. Sotion was one of the few Sextians,[11] the followers of Q. Sextius who developed a hybrid Neo-Pythagorean Stoicism in the time of Augustus. Much of our information about them comes from Seneca. Presumably he knew the founder of the short-lived school only through his writings, as in the pleasant scene where friends gather for dinner in the warmth of a hospitable fire and listen to the reading of one of Sextius' books.[12] Sextius "is really a Stoic, though he wouldn't admit it." His following—at any rate, Seneca's allegiance to him—resulted from his inspirational power to make a man see the greatness of the happy life without despairing of achieving it. He practiced Pythagorean self-examination at the end of the day, and Seneca goes on to tell how he himself does the same, acting as his own judge every night when the lights are out and his wife, knowing her husband's habit, falls silent (*Ira* 3.36.1–3).

Abstinence from animal meat was a Sextian principle, but the reasons for it varied (*Ep.* 108.17–21). Sextius himself was convinced by moral and hygienic arguments, believing that slaughter encourages cruelty and that variety of diet is luxurious and unhealthy. Sotion held the traditional Pythagorean view that the soul transmigrates from one form of creature life to another in a cycle of reincarnation and that thus all creatures, animal and man, are interrelated through the possession of soul. Sotion's position of course involves an un-Stoic conception of the soul as nonmaterial, but this seems to have been Sextian dogma, for a Christian writer of the fifth century quotes directly the view of both Sextii, father and son, that the soul is a wholly incorporeal force that holds body together (Claud. Mam. *Stat. An.* 2.8).

The Stoic orientation of Sextianism is evident in ethical matters. Sextius uses the simile of an army advancing in square formation to describe the action of the wise man (*sapiens*) always on guard against enemies—poverty, grief, disgrace, pain—that may appear from any quarter (*Ep.* 59.7–8). Seneca's second Sextian teacher, Fabianus Papirius, was well known for his moral diatribes. He was greatly admired by the elder Seneca, who devotes one of his prefaces to Fabianus' transition from rhetoric to philosophy (*Contr.* 2. pref.). The son recalls his teacher's rousing lectures for public audiences, which were so impressed with the dignity of the speaker that they interrupted with only an occasional cry of approval (*Ep.* 52.11). Apparently one of his favorite themes was the necessity of waging war against the passions, a theme developed from a full arsenal of military language (*Brev. Vit.* 10.1).

The development of Seneca's ideas cannot be traced precisely, but what we know of Sextianism seems to reveal at least an initial model of what his thought was to become. The following three points are noteworthy. The Sextians' preoccupation with ethics, particularly applied ethics, is apparent in the militant, idealistic teaching attributed to Sotion and Fabianus. Seneca was exposed to the conception of soul as nonmaterial spirit early in his studies and, whether there is a causal connection or not, at times stretches the Stoic corporeal definition about as far as it can go. The practice of self-analysis learned, he seems to imply, from Sextius is obviously related to the introspection characterizing his life and writings.

Attalus, the third teacher, has been called a Sextian,[13] but there is no evidence that he was not an "orthodox" Stoic. In him also Seneca found the inspiring qualities that he sought:

> I remember that Attalus gave me this advice when I haunted his school, being the first to arrive and the last to leave, and challenged him to some discussion as he walked about. He was not only ready for students, but volunteered himself to them. . . .
>
> When I heard Attalus condemning the vices, delusions, and evils of life, I felt pity for mankind, and considered him exalted higher than a human can rise. He would say that he was a king [in the Stoic paradox that only the philosopher is a king], but I thought him more than king since he could censor kings. (*Ep.* 108.3, 13)

Ironically, Attalus did indeed rise high, so high that he fell victim to the schemes of Sejanus, Tiberius' Prefect of the Praetorian Guard, and went into exile (*Suas.* 2.12). These could be dangerous days, even for philosophers.

The fact that Seneca presses Stoic materialism to its outer limits and exceeds traditional Stoicism in his religious ideas makes one look for explanations more specific than the widespread eclecticism. For one thing, his years in Egypt raise at least tempting speculation. From perhaps the middle twenties A.D. until the year 31, he was with his aunt and her husband C. Galerius, Prefect of Alexandria and Egypt for sixteen years.[14]

The only direct evidence of what he did there seems to be the one surviving fragment of his essay *De Situ et Sacris Aegyptiorum*. It tells how Isis found and buried the remains of Osiris at Philae on the upper Nile and thus was appeased in her wrath against the Egyptians.[15] The topic of Isis' anger calls to mind criticisms of superstitious religions found elsewhere in Seneca. His lost dialogue *De Superstitione* ridiculed the irrationality of religious beliefs and practices among the Romans, Egyptians, and Hebrews and therefore was used by Christian apologists as a source of propaganda against other religions.[16] For this reason, St. Augustine discusses, and so preserves, parts of Seneca's dialogue (*Civ. Dei* 6.10–11). Seneca decries senseless and indiscriminate deification, self-mutilation to appease wrathful gods, emotional gyration from grief at the fictitious death of Osiris to joy at his fictitious resurrection, various Roman mummeries—for example, when women at some distance from the temple manipulate their fingers to mimic dressing the hair of Juno and Minerva—and the idleness of the Jewish Sabbath. Presumably the self-mutilation is the emasculation performed in ecstatic state by the Galli, priests of the Anatolian Cybele or Magna Mater.

Whether this iconoclasm was related to his years in Egypt is hard to say. It is usually and reasonably assumed that the Egyptian piece, as well as the essay *De Situ Indiae*, was written at or near this time.[17] All the beliefs and practices disparaged in the *De Superstitione* could have been observed right in Rome, but they all also would have been very prominent in Alexandria, a city where the variety of cults matched the cosmopolitan population.[18] It is unbelievable that Seneca was not exposed to these cults during a number of years in the province, and a young mind trained in the rational tradition would naturally react in the form of the ridicule reported by St. Augustine.

De Superstitione was probably written during this period, but persistent memories of the Egyptian experience appear also in later writings. In Seneca's treatment of natural history, material about the Nile not only is fuller than the information about any other river but also contains what may be bits of firsthand experience. The half-preserved book on the Nile in the *Quaestiones Naturales* includes a vivid picture of the river passing violently through the Cataracts, a local story about pairs of natives braving the wild waters in a small boat (one rowing, the other bailing), and an appreciation of the beauty of the flooded land (4.2.4–6, 11). Firsthand memory may be working again when he contrasts the silence of true reverence with the noisy rites of Isis: the shaking of the rattle, the shrieking of a woman crawling along the street, and a linen-clad old man, with laurel branch and lamp at midday, howling that some god is angry (*Vit. Beat.* 26.8). The same passage mentions a worshiper slashing his arms.

The evidence is dim, but Alexandria is the most likely source of such memorable, moving scenes: the wild alternation of grief and joy, piercing cries of worshipers, abject human figures. It may well be true, as has been suggested,[19] that the vehemence of Seneca's protest and the nightmarishness of the memories show a susceptibility to the power of emotional religion. He remembers because he was deeply affected and deeply disturbed. Such sensitivity would have the double effect of intensifying his rational resistance to religious emotion and of opening his mind to the significance of suprarational experience.

The likelihood that Seneca continued studying philosophy in Alexandria is equally interesting—and even less supported by evidence. He may have had personal connections with philosophers there. Apparently Sotion was from Alexandria, though there is some difficulty in identifying different persons of that name.[20] Another Alexandrian whom Seneca must have known, at least later, was Chairemon,[21] Stoic philosopher, grammarian, head of the Alexandria Museum, and sacred scribe in the Egyptian priesthood. He and the Peripatetic Alexander of Aegae became teachers of the boy Nero after the year 49, probably shortly after Seneca himself undertook the same kind of post in the imperial court. It could well be that Seneca and Chairemon had been acquainted earlier. Our little information about Chairemon gives a picture of typically Alexandrian activity. He belonged to a movement that romanticized the Egyptian religious tradition in terms of contemporary philosophy. Thus the priests of old Egypt were represented as ascetics who fulfilled the ideals of Stoicism, and their religion became an allegory of the worship of nature.[22]

Chairemon is an example of the Egyptian-Alexandrian syncretism that set in strongly during the first century B.C., a fusion of Eastern religious traditions and eclectic forms of Greek philosophy (a revived Platonism, Neo-Skepticism, Neo-Pythagoreanism, Neo-Stoicism).[23] It was a time of insecure restlessness, of widespread searching to satisfy intellectual and spiritual needs. The uncertainties of existence had to be tolerated or transcended. Searchers modified and mixed established philosophical systems. They felt the pull of liberating mysticism. They bridged the gap between rational thought and suprarational experience by converting religious tradition to philosophical ideal, as Chairemon and his kind did, or conversely by using philosophical ideas to analyze the power of traditional religion, as in the writings of Philo the Alexandrian Jew. Because the whole drive was essentially spiritualizing, the strongest ingredient was the Pythagorean-Platonic-Stoic dimension of Greek philosophy. Alexandria was a natural center of this syncretism, for there in the lecture halls, libraries, temples, and synagogues West and East streamed together.

Philo was a highborn, well-educated leader of the very large Jewish community in Alexandria.[24] His official status is not known, but he was influential in both politics and intellectual life. He was chosen to head the embassy of five Jewish representatives sent to Rome for negotiating with Caligula after the brutal, politically maneuvered pogrom in the summer of A.D. 38 threatened the survival of the Alexandrian Jews. The real issues were their refusal to worship the emperor and their claim to Alexandrian citizenship. Philo's treatise *The Embassy to Gaius* (Caligula) is a masterful presentation of the Jewish position.

Philo's political realism is only the practical side of a very versatile mind. In his voluminous commentaries on the Jewish scriptures, he blends Greek and Judaic elements so thoroughly that the two are often indistinguishable. "He read Plato in terms of Moses, and Moses in terms of Plato, to the point that he was convinced that each had said essentially the same thing." He read "the Jewish Scriptures with Greek spectacles."[25] Although not a creative philosopher, he uses philosophy creatively, bringing Pythagorean-Platonic ideas and Stoic terminology to bear upon the Jewish texts.[26]

It is tempting to dwell on Philo's imaginative, searching, mystical, though often fantastic, meditations. Suffice it to say that his use of learning for spiritual ends is a fascinating example of the thinking that went on in Alexandria. His work not only spanned Greek and Judaic thought but also developed affinity between the Jewish and Christian traditions through its impact upon later thinkers like the Alexandrian Christians Clement and Origen.

Philo was at the peak of his career when Seneca was in Alexandria. The two would have shared a strong interest in Posidonius, but in this case also we have no hard evidence that the two were in contact. On the other hand, Seneca patently could not have failed to know at least about Philo's political role. During these years, Seneca was a member of the vice-regal family and so in touch with the problems of governing a country and a city where the interests of Roman officialdom, natives, Jews, Greeks, and others competed, and Philo was a leader of the most problematic group, constantly striving to preserve its homogeneity and status. The local political tensions obviously registered in Lucius' mind, for ten years after his return to Rome he describes his uncle's province as malicious and rebellious (*Cons. Helv.* 19.6). In the section of the *De Superstitione* used by St. Augustine to show Seneca's attitude to the Jews, Seneca may be following the official policy of the prefect's office concerning the Jewish Sabbath. Here the argument against the institution is that the Jews "lose in idleness almost a seventh of their life, and by failing to act in times of urgency they often suffer loss."[27] Philo himself attacks the action of a "recent governor"[28] who set out to abolish the Sabbath on exactly the same rationalization as Seneca's, arguing that the Jews are unable to cope with a sudden national or natural disaster.

Philo's Judaism could be fierce. His essay *Against Flaccus* presents the case against a prefect whom the Jews had reason to consider a Satanic figure. He had misgoverned, knuckled under to the anti-Jewish faction, and allowed the pogrom of A.D. 38 to develop. The treatise vividly tells how Flaccus fell out of favor with Caligula; he was arrested, tried in Rome, banished, and murdered by agents of Caligula on the island of Andros. Philo exults too much in the grisly details because he believes that Judaism is under divine protection and God punishes its enemies.

Roman rule was a comparatively recent imposition upon Egypt, and any prefect must have been suspect in the eyes of a Philo. The circumstances of Galerius' return to Rome, told by Seneca as an eyewitness (*Cons. Helv.* 19.4–5), raise a piquant question as to what Philo's version of the incident would have been. Galerius died during the voyage. When the ship was wrecked in a storm, his wife Helvia—with the courage of an Alcestis, Seneca comments—brought the body to land and so preserved it for burial. The retributive hand of God at work?

So at the age of about thirty-five Seneca was back in Rome. The evidence about his Egyptian visit does not take us very far, but scraps of information and reasonable assumptions may have yielded acceptable interpretations of some consequence. Exposure to the intricacies and chances of government in a motley and volatile section of the empire must have been invaluable training for the statesman-to-be. The firsthand experience of emotional religions in their own settings would collide with his training in rational thought, in some respects shaking it, in other respects reinforcing it, but certainly would enlarge the range of data to be comprehended by an inquiring mind. If he was ever inclined to restrict himself to any philosophical dogma, the syncretistic speculation of a Chairemon, a Philo, or some other Alexandrian, the blending of philosophy and religion, and the revisional fusion of philosophical traditions would make him more aware and more tolerant of other views.

These early stages in the development of Seneca's Neo-Stoicism can be isolated, but from here on no such distinctions are possible, and his thought must be treated compositely. Systematic and technical analysis is out of the question for a number of reasons. We have an approximate chronology of his prose writings,[29] but it is not exact enough for close analysis. The writings of greatest philosophical substance, like the 124 *Epistulae Morales*, date from the last years of his life. Therefore developmental process is not visible. His early contact with Sextianism, and probably also his experience in Egypt, made it unnatural for him to conform absolutely to any philosophical tradition. For the most part, he was not interested in being a systematic philosopher writing technically about logic, physics, and ethics. Typically he addresses himself to an ethical situation, and the use of technical and nontechnical points is controlled by the flow of his thoughts about the ethical problem.

The Stoic Tradition

In recent years, study of the Stoic tradition has made great advances. Stoicism is no longer treated as a derivative product, as a Hellenistic patchwork of earlier and later philosophy put together to meet current concerns. Scholars trained in both philology and philosophy are examining Stoicism scrupulously as a system of thought and have greatly refined our understanding of its consistency and development.[30] In particular, the modifications introduced by the so-called Middle Stoa and Late Stoa are now becoming clearer.

Seneca as a philosopher, like Seneca as a man or Seneca as a dramatist, has often been treated condescendingly or contemptuously. A more impartial appraisal of his version of Stoicism, attuned to the moral and psychological needs of his time, will be attempted here. But the first point to make is that what he chose to do philosophically was the choice not of an amateur in the field but of a remarkably well-versed student of Stoicism. He has been called "the last Roman who made a systematic study of Stoicism in the original authorities, and thus grasped the system in its full extent."[31] The total picture is shown by the fact that his prose writings contain almost one hundred references to the older Stoics Zeno, Cleanthes, and Chrysippus and the Middle Stoics Panaetius and Posidonius, as well as sixty-odd to the school generally and a sprinkling of eight or ten minor Stoics.[32]

He handles technical material in the Stoic literature competently. Much of the specialized matter involves the "scientific" theories of applied Stoic physics that interested him specifically in the *Quaestiones Naturales*: earthquakes, rivers, comets, thunder, and other natural phenomena. But he also explores more strictly philosophical points and distinctions in his sources. For example, he summarizes the disagreement between Cleanthes and Chrysippus concerning the source of energy that causes the act of walking (*Ep.* 113.23). On the physical and logical distinction between material objects and declarations about them, important evidence concerning the term *lekton* is given from an unidentified Stoic source in disagreement with Peripatetic theory (*Ep.* 117.11–13).[33] He reproduces Antipater's refutation of a Peripatetic syllogism (*Ep.* 87.38–40). The process of *oikeiosis* by which man's instinct for self-preservation leads him to reject what is harmful in his environment and accept what is beneficial, and thus ultimately to make ethical distinctions, is illustrated from the animal kingdom, following Posidonius and Archedemus (*Ep.* 121). Clearly Seneca's mind was capable of philosophical precision when this suited his purposes.

The Stoics recognized the primacy of logic in philosophical construction, and their considerable technical achievements in this science, partially anticipating the results of modern logic, have been shown by recent study.[34] For the purpose of analyzing Seneca's Neo-Stoicism as the basic stuff of his drama, a sketch of their ideas about perception and knowledge suffices here.[35]

The school is dogmatic in holding that man, like the gods, can achieve knowledge. The senses, particularly sight, are major sources of information, but, to avoid error, qualifications must be made and safeguards applied. Sense perception operates like a nervous system through reciprocal impulses between mind-soul and the object sensed. For sense perception to be true, both mind and the sensory organ must be sound, and the object must be truly perceptible. Even so, some perceptions may be faulty. The validity of the perception is determined by two interlocking factors, the clarity of the sensation and a complicated process of mental assent to the sensation. If these conditions are fulfilled, the external world of objects and the internal world of mind are assimilated, and man through true perception of the external world develops comprehension and knowledge. Further, sense perceptions so validated are stored in the mind, and from them reason extrapolates other forms of knowledge by composing or opposing data according to their likeness or unlikeness. It is typical of Stoicism that knowledge comes from sense perception when the potential continuum between the external and the internal is realized.

This kind of epistemology has its problems, not the least being how to determine truth or how to ascertain at what stage in the development of reason certainty can be achieved. The final court of judgment is a spiritual affirmation of the clarity of evidence, a conviction that general concepts and sense perceptions are consistent and mutually confirming. "Proof" consists in a state of internal consistency, something like the demonstration in non-Euclidean geometry when projections from the original suppositions turn out to be harmonious with these suppositions. In its theory of knowledge, Stoicism shows the weakness as well as the strength of a dogmatic system.

To reinforce this somewhat leaky system, the Stoics have a complicated set of reasoning and rhetorical devices: a complete grammar, various forms of syllogism, methods of posing and resolving fallacies, principles of precise definition, verbal exactitude, and disciplined argumentation. The most popular hallmark is the catchy paradox, such as "only the (Stoic) wise man is free," or "rich," or "a king." Seneca was trained in these technical things but was contemptuous of them when pursued for themselves. "'Mouse' is a syllable. Now a mouse nibbles cheese. Therefore a syllable nibbles cheese. . . . How childish! How silly!" (*Ep.* 48.6–7).

Their reliance on the notion of a continuum between the forces outside man and those within him appears clearly and fully in the Stoic physics.[36] Sambur003ky begins his treatment of physics proper with the conception of "the dynamic continuum." The cosmos is a continuous whole, without void. It is saturated with the principal *pneuma*, a mixture of air (with caloric content) and fire, which makes matter cohere and produces continuity throughout the universe. The active *pneuma* is the chief agent in the universe. Only it or one of its components has the physical property of tension (*tonos*), the cohesive force enabling earth and water and the whole cosmos to stick together.

The tensive *pneuma* also produces the physical qualities of inorganic substances. Functioning as body and as force, like a magnetic or electrical field, it mixes with passive inorganic matter and through its cohesive power causes the bonding of structures, making them to be iron or stone or whatever, by dint of the proportion of air and fire in the mixture. Through the proliferation of this process, there are various *pneumata* permeating various substances and accounting for their various qualities. Structures so bonded are the highest order of inert substance in the sense that their organization is interpenetrating, unlike that of nonintegrated elements of lower orders. Here in the ordered system of inorganic materials we have the lowest rung in the continuous extension-ladder that reaches all the way to the divine mind.

The notion of a continuous and dynamic cosmos requires a subtle definition of mixture. We have just seen how the active *pneuma*, itself a mixture of air and fire, permeates a certain class of inorganic matter, creates its structure, and determines its qualities. This is the most important of three kinds of mixture in the Stoic theory. It lies between the sort of mingling in which the separate components can be distinguished and the sort of chemical compounding where the elements lose their identity and form another entity. In the continuous mixture, the components remain identifiable and theoretically separable but penetrate one another in an absolutely homogeneous blending.[37] By this theory of total mixture, the Stoics are able to establish the continuity of elements in the structure of the universe.

The mechanism of this coherent whole has already been introduced. In describing sense perception, it was said that mind-soul receives impulses from the sensory organs and transmits impulses to them. More technically, mind-soul is the *hegemonikon*, the governing element of the soul, and the impulses are *pneuma* at work. The *hegemonikon*, which is body functioning as force (and usually identified with the heart), governs seven faculties in the human: the five senses, speech, and the generative powers. It is the center of consciousness and is perpetually in motion because of the constant movement of *pneuma* to and fro between it and the faculties on the surface of the body.

In Stoic theory, physical bodies are what they are, in composition, texture, and quality, because they contain in total mixture a subtle, constantly moving force fluctuating tensionally within matter. Since the cosmos and everything in it are corporeal, the presence of *pneuma* is crucial for the cosmos to be what it is. As Chrysippus is reported to have thought, "Nature is made One by the pneuma which makes the Whole coherent and interacting (*sympathes*)."[38]

The rest of the system of thought follows essentially from these physical principles. Since *pneuma* creates order throughout the universe, it is identified with God, and the two are described interchangeably with characteristics of the other in phrases like "rational *pneuma*" or "God penetrating matter." In the original Stoic tradition, *pneuma* and God are two ways of naming the force that makes matter alive, capable of action, movement, and change. Another very significant consequence of the Stoic dynamic continuum is the notion of interaction and harmony among the parts of the universe (*sympatheia*). As proof of the unity of creation, Stoics frequently use the influences of external forces upon the earth, for example, the relationship between moon and tide. Such considerations lead to the view that the entire cosmos is controlled by the same laws even as it is unified by *pneuma*, that is, the idea of universal law.

The rigidity of the philosophy and some crucial logical problems are seen in their theory of causality. Since only corporeal substance can act and be acted upon, causation is only through direct contact of body upon body or of the corporeal *pneuma* upon body. Because of the interrelation of various forms of body and *pneuma* in the continuum, there will commonly be multiple causes of effects. Thus a given effect is the product of multiple conditions, and a set of multiple conditions will commonly produce a given effect. Also, in an interconnected universe the effect of bodily causation in turn operates as cause of other effects. So the Stoics have the idea of a continuous chain of causes and effects that ultimately comprehends the sum total of events in the universe. This nexus is interrelated, regular, and unbroken, and amounts to a conception of natural law.

The notion of a self-contained system in which no effect is without a cause has deterministic implications, which the Stoics follow partway. They etymologize the traditional term *heimarmene*, "human fate," to mean "strung together," and Chrysippus is quoted as saying: "Heimarmene is a natural order of the Whole by which from eternity one thing follows another and derives from it in an unalterable interdependence."[39] It is only a step further to view the term religiously and to equate it with *logos*, "divine system and arrangement."

At this point, the Stoics come to a classic impasse from which they do not escape convincingly. The pneumatic theory serves many philosophical purposes. It accounts for the structure of matter and for the functional relationship between matter and life in the entire cosmos. It provides the basis for the conception of a dynamic, rational, purposeful order. But the ethical aims of the school are very strong, and for a significant ethic the human will must be meaningfully free to act. So Stoics walk a tenuous line between the alternatives of automatic nature (Fate) and human freedom by using a distinction borrowed from Greek medicine, the distinction between "antecedent cause" and "active cause." The former is the working of nature and the latter the functioning of human will. When a man acts in a certain situation, the antecedent cause is the sum total of all the external events in nature that determine the situation and present it to the human mind. The active cause is the mind responding to the situation rationally or irrationally. It is "free" or, as the Stoics say, "within our power."

The distinction between the two kinds of cause is illustrated by the simile of a stone rolled down a slope. The initial push represents the antecedent cause, and the continuing movement of the stone in accordance with its nature is the active cause. Both causes, the initial impetus and the rotating nature of the stone, are naturally determined; however, the second is not subject to the first but is a free agency in this respect. So man acts in conditions that are fixed by the fate of nature, but he functions quite independently of the external conditions when he follows his innate, natural (i.e., "fated") impulse to act. In a situation where he acts, he is not free not to act. If he does not assent to the stimulus of the external condition and therefore does not act, he is not free to do otherwise. His freedom consists in functioning according to his own character as it is determined by heredity and environment.[40] By such subtilizing, the Stoics make room for a kind of human freedom, but obviously a very limited kind that is more controlled than free. Understandably their theory was ridiculed and rejected. It is apparent that they valued the stability and security of an ordered system more than uncontrolled freedom of the will.

The theory of causes has other consequences. One is the attitude of the school toward divination. Foretelling of the future was of course commonly practiced in antiquity, but the Stoics had special reasons for believing in it. They, like the Pythagoreans and Plato, could accept the idea that in a universe filled with divine mind certain men could gain knowledge of the future from their "association" with divinity. More importantly, if the future course of events can be divined from the observation of present signs and inductive reasoning from them, there is a kind of scientific validation supporting the theory of predetermined (and therefore potentially predictable) causation. Omens thus become pointers to the working of causal nexus.

These physical conditions are those of a cosmos that is completely integrated and self-sustaining. It is a closed system, for its completeness is the sum total of everything it contains and nothing else. The infinite void surrounding it has no effect upon it. Rocks, man, soul, God, animals, plants, the constellations, and the virtues of wisdom, justice, courage, and moderation—all are forms of pneumatic nature, all are interrelated through the presence of *pneuma* structuring and vitalizing.

These physical theories seem far removed from Seneca's drama, but they are the most likely explanation of the universe in which the drama takes place. Perhaps the strongest Stoic characteristic is the sense of the organic unity tying the individual thing to the whole universe, just as the moral obligation of individual man is defined in terms of his relationship to society as a whole. This sense of the unity of the part with the whole, and the interrelationship of part with part, is not only philosophical tenet but a way of feeling and thinking nontechnically. Thus Seneca's poetry contains masses of figurative language that fuse different levels of existence, like man and mountain, into a picture of a unified world. Hippolytus, in his reaction to Phaedra's passion, expects that a sentient, integrated universe will change its natural order in harmony with his outrage (*Phaedr.* 671–84). In the *Thyestes*, Atreus' villainy causes a universal hurly-burly (789–884). Oedipus has to accept his fate as a necessary concatenation of causes. Divination is very prominent in the drama. Often the sense of unity of part with part and of part with whole is used metaphorically: Medea's evil is a monstrous perversion of nature, equivalent to cosmic force; when Hercules goes mad, what happens in his mind is represented in terms of physical happenings in the universe (*Herc. Fur.* 939–86).

"*Psyche* is pneuma in its driest and hottest state."[41] This definition takes us from physics to religion and ethics, with rather disconcerting simplicity. As creative as Stoic physical theory is in its world of non-experimental speculation, it inevitably seems simplistic in comparison with the ethical system, and the mind boggles in moving from the notion of corporeal *pneuma* in stone to corporeal *pneuma* as divine and human soul. However, the unity of Stoicism is very powerful. Logic, physics, and ethics interlock, just as all parts of the universe are interrelated. Their ethics cannot stand without their physics and follows consistently from the theory of dynamic continuum.[42]

Since *pneuma* is the source of continuity, order, life, movement, consciousness, and soul, the universe is pneumatic and therefore "divine." Its divinity is synonymous with its order, rationality, and beauty. These qualities are ubiquitous. The regular movement of the heavenly bodies; the beauty of the sun and moon or of mountain and valley; the continuous metathesis among the four elements from fire to air, from air to water, from water to earth, and back again through this series—all such features are aspects of a cosmos that is organized in the "best possible" way. Even the idea that the universe is periodically consumed in fire follows from the natural metathesis of the elements, for fire as the most active element gradually predominates.[43] In the conflagration, Nature restores itself phoenix-like and prepares for another period.

However, the Stoic cosmos is not merely a system or a mechanism but a self-creating sentient being. Since it is divine and conscious, the natural law by which it operates can be conceived of also as the activity of God or gods. Although the Stoics accommodate the traditional gods to their philosophy, the overriding tendency is to identify the natural order with the function of a god or divine soul. Thus cosmic order is viewed as the product of divine Providence. To it are attributed, for example, the creation of the universe and divine concern for humankind. Providence is, however, limited in that it does not transcend natural law, but is only commensurate with this law, and cannot operate to alter the way things are, including the necessary existence of evil.

So the Stoics assimilate traditional ideas to fit their theory of pneumatic nature. In effect, they create a glossary of nearly synonymous terms, approximate equations that refer to the one and only reality under different guises: Nature = Reason = Logos = God = Providence = Fate = Fortune. To them Fate is the system of causal nexus or Nature "seen as the order of events in time."[44] Providence is the order of events seen as the product of divine personality. Fortune denotes the unceasing change going on in the universe, of which the true causation is not understood or cannot be understood by man. To indulge in the Stoic kind of etymologizing, "chance" is not chance but "change."

Acceptance of the traditional gods by the Stoics is a good example of their capacity to expand the scope and the influence of the philosophy without serious compromise. In the early stage of the school, represented by Zeno and Cleanthes, the old gods and their paraphernalia are rejected. The aim is to replace the morally faulty traditional system with belief in a normative deity whose goodness, wisdom, and benevolence match the rationality and order of the cosmos. The old gods must give way before a divinity whose nature is identical with that of the universe morally as well as physically.

Chrysippus and his successors are less intransigent and more willing to utilize what is acceptable from the mainstream of religious belief and practice. So the syncretism develops. The Stoic God can be referred to as Zeus. The Stoic Jupiter is truly *optimus maximus*. Other gods and heroes, like Hercules, are assigned to different levels of Stoic divinity. However, it is significant that in the adaptation only the supreme God, only Zeus or Jupiter, is immortal in the sense that the universe is immortal and that the traditional gods still function primarily in their old identity as naturalistic beings representing physical aspects of the universe. Jupiter is the upper fiery air, Ceres the cornfield, Apollo the sun, Neptune the sea.[45] The whole drive of Stoic "religion" is toward a *deus* who transcends tradition, whose nature is cosmic nature, who is rational, beneficent, and a model of morality, so that in the old Platonic sense man is perfected by "becoming like God."

The human being can become like God. In the words of Diogenes Laertius reporting Chrysippus, " And this very thing constitutes the virtue of the happy man and the smooth current of life, when all actions promote the harmony of the spirit dwelling in the individual man with the will of him who orders the universe."[46] The dream is presumptuous, but it can be dreamed because *pneuma* is pervasive in the continuum. As *pneuma* is the source of the rationality of Nature, as it in rarefied form constitutes the *psyche* of divinity, so it is the essential ingredient of the human soul. Achieving the harmony of which Chrysippus speaks is the realization of an identity.

But the faculty of reason that man has as a gift from Nature is initially incomplete. It may advance through more complete levels and be consummated as truly the nature of the mature individual only by a long process of self-conditioned responses to his total environment.[47] The governing element, the "brain" as it were, transmits the other parts of the soul as pneumatic impulses to the seven faculties. It also moves pulsations to or from stimuli outside the body of which impressions are received. Whether *pneuma* is moved toward or away from the stimulus, seeking or rejecting the thing sensed, depends upon the presence or absence of a condition called *oikeiosis* or "affinity."[48] Here again cosmic system is working. As an instrument of self-preservation, an animal or a man has an innate sense of self and of that which is *oikeios*, "his own," "proper to his own nature." The creature seeks what is beneficial in his environment and rejects what is harmful. It will thus respond to stimuli indicating the presence of that which is *oikeios* and will act upon this assent.

For man, *oikeiosis* is complicated, crucial, and lifelong. In his early years, he resembles an animal: he seeks the satisfaction of physical needs in the environment. But his governing element, unlike that of the animal, has the faculty of reason, which develops during the second decade of life and radically alters the *hegemonikon*, not eliminating the innate animal impulses but absorbing them into a higher structure. It is according to Nature that the animal behaves in its way, but it is according to human nature that physical needs become subordinate to moral and spiritual needs and that man's affinity is with environment in the broadest possible sense, that is, with the total rational cosmos. The human quest for Virtue is more significant than the animal's hunt for food, shelter, and procreation, but no less natural.

We can reach perfected reason by following the path of assenting to what is according to Nature at every level of experience. But the Stoics are fully aware of the pitfalls to be avoided, and tirelessly try to cope with them. Why do we give assent to irrational emotions like anger, fear, and greed? Surely all our assents and acts are rational in a sense, for they result from movements of the *hegemonikon*, which in maturity is rational. Then how can "rational" beings be capable of nonrational behavior?

The somewhat less than clear answer is that, although our nature is rational, reason may be perverted. The governing element may make wrong choices. There is "right reason" and "wrong reason." By essentially circular definition, only the good man has right reason. His *hegemonikon* functions as a healthy muscle of proper tone does. If the governing *pneuma* is not steadily in a proper state of tension (*tonos* again), the governing element may at one moment function healthily and with knowledge of what is according to Nature, at another, function imperfectly and in ignorance. Reason and passion are both products of the *hegemonikon*. They are radically opposed not as discrete entities but as healthy and diseased fruits of the same tree; they are different not as apple and onion but as good apple and rotten apple. Since the mechanism of assent is single at any one given time, our instability may cause us to assent now to this, now to its opposite.

We have just used the phrase "knowledge of what is according to Nature." What *is* according to Nature? In the extension of *oikeiosis*, man's instinct for "his own" in the environment ideally expands into the perception that "his own" is identical with the rationality of the universe. However, human needs and desires often intervene. Stoicism is commonly criticized for its rigidity in reducing human behavior exclusively to rational or nonrational terms. Yet it is not as insensitive to humanity as might appear from this absolute distinction. The category of nonrational includes behavior that is not merely contrary to reason, and therefore foolish, but also characteristically and deeply human. Much Stoic argumentation has to do with situations where the operation of nature is bad from the viewpoint of a man and conversely with situations where we regard as good and desirable things that, viewed Stoically, are insignificant or worse. The philosophy fully recognizes the normal human attitudes that must be transformed for the attainment of reason.

The Stoics do not go so far as to deny that cosmic evils like flood, drought, and disease are somehow "bad," but their view that this is the best possible world puts them in the position of having to make dogmatic assertions about such phenomena rather than grappling with them freely as, say, outside of Nature or as non-Nature. In their system, the problem of evil is insoluble philosophically, and acceptance of the dictum that what seems to be bad results from the operation of Nature for the good—including the good of mankind—is an act of acquiescence and faith rather than the result of demonstration. For this very reason, Stoic literature contains a battery of rationalizations designed to account for the experience of evil in a beneficent universe, arguments that have been drawn on over the years by many apologists for optimistic systems, including Christianity: evil is designed by Nature to challenge, test, and develop the human capacity for reason; immediate evil is ultimate good, and so on. In one way or another, apparent evil is to be subsumed under the universal of rational order. Even moral weakness, the only true evil, has to be considered part of Nature's good purpose, no matter how unfathomable this purpose may be.

Another problem involves the ordinary things prized by human nature. By disposition, we prefer to be healthy, financially secure, beautiful, and popular rather than ill, poor, ugly, and lonely. In the rigid Stoic system of values, all such physical, material, and social conditions of life are neither good nor bad in themselves but "indifferent." Only Virtue and Vice, only reason and unreason are good and bad. The human importance of natural advantages like health and of disadvantages like poverty is, however, recognized. The former "indifferents" are considered "preferable," the latter, "nonpreferable." But all these conditions, whether benefits or handicaps, are morally significant only in that they provide situations where we may exercise reason or fall into irrationality.

For the problem of "indifferents," many examples were to be found in the traditional dramatic material, the tradition of highly placed, violent families and heroes who experienced conditions of power, wealth, rivalry, exile, conquest, captivity, and so forth. Seneca the Stoic dramatist exploits the opportunity fully. In the *Medea*, Creon uses his power evilly, and Jason forsakes Medea because he wants power and security. Lust for power in Atreus, Thyestes, and the young Tantalus causes the horrendous catastrophe. The *Troades* turns on the Greeks' irrational use of victory and the Trojans' rational behavior in defeat. Similarly, the *Agamemnon* contrasts the Greeks and the Trojans in respect to Fortune. Hercules' quest for glory is finally realized in spiritual terms. "Indifferents" are a major theme of the drama.

Within the limit of man's conditional freedom, he is a free moral agent acting in terms of his character. His status in relation to Virtue is like being on the lowest rungs of a long ladder that reaches all the way to complete harmony with Nature. He may climb steadily to the top—somewhat like the progression to absolute Beauty in Plato's *Symposium*—climb partway, or fall off altogether. The first steps upward have been guided by Nature, which gives him the instinct to preserve himself and to seek what is appropriate to his nature, rejecting the opposite. This instinct and the moral states that follow it by stages are not left behind but are enlarged into increasing strength of character until full reason is achieved. Beginning at the age when reason is developing, man's own efforts in moral choices come increasingly into play. His selection of "his own" becomes more or less a reasoned rather than instinctive act. Next, he practices rational discrimination continuously. Finally, as the culmination of qualitative development, rational choice becomes not merely continuous, not merely exhibited in each act at each time, but absolutely the characteristic of his completed nature. He knows the absolute primacy of Virtue. He is in complete harmony with Nature.[49]

The Stoic view of the human situation is impressive in a number of ways. It sees a development in which animal and more-than-animal qualities are in functional relationship. Man's nature is not static but evolves through a complex set of responses to those aspects of environment to which he is able to respond at each stage. Here too the dynamic continuum is at work. Also, there is understanding, if not tolerance, of limitations and conflicts. When a man acts, what matters is his intention, not his accomplishment. His preferences for "the good life" are natural, even though they must be converted to moral terms. The goal is so high that at best most men only come close. The essential role is to be a *prokopton*, "one who is making progress," "one who is hacking his way forward."

Several of the dramatic characters fit this category. Thyestes, though unable to reject the temptation of sharing the kingship, has been chastened by exile. In the *Troades*, Agamemnon has learned the transience of power. The most significant example is Hercules. As a hero, he can progress both humanly and divinely, in the *Furens* to a human kind of wisdom and in the *Oetaeus* to godhead.

Nevertheless, Virtue is a very long way off from the animal instincts of early childhood and is unconditionally exclusive. Any falling away from it is Vice. "In Stoic ethics a miss is as bad as a mile."[50] The ideal of consistently rational behavior is so rigid and uncompromising that it disparages humane emotions like sympathy and grief. It is inhuman also in the view that Virtue and happiness are synonymous, that the human being for his welfare and joy requires absolutely nothing more.

For the purpose of moral instruction at the practical level, Virtue may be subdivided into a varying number of component virtues,[51] the most common tradition being the four "cardinal" qualities of wisdom, justice, courage, and moderation, but again the Stoics are absolutist in holding that Virtue is unitary. A man who is virtuous has achieved all the qualities that comprise Virtue. More exactly, if he has achieved any one component, he possesses the entirety, and failure to achieve any one component means the absence of Virtue itself. If he is subject to anger, he is totally irrational. We may at this point turn back to the physical theory and recall that *pneuma* through total mixture produces cohesive unity in physical bodies. The same principle of interpenetration and interdependence applies as well to the ethical entities that also are functions of *pneuma*.[52] Virtue and its "parts" are all mutually interrelated. Their unity is indissoluble.

Seneca's Neo-Stoicism

That the tradition of Stoic thought just sketched is fully known to Seneca can be demonstrated at many points scattered through his prose writings. Though impatient with formal logic and physical theory as such, he is truly Stoic in following the definitions and axioms of the school. For example, he discusses the role of analogy, the combination of observation and inference by which the seeds of knowing what is good, planted in men by Nature, grow into comprehension of Virtue (*Ep.* 120.3–4). He affirms the corporeality of both vices and virtues, as well as of the soul itself, and highlights the idea that good and bad emotions, like courage and anger, alter and are mirrored in the physical appearance of those affected—an idea that will turn up later in discussing the physiognomy of characters in the drama (*Ep.* 106.3–10). The theories of mixture are reflected in his differentiation among continuous bodies (man), composite bodies (ship, house), and collective bodies (army, senate) (*Ep.* 102.6; *Q.N.* 2.2.1–3). He explains the tension and cohesive strength of *spiritus* (*pneuma*) (*Q.N.* 2.6.3–6). He points out that the metathesis of elements works not through discrete stages, but by gradation from one element to another (*Q.N.* 2.14.2). Less obviously, a moralistic essay like the *De Constantia Sapientis*, which gives the impression of being written nontechnically, exemplifies the dependence of Stoic ethics upon the corporeality in their physical theory: the wise man is invulnerable to injury and insult because the corporeal state of Virtue, filling and possessing his whole nature, blocks the intrusion of harmful effects.[53]

If it were not for the tendency to consider Seneca as much eclectic as Stoic,[54] there would be no need to affirm that his ethics and religion are essentially orthodox. From his writings it is quite possible to construct a comprehensive vocabulary of the technical terms and concepts by which Roman Stoics absorbed and maintained the Greek tradition, as a recent treatment has done for two of the *Epistulae Morales*.[55] His prose is saturated with the basic doctrines. "Everything you see, including the divine and the human, is one; we are parts of a great body" (*Ep.* 95.52). The first cause is "reason creating, that is, God" (*Ep.* 65.12). Jupiter can be called Fate, Providence, Nature, the universe (*Q.N.* 2.45). Fate "is the necessity of all things and acts which no force can break" (*Q.N.* 2.36). "Cause depends upon cause, things private and public are determined by a regular succession of events" (*Prov.* 5.7). The universe and God are the ideal standards for man to imitate (*Ira* 2.16.12). "Reason is nothing else than part of the divine spirit planted in the human body" (*Ep.* 66.12). "Reason is common to gods and men; in them it is perfected, in us perfectible" (*Ep.* 92.27).[56]

What is new in Neo-Stoicism? In several significant respects, the new version is the sequel of the work of Panaetius and his follower Posidonius in the second and early first centuries B.C.[57] Stoicism was already influential in Rome and was taught there by them. These distinguished Greek Stoics reexamined and partially revised the doctrines of the school, probably in reaction to criticism of its intransigence and impracticability. Stoicism had eclectic tendencies from its beginning, and the Middle Stoics continued this tendency by subjecting the philosophy to the test of other ideas, including Platonic and Aristotelian concepts. It is often said that this second stage of Stoicism moderated the rigor of the older tradition, but its accomplishment was more substantive and intellectual than this description indicates.

Unfortunately, our information about Panaetius and Posidonius is limited, but some of their modifications and innovations are becoming known more or less exactly. Panaetius had his doubts about the periodic conflagration of the universe. He also rejected the doctrine that astrology and divination reveal signs of the future given by the gods for men to interpret, but there is no evidence that this rejection challenged the orthodox view of the causal nexus predetermined by Providence. Apparently he leaned toward Aristotelianism in considering wisdom an intellectual as well as a moral virtue, and he may have anticipated Posidonius in modifying or rejecting the traditional Stoic conception of the soul. The extent to which he revised the ethics is disputed,[58] but it is clear enough that he brought his trained mind to bear on Stoic ethics at the level of practicality. No doubt like any Stoic he was concerned about the absolutist view of Virtue, the exclusiveness of Virtue and Vice, and the ideal of the sage whose reason is perfected. But he was equally concerned about those who "are hacking their way forward" toward Virtue and are achieving intermediate stages of Virtue as well as their individual natures allow. Cicero is probably reflecting the views of Panaetius when he speaks of the "good men" who are to be cherished because their actions show "images of Virtue" (*Off.* 1.46). We know that Seneca was sensitive to this characteristic of Panaetius' thought: "I think that Panaetius very nicely answered a young man who asked whether the sage should be a lover. 'About the sage,' he said, 'we shall see. You and I, who are still a long way off from the sage, must avoid falling into a condition which is disturbed, uncontrolled, sold to another, cheap in its own eyes'" (*Ep.* 116.5).

Both Panaetius and Posidonius had wide-ranging interests that exposed them to various sources of knowledge and may have made them less doctrinaire about their Stoicism. Posidonius was particularly versatile, following interests in astronomy, mathematics, history, geography, politics, and other fields. So he was in a position to reestablish the relationship between philosophy and science that had been so fruitful in the Greek tradition but had lapsed in the Stoicism of his day. His convictions that the philosopher must seek causes for everything and that philosophical theory must be responsive to known facts probably caused his well-known disagreement with Chrysippus about the nature of the soul and the causes of the passions.

We have seen that the older Stoicism is uncompromising in holding that both reason and passion are products of the *hegemonikon*; that there is no conflict between reason and passion when the *hegemonikon* functions healthily; that emotional disturbance is caused by the failure of the governing element to function healthily and fend off irrational external influences; and that irrational behavior is primarily a disease of the intellect and is not to be attributed to a nonrational component of the soul. Posidonius apparently thought that this theory does not square with what is known about human behavior: men do not make moral progress simply by the exercise of reason but by resolving an inner conflict between rational and irrational faculties. A sounder theory was to be found in Plato's tripartition of the soul into appetite, reason, and the spiritual element, which must side with reason if behavior is to be rational. Similarly, Posidonius held that there are three distinct capacities of the soul: irrational, emotional, and rational.[59]

This radical shift from the monistic Stoic psychology to a dualistic opposition between rational and irrational faculties has some very significant consequences affecting the later history of Stoicism. If, by the new theory, moral conflict is "natural" in the sense that it stems from conflicting elements in man's nature, if the causation of evil lies within man, the role of the Stoic philosopher is changed. The old doctrine that man is potentially rational in a rational universe is as important as ever, but the potentiality of human reason is now more complicated and more seriously conditional. The traditional tight parallelism between the cosmos and man is breached, becoming now a parallelism between an absolute and a deeply conditional state. Ethics must not only discipline the intellect but also analyze, purify, and "treat" the emotions as the main ally of reason or its main enemy. The philosopher is called upon to cure passion as a natural propensity and becomes as much physician as philosopher.[60]

One specific feature of Posidonius' psychotherapy must be mentioned. The rational faculty can be taught, he argues, but the irrational and the emotional capacities can be moved only by the irrational, only by means that appeal to our emotions, such as music, rhythm, and poetry, in a kind of homeopathic treatment.[61] It has been suggested that Senecan drama is "a practical Stoic example of the poetic purgative that Posidonius had in mind."[62]

Posidonius' tendency toward dualism did not end with his Platonizing psychological theory and probably did not begin with it. There is evidence, difficult to interpret,[63] that he also changed traditional physical theory, and here again in Stoicism the ethics may have followed from the physics. Posidonius, rather than identifying God and Nature, distinguishes between them. God becomes more explicitly the active principle in the universe and Nature the passive principle. God or world soul (*pneuma*) works in two ways. It permeates the entire universe with its cohesive power but is localized around the circumference of the cosmos more specifically and more importantly than in earlier Stoicism. In this location, it is both a physical band around the universe and an active force making the cosmos spherical. The presence of world soul both within Nature and at the borders of Nature, and its function of giving form to the universe, tend to make Nature the body of the physical world acted upon by God. That is, these ideas tend toward a dualism of body and soul.

Reconstructing the connection between this differentiation of God and Nature and Posidonius' view of the human *psyche* is problematic. The idea of world soul as the governing limit of the cosmos and the conception of conflicting rational and irrational faculties of the human soul appear to be at odds. They must have required an alignment between world soul and individual soul that was different from the earlier theory that the two are entirely compatible. One logical interpretation is that the *hegemonikon* of the world soul as governor of Nature would be aligned with the *hegemonikon* of man as the good *daimon* within him, in contrast to the evil *daimon* of irrationality.[64] In this way, the cosmos and man are brought into a potential harmony that is still viable as Stoic doctrine. However, a greater qualitative distance now separates God and man.

Despite these innovations and their implications of dualism—rational-irrational, soul-body—the evidence indicates that Posidonius did not qualify the Stoic position that soul is corporeal, even though the logical problems of corporeality are increased by his innovations. The theory once held that the Middle Stoic went further with his Platonizing, that he believed in the existence of the individual soul before birth and after death, and was even a forerunner of Neo-Platonism, is now firmly rejected.[65]

Seneca's relationship to the Middle Stoa is indicated by his citations of Panaetius and Posidonius.[66] The references to Panaetius are few and perfunctory, except for the quotation of Panaetius' answer to the young man, given above. Posidonius appears more frequently and much more substantively than any other Stoic, unless we count the old Stoic hero M. Porcius Cato the Younger, who figures in history as well as in philosophy. Seneca's references to Posidonius must be examined with some care, as part of the evidence warranting the conclusion that the specific concerns of Senecan Neo-Stoicism are much more Posidonian than anything else.[67]

Posidonius does indeed appear as Seneca estimates him: "one of those who have contributed most to philosophy" (*Ep.* 90.20). A number of his scientific theories (and also those of his follower Asclepiodotus) are used in the *Quaestiones Naturales*. He is of course recognized as one of the five great names in the history of Stoicism and is linked with Zeno the founder of the school and Chrysippus its systematizer, as teachers of Virtue (*Ep.* 33.4, 104.21–22, 108.38). In one passage where he is mentioned among the five great Stoics, Seneca is contrasting the static nature of Epicureanism with the free development of Stoicism, a dynamic conception of the history of philosophy that Posidonius held and followed.[68]

Posidonius figures in Seneca as a model of philosophical rhetoric. The Posidonian theory of psychotherapy, as we have seen, combines instruction to teach the rational faculty and emotional motivations to affect the irrational. So his method, which Seneca explains favorably (*Ep.* 95.65–67) and himself follows, employs the giving of precepts, persuasion, consolation, exhortation, examination of causes, and description of virtues and vices.[69]

Ideas that Seneca cites from his predecessor can be combined with his material from unnamed sources to show an impressive network of Posidonian thought in Seneca. A number of these ideas are on the general topic of the "indifferent" conditions that are "preferable," such as health, wealth, honor, friendship. Despite much argument to the contrary, there is no sure evidence that Posidonius changed the traditional doctrine that such states are not per se conducive to Virtue.[70] What probably did change is the role of "indifferents" as the result of the new Posidonian psychology.[71] In the theory of the Old Stoa, the intermediate conditions are neither good nor bad, and Virtue is achieved through right choices among them when the *hegemonikon* functions healthily. In the new theory, causation within the soul is complicated by the coexistence of rational and irrational capacities, and choices among the intermediates may presumably be made by either of the two capacities. So in this sense the "indifferents" are both positively good and positively bad in relation to causation in the soul.[72] In one passage under explicit Posidonian influence, Seneca uses terms familiar from Stoic physics to explain that wealth is an antecedent cause of evil, not an active cause, that is, that wealth causes evil not because it does evil but because it motivates men to do evil (*Ep.* 87.31).

Explanation of the network of Posidonian thought can begin with letter 78. Here Seneca consoles Lucilius, who is ill, recommending the usual Stoic prescriptions of study, association with friends, scorn of death, endurance, and so forth. He concludes with anticipation of their reunion and a quotation from Posidonius: "For educated men [i.e., Stoics], one day is longer than the longest time for the uninformed" (78.28). Letter 74, in which Posidonius is not mentioned, sets Virtue against external goods distributed at the whim of Fortune. The virtuous life is so complete in itself that it is not affected by duration of time. Its self-sufficiency is described in the same Posidonian image: "Reduce the virtuous life from a hundred years to as little as you wish, even to one day; it is just as virtuous" (74.27). The fact that Seneca has Posidonian language stored in his mind makes it likely that the letter contains other Posidonian material. In turn, letter 76 makes references back to 74.[73]

The place of Posidonius in Seneca is hard to locate exactly because, as in the preceding example, Seneca treats his predecessor so familiarly. However, there are signs of an extensive and functional role. One scholar is convinced that 102, on the topic of renown after death, derives not merely ideas but the whole process of discussion from a Middle Stoic source in which the ideas of Panaetius are defended by Posidonius, although neither is mentioned in Seneca's letter. The theme of friendship in 109 may come from a similar Middle Stoic source.

Citations involve other topics also. Letters 83 and 87, on drunkenness and luxury respectively, name Posidonius and appear to use him as a source of both objections in the argument and refutation of the objections. The main origin of 90, on the place of the philosopher in early society, is clearly Posidonian. Posidonius and Archedemus appear at the head of 121, on instinctive behavior of animals.[74]

There are several more. In 88 the distinction between conventional studies and liberal studies (that is, those that free a man for Virtue) is based explicitly on Posidonius' classification of the arts into four categories (88.21–28). In 94, discussing the relative value of dogmas and precepts in philosophy, Seneca disagrees with Posidonius' criticism of Plato for adding preambles to his *Laws* (94.38). Letter 113 quotes him concerning moral protection against Fortune (113.28). The range of topics on which Seneca introduces his predecessor obviously is very comprehensive.

In 92 (3, 10, 24–25, 1, 8, 29) we have a clear link between the two Stoics that is by far the most significant for an understanding of Seneca's Neo-Stoicism in all his writings, including the drama. The subject is happiness, defined as "security and everlasting tranquillity" resulting from living in tune with reason. The alternative of living for pleasure merely caters to the flesh, which, "as Posidonius says," is suitable only for taking in food. Elsewhere in the letter, Seneca uses the Posidonian theme noted earlier: "Virtue is so great that it does not feel those little assaults, the shortness of life, pain, and the various indispositions of the body. . . . It has no need of the future and does not count up its days; in the smallest possible time it completes everlasting good." The argument of the letter is based on Posidonian psychology: "In the *begemonikon* [*principale* in Latin] there is something irrational and something rational. . . . The irrational part of the soul has two parts, one of them spirited, ambitious, headstrong, centered in the emotions; the other is base, spiritless, and given to pleasure. Other philosophers have ignored the former part which is better—even though unbridled—and surely stronger and more worthy of a man." Seneca concludes, "Through reason man can lead a life which he need not regret, but in unperfected man there is a certain force of evil because his soul moves easily to evil."

The theory also appears in 71 anonymously and in an interesting way. Virtue "can be neither shortened nor lengthened, any more than you can bend a ruler used to prove a straight line. . . . Virtue also is straight and does not allow bending." Even the wise man "is composed of two parts. One is irrational; it is hurt, burned, and feels pain. The other is rational; it keeps its thoughts unshaken, is fearless and invincible. Here that supreme good of man resides. . . . Virtue is located in the better part of us, that is, the rational part" (71.19–20, 27, 32). It appears to be more than a coincidence that the summum bonum is described here in the image of a straight line and in the image of a circle in 74; the circle may be larger or smaller, but its form is absolute (the straight line also is mentioned). The image of circle leads into the Posidonian language about the completeness of Virtue even in one day, mentioned above (74.27). Posidonius was well trained in geometry,[75] and we know that he thought of the world soul, which makes the world spherical, in mathematical terms.[76] Thus it is logical that he would also conceive of Virtue in terms of geometrical absolutes, the circle and the straight line. If this speculation is correct, it means that Seneca in letters 71 and 74 is reflecting Posidonius' use of mathematical logic and that he read Posidonius closely and perceptively.[77]

However, most of the references to Posidonius appear in the latter part of the collection, in letters 71–121. The collection as we have it seems to reflect the order of composition at least approximately. It is likely that Seneca was consulting Posidonian texts closely at that time, when he was writing his own *Moralis Philosophia* (106.2, 108.1, 109.17). Letter 92 is the only extant text in which he clearly commits himself to the basic principles of the Posidonian revision. So one may ask, what is the significance of Posidonius in Seneca's Neo-Stoicism as a whole?

The effects of the new moral psychoanalysis are evident throughout.[78] In the second earliest extant piece, the essay *De Ira*, Seneca defines the motivation of anger almost exactly as Posidonius did, according to Lactantius.[79] He implies the dualistic conception of soul when he describes anger as "the enemy of reason, but a passion which appears only where reason is found" (in contrast to animals, whose *principale* does not reach the level of reason).[80] The soul can reach heights of both happiness and misery (*Ep.* 39.3–6). Human predisposition to evil as a function of psychic nature is a commonplace. "The mind does not have to be aroused to avarice, complaints, discord; it moves to these spontaneously" (*Ben.* 3.14.4). Youths learn vice even without bad examples (*Cons. Helv.* 10.10). Wickedness advances of itself and needs no teacher (*Ep.* 97.10; *Q.N.* 3.30.8). Another very frequent commonplace is the notion of the sick mind, a thought not new in Stoicism but certainly a hallmark of the Posidonian theory of soul. Seneca distinguishes between passions and diseases of the soul: passions are offensive impulses of the mind that have occurred so frequently and been untended so long that the mind is chronically diseased (*Ep.* 75.12). All chronic vices are diseases of the mind: ambition, avarice, cruelty, folly, intemperance, and the like.[81] These examples could be multiplied manifoldly but suffice to show that Posidonian psychology pervades Senecan Neo-Stoicism and indeed that the most persistent Senecan themes, emotional security and emotional disturbance, are basically the product of his model's view that "understanding of the nature of emotions is the basis of all ethical philosophy."[82]

If we had more exact knowledge about the contributions of Panaetius and if Seneca had cared more about recording his sources, Panaetius would probably be more prominent in our account of Neo-Stoicism. Certainly in Seneca, as in Panaetius, the absolute ideal of the sage no longer dominates Stoic ethics. "Instead of the best man, let it be the one who is least bad" (*Tranq.* 7.4). Now that the propensity toward evil is recognized as part of the human condition, the ideal is even more difficult to realize, and the theme of the "one making progress" toward Virtue (*proficiens* in Latin) becomes central in the practical moral teaching of Neo-Stoicism. The relationship between the philosopher and his audience is changed, becoming less that of teacher to learner and more that of the still struggling counselor to fellow strugglers.

The influence of the Middle Stoa upon Seneca as the leader of the third stage of Stoicism has other important implications. The stereotype that the Roman is a rhetorical moralist rather than a creative philosopher has to be qualified by considering his place in the tradition. It has been argued that Posidonius' revision was the beginning of the end for Stoicism as a unique philosophical system.[83] Certainly his psychological dualism implies the priority of curing the human soul of its natural evil and so leads directly to moralism. Yet the revision was a response to intellectual problems and psychological needs. The moral teaching of Seneca of course had its own motivations in his life and time, but the foundation of his moralism had already been laid. In this respect, he did not degrade his school but was being responsive to its history and development.

Both Panaetius and Posidonius probably were eclectic Stoics. In this respect also, Seneca is their follower. There is no intention here to equate Posidonius and Seneca, for obviously Seneca is no more, if that is the right phrase, than a remarkably well-read student of Stoic and other philosophical literature. He is intensely, painfully concerned about his own and others' moral problems, is a confirmed believer in the therapeutic value of Stoicism, and writes eloquently about both the problems and the therapy. But his groping for answers and remedies is only an extension of what Posidonius did. Seneca seeks them wherever they can be found, so long as they are consistent with Stoicism.

His selectivity results from a conscious conception of philosophical experience and method. In the early essay *De Brevitate Vitae*, he values his intimate "friendship" with Socrates, Carneades, Epicurus, Stoics, Cynics, Zeno, Pythagoras, Democritus, Aristotle, and Theophrastus (14.1–2, 5). He justifies quoting Epicurus with a general principle: "What is often done in the senate, I think should be done also in philosophy. When someone has made a motion which I approve in part, I ask him to split the motion; and vote for what I approve" (*Ep.* 21.9). He chooses independently because he is aware that philosophy is an ongoing search: "Of whatever quality my books are, read them as if I did not know the truth, but were still seeking it, and seeking stubbornly. For I have not bound myself over to anyone, I am no one's disciple. I have much confidence in the judgment of great men, but I claim some place for my own. For they too have left to us not discoveries, but inquiries" (*Ep.* 45.4). He does not tie himself to any one of the Stoic masters and follows Zeno or Chrysippus by his own judgment (*Vit. Beat.* 3.2; *Ot. Sap.* 3.1). Zeno's syllogism about death is absurd (*Ep.* 82.9). Chrysippus wasted time on mythological subtleties—he was a great man but still a Greek! (*Ben.* 1.3.8–1.4.6). Quotations of Epicurus are common, often as fillips at the close of letters to Lucilius. Despite Seneca's radical disagreement with Epicureanism, he is able to extract bits of moral substance that suit his purposes because he understands the rationalism of Epicureanism and knows that it is commonly corrupted to justify moral weakness.[84]

Another link is with the Cynic Demetrius, a colorful and fiery anti-monarchist who was in and out of Rome—and trouble—during the period from Caligula to Vespasian. Seneca seems to have been very much attached to him. He reports how Demetrius exhibited his philosophy by his way of life—half-naked, sleeping on the floor—and quotes his famous remark about Caligula's attempt to influence him with a huge sum of money: "If he wanted to tempt me, I should have been tested with his whole empire" (*Ep.* 62.3, 20.9; *Ben.* 7.11.2). The Cynic's extreme rationalism, rejection of convention, and scorn of luxury must have impressed Seneca. There is some reason to believe that the traditional Cynic form of the diatribe influenced the technique of the Senecan moral essay.[85] At one point, Seneca imagines what Demetrius would say if he were offered great wealth on condition that he keep it and has him refuse in a vehement "diatribe" against riches (*Ben.* 7.9.1–7.10.6).

In conclusion, certain extremes, absolutes, and tensions in Seneca's Neo-Stoicism must be noted.[86] To one degree or another, most of the stresses are related to the conditions of Neronian Rome. These tortured and paradoxical conditions will appear in the chapter about Seneca's public career, but the general image can be called up by some descriptive phrases: spiritual groping, criminality and psychosis in high places, vulgarity of taste, extravagant luxury, brave intellectuals, sexual license, skepticism and superstition, autocratic power, idealistic senators, slander and execution for profit, competent statesmen, the cult of suicide, court intrigue, transcendental creeds, the satiric spirit—and so the list might go on.[87]

When these stimuli prick the thin skin of a vulnerable and sensitive Seneca, the response is deep insecurity. He whistles in the dark, trying to affirm the security of inner peace against the threats of society. "There are three types of fear: of want, disease, and what comes from the violence of one more powerful than we. Of all these nothing shakes us more than the threat of another's power" (*Ep.* 14.3–4). "We have to be wary, how we can be safe from the mob" (*Ep.* 14.9). "To be wary" is *circumspicere*, to keep the eyes on the alert for assault from any direction. Death can come from any source (*Ep.* 74.3). "Nothing is so treacherous as human life, nothing so dangerous" (*Cons. Marc.* 22.3). "Are men only ungrateful? They are also—all of them—greedy and malicious and cowardly, especially those who seem to be bold. Also they are all self-serving and godless. But this is nothing to get angry about. Pardon them, they are all mad" (*Ben.* 5.17.3). Page after page of Seneca evinces "l'angoisse du temps."[88]

The degradation of "all of them" includes Seneca himself. On the surface he is diagnosing human sickness generally. "In his philosophical writings Seneca in agreement with Posidonius asks that the physician of the soul examine the disease and draw it to the light of day, for only then will he be able to heal."[89] But the diagnosis is at once altruistic and introspective. The Stoic philosopher never writes as one who is a sage and always holds to the view that the imperfect man is still evil as long as he is not virtuous. Seneca's moralizing must often have been a confessional for his own sense of inadequacy and guilt, and sometimes we can read between the lines. It is obvious, for example, that the growth of his inherited wealth to huge proportions, which was not unusual for one of his status but became a weapon in the hands of political enemies, was a moral issue that rankled deeply in him. Only one who feels caught in a conflict between principle and wealth would write about it so often and at such length.[90]

More important than this specific kind of stress is the moral tension that saturates all of Seneca's Neo-Stoicism, the opposition between the degradation of men and their nobility, the sharp dichotomy of joy and pain. In accounting for this antithetic quality, his temperament and his rhetorical intensification must be reckoned with, but the fundamental motive power is Stoicism itself and in particular his brand of Stoicism. The antithesis reason versus unreason is of course the staple of the tradition. Clearly this confrontation is accented when Posidonius localizes it in the natural mechanism of human behavior. Our better side and our worse side are now locked in a moral-mortal combat.

This combat is the scene on which the drama is played. All the dramatic events and experiences result from various stages of moral disease and health. Even an initial or temporary passion may be morally fatal, for the destructiveness of passion is progressive. Reason and passion cannot mingle; reason becomes contaminated and loses control (*Ira* 1.7.2–4). Once the disease has become chronic, not even philosophy can cure it (*Ep.* 94.24) unless the patient's natural quality is still alive (94.31). On the other hand, the curative power of reason is invincible (*Ira* 2.12.3).

The ultimate in despair is seen in Seneca's thinking about suicide.[91] Among different Stoics, ideas vary somewhat in detail, but the tradition accepts and justifies self-destruction when either the external or the internal conditions of a man's life make it impossible for him to live in accord with Nature, when he can no longer perform his moral function. "By his death he confirms the truth for which he has been living, namely, that his true being is nothing but reason."[92] Seneca too would agree with this logic, but it does not define his thinking adequately. The soul-destroying conditions of Roman society in the first imperial century, particularly the "higher" society in which Seneca moved, put pressure into the concept. Seneca rejects anything like a death wish (*libido moriendi, Ep.* 24.25). Suicide must not be an escape from one's moral self, nor a passionate impulse, but meaningful and rational. However, the value of freedom, especially moral freedom, is increased by the autocracy under which he lives. Suicide becomes not simply a resort available when man *cannot* do something morally but a free act that he *can* perform, that is, it is the ultimate, perhaps the only, affirmation of freedom. Some have said that men should not violate their own lives. "He who says this does not see that he is cutting off the road to freedom" (*Ep.* 70.14).

Another extreme is a visionary quality. Brutal reality can be swept away by the vision of Virtue and the wise man. The path to Virtue is an upward journey to a summit elevated so high that it towers above Fortune (*Const.* 1.1). Contemplating wisdom is as astounding as looking at the sky through the eyes of one who has not seen it before (*Ep.* 64.6). A soul in love with Virtue is a god (*Ep.* 82.1). To look into the soul of a good man is like being transported by an encounter with divinity (*Ep.* 115.3–4).

Such visions inspire thoughts about human affairs and relationships that have a long history in the Stoic tradition, but they reach new levels in Seneca. He still uses the traditional metaphor describing the universe as a political entity, a commonwealth where men are fellow citizens under the constitution of the world soul (*Cons. Helv.* 8.5–6; *Vit. Beat.* 20.5; *Ot. Sap.* 4.1–2; *Ep.* 102.21), but this analogy is expanded to include the idea that men are related to one another and to God as members of a single body, a corporeal union. "Everything you see, including the divine and the human, is one. We are parts of a great body" (*Ep.* 95.52).[93] The civic metaphor, which derived from the Greek sense of *polis*, is no longer adequate, presumably because in the Hellenistic times of Panaetius and Posidonius, and certainly in early imperial Rome, the significance of being a citizen has faded before an autocratic structure of power.[94] The new image is a compound of two elements. It starts from the standard Stoic conception of corporeality but establishes a kind of identity between man and man and between man and God that is little short of mysticism.

This more thoroughly religious way of thinking about human unity reduces the importance of social and economic conditions by which men differ and creates an idealistic social ethic. The process of *oikeiosis*, man relating to his world, is fully extended. *Humanitas* is no longer merely the quality of having general refinement and social culture but the quality of being a human attuned to all other humans as brothers under God. "*Humanitas* forbids arrogance toward comrades, forbids greed. In word, act, and feeling, it shows itself kind and courteous to all. It considers no evil as merely another's. Rather, it loves its own good for the very reason that it will become another's good" (*Ep.* 88.30). Any disruption of natural human relations is madness. "The human race, mildest of all by nature, is not ashamed to glory in others' blood, to wage wars and pass them on for their sons to wage, while even dumb animals share peace. Against this violent and far-flung madness, philosophy toils mightily" (*Ep.* 95.31–32). In egalitarian thinking about slaves, Seneca goes farther than any other Stoic source preserved to us[95] and makes often-quoted, stirring statements. "Remember that this one whom you call your slave was born of the same seed as you, finds joy in the same sky, and equally with you breathes and lives and dies" (*Ep.* 47.10).

The ultimate dream is religious. Seneca tells Lucilius that his letter has interrupted "a very beautiful dream." "I was enjoying myself meditating about the immortality of souls or rather, by heaven, believing in it. For I was submitting readily to the thoughts of great men who promise, more than prove, this very desirable state" (*Ep.* 102.2). The format of dream is apt, for Seneca's thoughts about survival of the soul lie somewhere between belief and hope, and are not consistent.[96] He ranges all the way from viewing death, like prebirth, as nonbeing, through the more common Stoic idea of limited survival, to the conception that the purified soul rises to the company of the gods.[97] The evidence does not allow us to say that Seneca exceeds Stoicism in this respect but only that he has his dream.

However, he does press Stoicism to its outer limits in his thinking about the function of God and about the relationship between God and the human soul, although technically he does not break the doctrine of corporeality. Neo-Stoicism shows a strong religious trend in the sense that God is viewed not merely pantheistically but as a personal divinity.[98] He is still rational *pneuma* activating the universe but is related to man as father to son. Man is God's "pupil and imitator and true offspring. The glorious parent, enforcing the virtues strictly like a stern father, rears him severely" (*Prov.* 1.5). Seneca's language about the relationship goes considerably beyond mere metaphor when he speaks of the indwelling of God in man, clearly implying a union of divine and human identities. "God is close to you, is with you, is within you. I tell you, Lucilius, a holy spirit lives with us, watching our evil acts and our good acts, and guarding us" (*Ep.* 41.1–2). As for the human body, Stoics always consider psychic health of higher priority than physical health, but Seneca shows "a quasi-Platonic contempt for the body"[99] as a prison or a chain that shackles the soul.

Similar theistic implications are found in the functions of conscience and prayer. The great soul can open its conscience to the gods (*Ben.* 7.1.7). The gods answer good prayers (*Ben.* 4.4.2–3). Such supra-Stoic thoughts and feelings are chief among the reasons why early Christians appropriated Seneca to their creed as one who was Christian at least by nature and why an inventive student of the fourth century A.D., familiar perhaps with the probability that Seneca came to know St. Paul in Rome, wrote a correspondence of eight letters from Seneca to Paul and six from Paul to Seneca.[100]

Exactly what produced these dualistic and theistic tendencies in Seneca will probably never be known, but there are several clearly possible sources, which may have merged in his thought. His early study of Sextianism brought him into contact with the Pythagorean-Platonic tradition. For that matter, his writings contain considerable evidence that he knew basic Platonism rather well.[101] The large Middle Stoic influence on Neo-Stoicism suggests the explanation that Seneca extends the dualistic trends in Posidonius. When Posidonius interprets human behavior as the product of a natural internal conflict between reason and passion and when he elevates the role of God as an active force shaping the world, the effect is to emphasize the potential of man for evil and the potential of God for good. From this emphasis it is not a long step to the Senecan view of a personal divinity helping man overcome his propensity to evil. Also, we have seen that Seneca was acutely aware of the emotional power of religious experiences that he could observe in Rome and Alexandria, and he must have been familiar, through Chairemon and others, with the synthesizing of philosophy and religion typical of his time.

Seneca's Neo-Stoicism shows the mind and heart of a man who despairs about the moral problems of human life in general and of his time in particular, including his own. But his energy and vehemence are too characteristic of him to be only negative. The depth of his distress is matched by the height of his aspiration to such an extent that he stretches his chosen philosophy to a new dimension of religious feeling.

The impact of the philosophy upon the drama is manifold. We have seen how some of the traditional Stoic ideas function in the drama: the concept of a bonded, responsive universe; the moral significance of "indifferents"; the human struggle to achieve rationality. But the most important impact comes from the new orientation of Neo-Stoicism, the new interpretation of the human situation that apparently sprang from Posidonius and became the center of Seneca's moral philosophy. Irrationality, the source of human violence and pain, no longer is to be explained by an obscure technical distinction between right reason and wrong reason. Human frailty lies not in an intellectual malfunction but in the depths of the soul, where behavior is determined by the interaction of the three elements, where reason and passion compete for the support of emotional spirit to motivate rational or irrational action. This psychic struggle and the victory or defeat that results are the matrix of Seneca's conception of drama and dramatic character.

4. PHILOSOPHICAL DRAMA

The centrality of Stoicism in the drama is now acknowledged in most of the scholarship, but some essential problems remain. The dramatic function of the philosophy has often been restricted to the obvious conflict between reason and passion and so oversimplified.[1] The extent and the particular nature of the Stoicism involved have not been analyzed with as much precision as is possible. Beyond this, the overriding question is the relationship between the philosophy and the dramaturgy. In order to analyze the drama as drama, we need to see how the Neo-Stoic Seneca functions both as philosopher and as dramatist in writing the plays.

Traditionally the Stoics recognized that poetry could serve their moral purposes and were therefore favorably disposed to it. They wrote their treatises on poets and poetry, complete with theories about language, meaning, and the conversion of philosophy to poetry.[2] Most of the Stoic poetics is adapted from the mainstream of ancient literary criticism, such as the doctrine of imitation, the double function of poetry to please and to instruct, the theory of emotional catharsis, the teleology of art, and the use of myth, but all the ideas are focused on the Stoic purpose to develop reason and destroy vice.

So in respect to the effect of poetry on the emotions, poetry affects the nature of the hearer by inducing pleasure and fear, which in Stoicism are passions. But good poetry transforms these passions into moral benefits when the pleasure experienced brings moral elevation and the fear experienced is the fear of passions. Essentially art is the servant of morality. Yet the conception is not entirely moralistic, for it recognizes the peculiar power of poetry and music to amplify what is heard and to move the hearer with increased effect. This effect is particularly important when the hearer is a learner of philosophy, a *proficiens.*

The Stoic definition of imitation is crucial for the understanding of Stoicizing poetry. Posidonius defines poetry as "significant poetic diction, containing an imitation of things divine and human."[3] Stoic "imitation" can be several things.[4] The poem as a whole can directly represent divine and human affairs. Or a poetic detail, such as a reference to the action of a god or hero, can convey a truth symbolically or allegorically. Or even single words can signify the nature of what they designate when they are etymologized in the Stoic fashion. The indirect methods of expressing meaning lead to a heavy Stoic use of allegory and other figurative transfers like metaphor, metonymy, and analogy. A poet trained in Stoicism uses conventional means, like traditional myth, to figure the insights of his philosophy. This is exactly what Seneca does in his drama.

The use of myth for philosophical purposes is a major point in Stoic poetics.[5] Significant poetry is a mixture of *logos* and *mythos*, of rational truth and false fable, but the fable must be so disposed as to lead to rational truth. Thus the narrative of a myth may be convertible to philosophical purpose when it functions protreptically to encourage a virtuous course of action or apotropaically to discourage an evil course. Under the right conditions, poetic myth becomes philosophical *exemplum*.

The more technical aspects of this poetics might not interest Seneca, but his ideas are consistent with it.[6] The moral nature of poetry is equivocal. Poetry can merely put the torch to our passions (*Ep.* 115.12). But he also recognizes that poetry is packed with lofty statements (*Ep.* 33.2) and mentions tragedy as a source of serious ideas (*Ep.* 8.8). The technical study of literature is barren, but reading can be coupled with philosophy as an approach to happiness (*Ep.* 108.35). Poetry—he mentions poetry of the theater—has a unique power to affect the mind and reinforce the impact of philosophy: "Words are heard more inattentively and with less impact when expressed in prose, but when meter is added and its regularity compresses a great thought, the same idea is hurled with more muscle" (*Ep.* 108.8–10). Seneca considers tragedy foremost among dramatic forms for its severity and grandiosity.[7]

These opposite conceptions of poetry are not contradictory but mean simply that the quality of poetry is determined by its moral content. The case is the same, of course, with myth. In itself it is false and immoral, the remains of an effete theology. When poets use myths like the story of Jupiter doubling the length of the night so as to enjoy Alcmena's bed longer, "What is this but to kindle our vices by attributing them to the gods and giving the example of the gods as an excuse for our own disease" (*Brev. Vit.* 16.5)?

However, Egermann has shown that myth as *exemplum* is fundamental to Senecan drama.[8] Seneca, as "a distinguished censor of vice" (Quint. 10.1.129) and an intensely serious moral educator, understood the educational power of vivid models. The *exemplum* gives "an imprint of common coinage, a rich complex of human behavior compressed into a 'spiritual form.'"[9] Its effect conveys abstraction directly. The device was an old one in rhetoric and philosophy, especially Stoicism, and Seneca was fully aware of its power. He advises Lucilius to seek models in active life "because men believe their eyes more than their ears, and the road through precepts is long, but short and effectual through *exempla*" (*Ep.* 6.5). The effect may be positive or negative. "Noble *exempla* spur us" to emulate them (*Tranq.* 1.12). "These things should be considered *exempla* to avoid, but the following are models to follow, moderate, gentle" (*Ira* 3.22.1).

His *exempla* are from various sources. The passage last quoted is surrounded by the negative models of Cyrus and Caligula and by the positive models of Antigonus, Philip, and Augustus. It was routine in rhetoric, philosophy, and literature to cull such figures from world history. Seneca was particularly fond of using the well-known Roman worthies who had become stock Stoic heroes: Mucius, Fabricius, Rutilius, Regulus, Cato (*Prov.* 3.4). Philosophers taking attitudes compatible with Stoicism—Antisthenes, Democritus, Diogenes, Plato, Socrates—frequently appear.

But of course the richest source, known to every educated person, is myth. The mention of Penelope calls up the image of chastity (*Ep.* 88.8); Ulysses, self-control (*Ep.* 123.12); Agamemnon, love of homeland (*Ep.* 66.26); Ajax, anger (*Ira* 2.36.5); Achilles, bravery (*Ben.* 4.27.2); Aeneas, piety (*Ben.* 3.37.1); Hydra and Chimaera, a unity composed of different elements (*Ep.* 113.9). Seneca uses such mythological references sparingly in his prose writings because he was a moral activist more interested in models from real life, but tragic drama of the great tradition drew its very life from myth.

Seneca in his prose makes references to poetry that bring us close to the symbolic procedure in his own poetic drama.[10] Poetry is good poetry when it can be converted to moral symbols. Seneca's ideal is writings that give "countless *exempla* of human vicissitudes, instability, and tears which flow from one cause or another" (*Cons. Polyb.* 11.5). *Sunt lacrimae rerum.* The wanderings of Homer's Ulysses warn us against straying from a true course; as he was storm-tossed, so are we beaten by spiritual storms; like him, we are tempted by the beauty of the Sirens and threatened by (moral) enemies, monsters, and shipwreck (*Ep.* 88.7). Virgil is the greatest poet (*maximus vates, Brev. Vit.* 9.2) because of the wealth of spiritual insights that can be drawn from his poetry. The last night of Troy symbolizes human life in the painful uncertainty of its own fall (*Ep.* 59.17–18).[11] The Virgilian line, *una salus victis nullam sperare salutem* (*Aen.* 2.354), is an *exemplum* for Stoic imperturbability (*Q.N.* 6.2.2).[12] Seneca's conception of tragedy is implied when he comments that Bellerophon in the Euripidean play was to pay for his greed the price "that every man pays in his own life-drama" (*Ep.* 115.15–16).

The function of *exempla* in the drama is probably to be linked with the Posidonian theory of catharsis. Posidonius' Platonizing view that the soul has three distinct capacities—irrational, emotional, and rational—carries over to the thought that the irrational and emotional capacities can be moved only by forces of their own nature. That is, they can be moved only by means that appeal to our emotions, like music, rhythm, poetry. This thinking is related, of course, to the Stoic recognition of the direct power of poetry and also explains the role of *exempla* in poetry. Positive *exempla*, whether in poetry or elsewhere, instruct the rational capacity. Negative *exempla* purify the nonrational capacities most effectively when they use the power of poetry homeopathically. They confront the "patient" with the experience of his own symptoms, which is conveyed in the *exemplum*.

The connection between the Posidonian theory of catharsis and Senecan drama has been proposed,[13] although the evidence for it is more circumstantial than concrete. In places Seneca adopts from Posidonius ideas that are compatible with the theory. In letter 88, based upon Posidonius' classification of the arts (88.21), he argues that the study of virtue is the only truly liberal art (88.2); the liberal studies, as practiced in his time, do not make a man good but they do "prepare the mind to receive virtue" (88.20). *Exempla* in poetry would be aimed precisely at this effect. Letter 95 refers to Posidonius' ideas about the technique of giving philosophical precepts (95.65–66). They include the device of *ethologia*, explained by Quintilian (1.9.3) as the art of depicting character.[14] *Ethologia* gives "the marks and signs of each virtue and vice" (95.65) by using exemplars or models. It obviously includes dramatic *exempla*. However, the best evidence for the connection is the fact that Seneca's thinking about psychology and psychotherapy is essentially Posidonian and that most of his dramatic characters are apotropaic models.

Recognition of the Stoicism in the drama has been a long process. It began early in this century indirectly. Ackermann, arguing for the authenticity of the *Oetaeus*, saw that the character Hercules in the two plays is a philosophical model and that the *Oetaeus* is the complement of the *Furens* and does not deviate from Seneca's Stoic creed.[15] Edert disagreed, thinking that the portrayal of Hercules in the *Oetaeus* is not consistent with the philosopher's view of him in the *Furens*, but he accepted the proposition that the philosophy in the dramas is uniform and harmonious with the prose writings.[16] At the same time, Schaefer resisted Leo's view that the purposes of the dramas are purely rhetorical and held that Seneca uses the mythological material for philosophical illustration in a new kind of tragic art;[17] this disagreement is significant because it highlights two major components of the drama that must finally be reconciled. It had now become customary to recognize the role of Stoicism when analyzing the dramaturgy.[18]

Regenbogen and Egermann contributed the most. The former's monograph[19] lays the foundation for a more substantive understanding. It uses Seneca's preoccupation with suffering and death as the focus of a sketch of the philosophical and cultural orientation of the drama. "Regenbogen finds in the Senecan tragedy a new form, partly ethical, partly psychological, stamped by the reflections on suffering and death, freedom and tyranny, to which the Neronian epoch gave rise."[20] Seneca's originality lies in his dramatization of the pathos of emotional experience. Scenes like the confrontation of Andromache and Ulysses in the *Troades* (524–813, approximately one-fourth of the play) or the psychological anguish of the adulterous Clytemnestra in the *Agamemnon* (108–225) show new insights into the tearing force of emotions, insights not found in Greek tragedy. The motto of all Senecan plays is found in the *Oetaeus* (*formas dolor/errat per omnes*, 252–53: pain in all its forms). The new insights are motivated by general and personal factors combined: "Stoic psychology and ethic, Roman blood and Roman passion, Seneca's personal place as a Roman of the time of Caligula and Nero."[21]

The Senecan hero, Regenbogen continues, faces pain in the Stoic posture of imperturbability, an ideal of human behavior often demonstrated in the life of the time. Since the Stoic universe is unified and sentient, human pain and the horror of the earthly occurrence are set in a wider context, being projected from earthly chaos to the cosmos, which reacts sympathetically. For example, springs lose their water, trees drop their fruit, and so forth in reaction to the evil ghost of

Tantalus (*Thyest.* 103–21). Another aspect of Seneca's psychological power is his portrayal of fantasizing, hallucinating pathological emotion, best seen in his Medea, who, in contrast to the Euripidean figure, is womanly pain in all its dimensions (*dolor*), raised beyond human limits to represent the paroxysms of a world transformed by the voyage of the Argo (and the early Roman Empire).

The ultimate degree of pain and the first step out of it is death.[22] Some mythological scenes of Hades (*Herc. Fur.* 658–829; *Oedip.* 530–658) are designed to intensify the horror of death in a kind of plastic painting of this principal source of human terror. Other treatments of the theme of Hades (*Troad.* 371–408) are quite serious in the sense that they express the fact of death at the end of life. In both cases, death, like pain, becomes a matter of subtle dialectic. Seneca is so much interested in the pathological that he portrays all the horror of a bloody death to the last detail, as in Astyanax's leap from the Trojan walls (*Troad.* 1068–1117). But death is also glorified as the first step into a new freedom, to be taken in an ecstatic Stoic courage. As in the case of pain, the effect of death flows into the cosmos. The chorus of the *Thyestes* (789–884) even fears the death of the universe. As Medea is the epitome of total pain, so Hercules in the *Oetaeus* epitomizes the whole phenomenon of destruction and salvation in death.

Regenbogen's summary[23] points out that Seneca, in his portrayal of emotion and the pathos of pain and death, achieves a new conception of the tragic, a conception unlike the orientation of Greek tragedy, which often is not tragic in the modern sense. Seneca's version is simpler, perhaps more primitive, more specific and transferable to the audience because it concentrates upon a hero and his emotional state, approaching the *Trauerspiel* ("tragedy") of modern practice.

The creativity achieved in this new synthetic form of tragedy is clarified by Seneca's achievements in the prose writings. The prose and the tragedies show the same features: spiritual analysis, clear insight into the mechanism of spiritual suffering, the plastic picturing of sickness and passion (which in the Stoic view are identical). Senecan drama is a contemporary form for it fuses Stoic psychology and ethic with Roman pathos and the preparedness for death characteristic of Seneca's century.

Actually, Regenbogen concludes, even the most horrible Senecan tragedy contains less pure rawness than an early Shakespearean play like *Titus Andronicus* because behind all the Senecan horror lies a standard of life that holds the middle ground between philosophy and religion and derives from the dramatist's own formal view of life. In its interlacing of human pain and longing for freedom, Senecan drama is the right expression of the need and passion of its time.

Schmerz und Tod has inspired the most productive philosophical interpretation of the drama. Its ideas are oversynthesized and romanticized, the concept of "tragic" causes difficulties, and much more can be learned about Seneca's motivations and purposes. But it remains the most important item in the bibliography of the drama.

Egermann's work[24] is less comprehensive and more precisely analytical of the philosophy in the drama. In general, he holds that Seneca's whole career was the expression of a spiritual personality, so that there was no difference among his roles as statesman, poet, and philosopher. All his activities show him as the *proficiens*.

In the tragedies, Seneca subordinates poetic art to the demands of a worldview, using the mythological *exemplum* as a means of education. The philosophical education is centered on the technical matter of "indifferents," the external conditions of life which are morally significant only in human attitudes toward them. Egermann believes that the central theme of the drama is the evaluation of external things: humans become wretched when they passionately desire "indifferents," happy when they judge them correctly.[25] Teachings about the ideal of "life in accord with nature" appear in the words and actions of characters in the drama and frequently are expressed by the chorus, which stands above the dramatic events, not deriving insights from the events, but giving insights to them.[26] In handling myth, Seneca suppresses detail that is not essential to his moral purpose.[27] He shapes myth and its figures to evoke the characteristics of persons and events in his own time.

Seneca's second main purpose is to engage the reader deeply, to affect him lastingly. According to Egermann, Senecan tragedy is unique because it combines the conscious use of the power of poetry to instruct with interpretation of the dramatic events according to the Stoic viewpoint. Seneca was not the creator of this kind of tragedy for the Cynics Diogenes and Crates practiced it. Seneca also followed Ariston of Chios (an independent Stoic with Cynic tendencies, third century B.C.) and his theory about poetry as Stoic teaching. So Senecan tragedy is derived from established Stoic theory. Epictetus refers to this theory later when he asks (*Fr.* 1.4.25–26), "What are tragedies but the portrayal in verse of the passions of men who have completely fallen victim to external things," like Priam, Oedipus, and all the other greats?

There are no moderate emotions in the drama because the Stoic knows that passion disorders the balance of the soul and its destructive course is hard to reverse. Therefore he portrays emotion extravagantly in all its potentiality for evil in order to cure it. Because passion threatens most humans, combating it requires the total effort of the philosopher-dramatist, and so it has a pervasive role in the drama. But the portrayal of passion is not an end in itself. Destructive emotion is a response to falsely valued external things, and overcoming this false evaluation leads to the goal of imperturbability, the prized freedom from passion. The tragedies take their place in Seneca's entire philosophical lifework.[28]

Egermann emphasizes the role of "indifferents" too exclusively, but he has identified an important specific respect in which the thought of the drama is Stoic. Actually his work can be reinforced and refined by seeing that the thought is distinctively *Neo*-Stoic. As we have seen, Seneca follows the Posidonian theory that the struggle for personal order is a struggle between rational and irrational faculties, and, apparently, the Posidonian view that "indifferents" are both positively good and positively bad in relation to causation in the soul. "Indifferents," then, are morally ambivalent and a major battlefield for the struggle.

To show the wide range of thinking about the philosophy in the drama, several other views may be mentioned. Roman elements in the tragedies are defined in terms of the fact that "the ethical and the political tone is the same for his prose as for his tragedies, and in the latter are a number of passages which accurately describe conditions under the emperors, especially under Nero."[29] A distinguished critic sees in Elizabethan tragedy and Shakespeare the organic effect of Senecan Stoicism, transmitted from the drama both directly and indirectly: "the self-consciousness and self-dramatization of the Shakespearean hero, of whom Hamlet is only one."[30] An eminent historian of Stoicism observes a trait that tells much about the nature of Seneca's drama: Euripides was Seneca's predecessor in the dramatization of passion, but he always sees the entire person from within whom the emotions rise, whereas Seneca gives emotions a life of their own and shows their outcome in illustrations colored by Stoic teaching.[31]

Another scholar believes that the teaching of Neo-Stoicism in the drama is specifically programmatic. Manuscript tradition E preserves the order of reading intended by the dramatist, moving from the passion of Hercules in the *Furens*; progressing through the *Troades* and

Phoenissae, which deal with the problems of life, death, and destiny, the *Medea* and *Phaedra* as studies of passions, and the *Oedipus*, *Agamemnon*, and *Thyestes*, which concern free choice, sin, and retribution; and finally reaching the climactic apotheosis of Hercules in the *Oetaeus*.[32] This analysis seems to go beyond the evidence but greatly illuminates the essential unity of the prose and the drama, as well as giving many specific insights.[33] In another view, the "metaphysics" of the dramaturgy, so to speak, is that "in his plays, evil is either externalized as the workings of fate or fortune which can be nullified by reason or endurance, or is thought to be caused by the deterioration of character which results when passion destroys reason."[34]

Posidonius' *ethologia*, giving the marks and signs of each virtue and vice, follows the Stoic physical theory that vices and virtues are corporeal and therefore are mirrored in the physical appearance of those affected. So in the plays physical description is patterned according to the inner state or nature of the characters.[35] Another scholar finds deep consequences in the composition of drama on the basis of Stoicism. Since the philosophy tries to minimize the importance of all external events for man, it eliminates the possibility of creating characters who suffer physically and morally without having subjective moral guilt, found in Greek tragedy and Aristotelian theory. The effect of the Stoicism is untragic or antitragic. Consequently, Senecan drama cannot be tragedy in the sense of the fifth-century drama but uses characters who are illustrations rather than living human individuals, in order to dramatize the pathology of the passions.[36] Yet despite all such analyses, an occasional skeptic does not believe that the drama is really Stoic.[37]

Medea

The dramaturgy of the *Medea* confronts the hearer with the *exemplum* of wrath abruptly. The prologue is cleverly designed to project the image of the destructive force in the play by a technique that communicates directly with us more than it creates a dramatic situation. Medea's curses (1–26) and self-exhortation to revenge (26–55) have bothered critics who find them more determined and violent than her later thoughts, but the problem is merely to understand what the dramatist is doing.[38]

Medea invokes the divinities connected with her past, particularly her marriage, and the avenging furies to destroy Jason's new wife, Creon, and the whole royal line. For Jason, she prays that he live, wander destitute in exile, and have children like their father and their mother. "Now I have my revenge, I have given birth to it" (25–26). She now wildly imagines a direct attack. Her mistreatment is so monstrous that surely her ancestor the Sun will leave his normal course and return to the east. She will drive his chariot and melt Corinth with its fire. Or she will enter the marriage chamber, slay the victims, and, if she still has her old-time strength, use the "entrails" (40, *double entente* for "children") as a means of revenge. Putting aside her womanly timidity and putting on the primitivism of her origin, she will outdo the crimes of her maidenhood now that her motherhood requires greater crimes (50). Through rage and total passion (51–52), her marriage begun in crime will end in crime.

This rodomontade cannot be interpreted exactly (despite the best efforts of editors) and is not intended to be. Medea speaks in distraction, not cunning.[39] At this stage, she has no plan of action. Her words are the first boiling over when she learns of the new marriage. The main effect of the prologue is to show the potential destructiveness of this explosive woman, who has killed for love in the past and will now kill for love rejected, who is human in anguish about her marriage but superhuman in her powers of revenge. A secondary effect is to remind the hearer of what Medea will actually do (kill Creusa, Creon, and her children) by foreshadowing that specifically plays upon the knowledge of the hearer. So we are fully prepared to experience the *exemplum*.

Chorus I is a rather pretty wedding hymn sung by Corinthian women (presumably; their identity is not specified anywhere) who are antagonistic toward Medea, taunting her with being a barbaric wife (102–4, 114–15). In Seneca she will receive no sympathy like that of the Euripidean chorus, which recognizes the tragedy of being a woman and a mother. The isolation of Seneca's Medea is absolute.

This choral ode even gives the illusion of being an entrance song. It is organic in the dramatic structure for Medea hears it (116) and moves from her distraught state into reality.[40] Thus begins the conflict between the rational and irrational faculties of her soul, between normal and destructive emotions. The process is dramatic because it goes on within a character of drama having a deep propensity to violence and philosophical because it illustrates Neo-Stoic psychology.

Episode I is transitional in Medea's movement from initial shock to total passion. The first scene is full of fustian about Jason's cruelty, her abandonment, and the inspiration to deeds of wrath she can draw from her previous crimes committed for love. However, Seneca makes her mental state still open to normal sensibilities. She recognizes that Jason has little freedom under the control of Creon (137–38), hopes that Jason will be safe with or without her (140–42), and centers blame on Creon (143). This more rational strain seems to continue when the nurse urges her mistress to restrain herself (150–51), but the effect is just the opposite because the nurse is pointing out that Medea is now without resources and must act covertly. The most significant feature of their brief exchange, done in Seneca's thrusting stichomythia, is the total foreshadowing resulting from Medea's use of her own name (166, 171) to signal the destructiveness traditionally associated with herself, as if the dramatic character is speaking directly to the audience. "Medea," the nurse starts to speak; "I shall become," her mistress interjects.

The following scene with Creon shows how the rigidity of the *exempla* inhibits normal dramaturgy. Seneca's Creon is a paradigm of the tyrant: cruel, unjust, imperious, cowardly. He fends off Medea with his bodyguard and savagely orders her into exile, having yielded to Jason's plea that she be banished rather than executed. Seneca has Medea plead her case so as to characterize the tyrant. She argues that she is being condemned without a hearing, that she knows the stubbornness of royalty from her own previous status as princess, and that the only enduring prerogative of kings is to help the afflicted, as she has done in saving Jason and the Argonauts. She confesses her guilt for crimes past and asks only that Jason be restored to her or that she be allowed to hide somewhere in Corinth. Creon ignores her requests and argues the political reality that Jason's enemies were made by her crimes and that he, disassociated from her, is innocent. Medea and her deadly magic must go. Nevertheless, Creon agrees to spare Medea's children and to adopt them as his own. Despite deep misgivings, he gives Medea one day to prepare for exile.

The scene is an unstable mixture of Neo-Stoic ideas and dramaturgy. The dramatist is using each of the principals to characterize the other as a negative model. Creon is the Stoically defined tyrant who uses the "indifferent" of power for evil, in radical contrast with the good king. "Our soul," Seneca writes (again in Posidonian psychology), "is now a king, now a tyrant. The king, with his eye fixed on the good, tends the health of the body politic entrusted to him and gives it no evil commands. But when the soul is unbridled, passionate, and weak, it passes over to that hateful and cruel name and becomes the tyrant" (*Ep.* 114.24).

Because Medea appears immediately in high emotional pitch (there is little gradation in the portrayal of her throughout the play) and because Seneca gives her language that foreshadows very explicitly, she is from the start a chronically irrational figure whose violent past is a precedent for a violent future, whose emotions of love or hate are indiscriminately destructive. The theft of the golden fleece, the betrayal of her father, the grisly slaughter of her brother, and the treacherous murder of Pelias are acts of a woman whose emotions, whether love or hate, are leagued with the irrational faculty of her soul.[41]

These paradigms are of such primary importance to Seneca that dramatic mechanics take second place. The fact and conditions of Medea's banishment have to be deduced by the hearer. Her reasons for requesting that the children be allowed to stay in Corinth are not at all clear, except for those known by the audience. Creon's decision to accept the children as his own is completely out of character. The exposition depends heavily on our interpretation of allusive signs that Medea is going to be "Medea."

The next two Choruses use the Argo theme interestingly as commentary on the dramatic action. Both are overburdened with mythological and other lore, but the learning has more dramatic point than usual. Chorus II is preparatory to III. In language reminiscent of Horace, it portrays the first mariner (of the Argo) as "excessively bold" (301) in venturing from his own land. He is contrasted with those of the Golden Age who lived in simple purity, without knowledge of stars and winds.

The dramatist is here introducing the idea that will be used to define the nature of Medea philosophically, that she is the negation of the moral order realized most perfectly in the life of primitive man. Tiphys, the pilot of the Argo, has boldly used his nautical skill to join lands previously separated according to "the covenants of the well-partitioned universe" (335, obviously Stoic language). So "the sea, formerly set apart, has become part of our fear" (338–39), that is, fear of the sea has become one of the passions that disturb the natural order of human life. Thus, the chorus continues, came all the perils encountered in the outward and homeward journey of the Argo. And the prize brought back was the golden fleece and Medea, who is "an evil greater than the sea, a reward worthy of the first ship" (361–63). Medea, like the sea, is a superhuman, irrational force that threatens and destroys.

At the end of Chorus II, the implications of destructive irrationality are seemingly carried over to Seneca's own time, when the sea has given way to any little vessel, "every limit has been removed" (369), and the geographical order of the world is totally confused. "Seneca's Corinthian chorus talks like a Roman surveying the ends of his empire."[42]

Choruses II and III are effectively placed after the scenes with Creon and with Jason. In the Creon scene, Medea is confronted with a tyrant whose intractability drives her to revenge. Chorus II elevates the status of her *ira* to that of a world force. At the beginning of Episode II, the nurse describes her mistress in Seneca's favorite metaphors, fire and sea storm. Medea rushes in like a maenad raving under divine influence, her face flaming with passion (387), or a boiling wave about to break (392). She speaks with the superhumanness indicated in Chorus II, using an inflated and truly Stoic oxymoron to say that her passion (*furor*, 406) will grow as long as the universe maintains its order. Her irrationality is commensurate with the universe.

She can still have normal reactions. Reacting to what she has learned from Creon, she muses that possibly Jason was afraid of Creon and his enemies in Thessaly. But not if he really loved her. Even if he was forced to yield to their pressure, he should have come to her with an explanation. He could have postponed her exile. However, her cosmically proportioned passion asserts, the one day she has "will accomplish what no day ever will fail to mention. I shall attack the gods and shatter everything" (423–25). She can be at rest only if she and the universe go to ruin together (426–28).

Medea's progressive mania is so strongly portrayed that the delineation of Jason is pale by comparison, and he has been variously interpreted.[43] Is he merely a pawn in the process of Medea's decision to kill the children? Or is he delineated in his own character and state of mind? The answer seems to be that Seneca skillfully combines both of these dimensions. When Jason appears and soliloquizes (431–44), he voices the fear and insecurity that Medea has attributed to him. Fate has always been cruel to him. Now he must either abandon Medea or run the risk that being faithful to her, as she deserves (434–35), will destroy both of them and their children too. Paternal concern for his sons has prevailed, and he thinks Medea will share this concern.

As Medea tries to persuade him to flee with her, in a torrent of memories of their violent past and her criminal service to him, other aspects of Jason emerge. He denies that he shares Medea's guilt (498–

99), is ashamed that he owes her his life (504), prizes the security that his sons will gain from the royal marriage (509), wants to disassociate himself from Medea (513), and—significantly—admits that he is exhausted by his troubles (518). When Medea asks that she be allowed to keep the children, Jason is moved but refuses because they are his very life (547–49). In an aside, Medea exults, knowing now how to hurt Jason most painfully (549–50).

Jason's state of mind is quite understandable in itself and is also designed to motivate Medea's final decision. He is worn out from the adventures and violences of the past, is unable to cope with new troubles, and wants only to enjoy the physical security afforded by marriage to Creusa under the protection of Creon. Heroism is gone. Security is preferable to principle. The "indifferent" conditions of safety and status have become the goals of his life.

Seneca achieves good dramatic variety in showing how the chronically irrational Medea is driven to passion by her reactions to both the aggressive nature of Creon and the debilitated state of Jason. Once she learns that Creon is unalterably hostile, her only hope is to persuade Jason to resist Creon's hostility. But she finds that Jason is completely enervated, that this last hope is empty, so she explodes in frustration. Her past crimes make her insensible to more crime (563–64). She will annihilate.

Chorus III completes the Argo theme. Its opening words use the standard metaphors (579–82): "No force of fire or swelling wind . . . is as fearful as the blazing passion and hate of a wife bereft of her marriage." The comparison of Medea to natural force is reinforced when the picture is amplified to include winter wind and flooding rivers as lesser forces (583–90). The fire of love fanned by hate is blind, is uncontrollable, and has no fear of death (591–94). The chorus prays that Jason safely survive Neptune's wrath caused by the Argo's victory over the sea.[44] But Phaëthon was punished for disturbing the path of the sun, and it is disastrous to stray from known ways, breaking the "sacrosanct covenants of the universe" (*foedera mundi*, 606, the same Stoic language used in 335). The rest of the ode describes the punishment of other Argonauts for their sacrilege against the sea and nature. The sea has been avenged enough; let Jason be spared.

The dramatic art of this whole section is typically Senecan in its merits and faults. The two choral odes are carefully articulated with the Creon scene and the Jason scene in a progression of emphasis and significance. After the impasse with Creon, the cosmic dimension of Medea's irrationality as a tool of the sea's revenge is suggested. After the decisive confrontation with Jason, the idea is worked out in detail: the violence of Medea's rage surpasses destructive forces in nature; other Argonauts have been destroyed, but Jason should be spared. So Medea's *ira* is an absolute evil commensurate with the absolute good of the universe.

The powerfulness so generated is grandiose and also impressionistic in the sense that it conveys the dramatist's realistic view of human passion without involvement in subtle inferences or logical details. For example, Medea is obviously aligned against natural order and stability because of her mania, but in the Argo theme she is aligned also with natural order and stability as the means by which the sea will be avenged against Jason for his violation of nature.[45] This antilogical quality results from Seneca's preoccupation with the philosophical impression, his main purpose.

The Argo odes are typical of many of the Senecan Choruses. The function of the Corinthians is not fully dramatic. They have no organic part in the action and no clear individuality, only general characteristics and attitudes, such as antagonism toward Medea, which attach them to this play. On the other hand, these odes serve the purposes of the kind of drama Seneca is writing, educative exhortatory drama demonstrating the destructive forces in human nature. The Argo theme is developed to show the absolute nature of the evil portrayed in Medea. Seneca is using the chorus for philosophical commentary on the significance of the action, communicating directly to the audience the lesson of the drama.

The rest of the play is a paroxysm of mania, so unimaginable that Seneca introduces it indirectly. First, the nurse reports what Medea is doing "off-stage" (670–739). By incantation, she is summoning elements in the universe that can be used for evil, feeding the fire of her passion to outdo her previous crimes: poisonous serpents and plants, their venoms and juices mixed with magic ingredients. Here again Seneca can indulge in complicated mythological and geographical lore that must have challenged the cleverness of his hearers (and sends the modern reader scurrying to the reference books).

But all this is not just for show. Serpents and plants from all points of the Roman globe, the constellation Draco, Python who attacked Apollo and Diana, plants growing from the earth in spring and winter, plants from mountains and rivers harvested at dawn or midnight, and so forth—it is no wonder that the nurse signals the appearance of Medea by saying, "The universe quakes at the sound of her incantations" (739). The dramatist is using his considerable powers to portray a monstrous perversion of Nature. The entire universe is turned to misuse as a weapon of evil, of Medea's *ira* grandiosely conceived as anti-Nature.

The second scene in Episode III is one of the most passionate and, in its fantastic way, exciting scenes in Senecan drama. Its importance in the dramatist's mind is marked by the poetic care put into it. The pace of the whole scene is accelerated by a series of meters unparalleled in Senecan poetry: trochaic tetrameters (740–51), iambic trimeters (752–70), iambic trimeter and dimeter couplets (771–86), anapests (787–842). The material about magic that generates the great power of the nurse scene and the Medea scene must have required careful study. In authenticity and variety, at least, it is not surpassed by any of its possible literary models.[46]

Seneca has taken the association of Medea with Hecate, which had become traditional since Euripides' version (*Med.* 395–97), and made it the focus for portraying Medea's demonic irrationality. In the Stoic view, Hecate as goddess of magic and the ghost world is the worst kind of superstitious humbug, and superstition is "the delusion of a madman" (*Ep.* 123.16). Medea's invocation of her and her hallucinatory appearance at the end of the scene contribute spectacularly to the view that Medea's passion is equivalent to cosmic force, for Hecate is such a cosmic figure herself, having powers in the sky, on the earth, and in the underworld. In effect, Medea becomes a human Hecate. We may fault the scene for its grotesqueness, but its power is terrific, and Seneca would not have written it this way except for its contra-Stoic implications.

In the first of the four metrical sections (740–51), Medea invokes the presence of the dead, the gods of death, the ghosts of the traditional criminals in Hades, and Hecate. She then recounts (752–70) how she has used her powers to overturn the processes of nature, causing dry clouds to rain, sending seas back to their bottoms, confusing the law of the sky so that the universe has seen the sun and stars together (757–58), and changing the course of constellations and the seasons. Such actions are all specifically anti-Nature. She offers Hecate gifts of bizarre mythological charms (the limbs of Typhoeus who threatened Jupiter's power, the blood of Nessus, etc.), items implying various evils like violence against the gods, treachery, and filicide (771–86). Finally, in hallucination she sees Hecate's chariot approaching with ghastly appearance and slashes herself to draw blood in a wild ritual welcoming the goddess. Now Hecate's powers become effective in her, and she prepares the poisoned gifts elaborately, anticipating their effect. Hecate barks three times and makes the altar fire blaze up. The chaos of Hecate's world—animalistic, violent, obscene, criminal, unnatural—is fused with Medea's *ira*. After Medea's nature and motivation have been formulated in this absolute way, no significant change hereafter would be credible. At most the dramatist can only retard the inevitable consequences of his own formulation in order to maintain dramatic interest.

The chorus agonizes about the impending climax: by nature, Medea cannot curb her anger or her love, and the two emotions are now joined in common cause (866–69). The catastrophe at the palace requires only a brief report because it has been anticipated in the incantation scenes. Only the final convulsion remains. Medea urges herself on to the ultimate revenge. *Medea nunc sum* (910). Her passion and maternal love are momentarily at odds. Seneca retards the rush of the action briefly by the conflict between her natural and unnatural emotions, but the latter have so dominated the former in her characterization that the conflict is more rhetorical than meaningful and serves only to emphasize the complete triumph of irrationality within her. Her absolute loss of reason is signified again by hallucination, this time of the Furies and the ghost of her brother. She satisfies their vengefulness by killing one child. Jason now appears, and Medea rejoices that the second child can be killed in his presence. She makes a witch's escape on a team drawn by serpents. The last words, spoken by Jason, must mean that wherever Medea goes there are no gods, for surely she has become antigod.

This analysis of the *Medea* as a dramatization of Neo-Stoic negative models is an unorthodox kind of dramatic criticism. It analyzes a pattern of thought imposed upon the dramatic material and thus departs from normal canons of criticism that assume that the dramatist creates action and characters with some kind of status and life of their own. More than one critic has objected to Stoic interpretations of the dramas as being artificial and exaggerated.[47]

However, the characteristics of the *Medea* as drama demand the Neo-Stoic interpretation. How else can we understand the preoccupation with irrational psychology in the characters of Medea, Creon, and

Jason? The subordination of dramatic realism to philosophical impres-
sionism to such an extent that dramatic details are obscured? The fact
that the dramatist moves the chorus in and out of the action, depending
on what he needs in order to develop the model of Medea? The Argo
theme as a kind of external interpretation? A system of foreshadowing
that keeps the hearer constantly aware of the consequences of Medea's
nature? Such dramatic features mean that Seneca asks us to accept his
system of thought and then dramatizes in ways to project his system.
The technique is undramatic in the sense that essentially the dramatist
is communicating directly with the hearer rather than communicating
through his construct of a semiautonomous dramatic world. As we
shall see later, this kind of relationship between the dramatist and his
audience is basically rhetorical.

Actually, in the case of *Medea* there is a clear parallel with the essay
De Ira. Comparison of the two shows the same conception of *ira* and its
progression from the initial sense of being offended to the ultimate
stage of insanity.[48] Yet Seneca is not simply dramatizing a philosophical
idea. The philosophy and the drama are so organically related that
characteristics of the dramaturgy and the poetry themselves can be
traced to the philosophy. For example, Medea shows the same physical
symptoms attributed to *ira* (insanity) in the *De Ira*[49] since both prose
and poetry are using Posidonian *ethologia*: aggressive appearance, melancholy, quick pace, changing complexion, agitated breathing, fiery
face, groans, and unintelligible speech (*Ira* 1.1.3–5; *Med.* 186–87, 446,
385, 862, 860–61, 387, 858, 390).

Similarly, the images used to describe Medea overlap the images
used in *De Ira*, where anger "is a monster like the fiction of poets, a
creature of fire, noise, and darkness; or a gathering storm and darkness"[50] (*Ira* 2.35.5, 3.10.2, 3.12.4, 3.27.2). This stylistic link is not
unique to these two pieces because the imagery used for irrationality
and reason is essentially the same in all of Seneca's writings,[51] but in
this case the link is especially close because the subject matter is identical. Seneca's repertoire of figurative language is used fully in the
Medea[52] because the play is so concentrated on showing destructive
personality in action. Massive verbal systems build the picture of a
world—not just the human sphere but the entire universe—thrown
into the chaos of dark, foul insecurity when the violence of human
passion is unleashed. The annihilating effect of Medea's rage is profusely conveyed in the metaphors of fire and sea storm. She is a flaming

storm of passion buffeting the cosmos. The theme of the absolute and cosmic nature of the evil portrayed in Medea is carried out in the total poetry of the play. Medea is the *exemplum* of a universal malady in human personality. "We shall always have to declare the same verdict about ourselves, that we are evil, have been evil, and . . . will be evil" (*Ben.* 1.10.3).

Phaedra

The Senecan plays share so many patterns that analysis of them individually becomes repetitious. From here on, important variations of theme and singular features will be emphasized.

On the surface, the *Phaedra* seems much like the *Medea*, a case of mania in an emotional, nonrational woman. However, Phaedra's passion is lust rather than anger and in some sense is due to her origin. Her unnatural desire for stepson Hippolytus is traced back to her mother Pasiphaë, who bore the Minotaur to the Cretan bull (113–14). Seneca makes her so gross as to allude to the bovine contrivance invented by Daedalus so that Pasiphaë could indulge her lust (120). Phaedra blames her obsession on a curse that Venus has put upon women descendants of the Sun to avenge the disgrace of being revealed in adultery with Mars (124–28).

If Seneca is interpreting the legend Stoically, he cannot mean that Phaedra's obsession is strictly hereditary and the result of a divine curse. One scholar points out that Seneca as a Stoic has rejected the traditional mythology and has borrowed from Euripides' lost play the idea of a hereditary curse, thus falling into inconsistency with his own Stoicism.[53] It is unnecessary to entangle Seneca in such a hypothesis. Whenever the Stoic poet uses such traditional mythology, the most likely explanation is that the use is figurative, that the dramatist is saying something Stoic indirectly. True, the idea of innate evil is not Stoic. "You are wrong if you think that faults are born with us. . . . Nature does not commit us to any fault; she has made us pure and free at birth" (*Ep.* 94.55–56). But Seneca adds that "faults are imposed upon us from outside ourselves." So most likely the dramatist means that Phaedra's weakness is due to the environment of her birth and her inability to overcome it. We shall see that his Hippolytus is characterized similarly.

The first scene is mostly a display piece.[54] In preparation for the hunt, Hippolytus gives to his company directions that resemble a cynegetic catalog. The only specific dramatic touch in the whole scene comes when he invokes Diana as a "divine virago" (54), a hint of his male monomania. Here again, as in the *Medea*, the opening scenes introduce the destructive force in the play, the radical conflict between the obsessions of the two principals. After Hippolytus has shown his complete preoccupation with the hunt, in the second scene Phaedra and her nurse agonize. Phaedra speaks of Theseus as an enemy, who is off on a madcap venture to Hades in his usual role as an adulterer (89–98). The nurse urges restraint but already knows the fact and the intensity of Phaedra's craving for Hippolytus (not even this knowledge is developed dramatically). She asks the ultimate ugly question, whether Phaedra will produce another minotaur from the mixed breed of Theseus and Hippolytus (171–72) and so overturn Nature (173). Phaedra's pathological state is an absolute negation of physical and moral order. She knows her guilt but protests helplessness. "What can reason do? Passion has won" (184). So already the action reaches the irreversible point after which no major change in her role would be credible.

Obviously this drama is poor in conventional terms of dramatic development, apparently because philosophical idea takes precedence over dramaturgy. It has been noticed that in the relationship between reason and passion, so closely analyzed in Neo-Stoic psychology, Phaedra is one who shows that reason can combat only the initial arising of passion, not the established passion that arises against its will (*Ep.* 85.9). She recognizes her perversity but cannot control it. She is not like Medea, who puts aside the consciousness of wrong, or like Theseus, who submits to passion blindly.[55] Perhaps this is the reason why Phaedra is a more sympathetic character than Seneca's other destructive characters.

However, the main purpose is to dramatize the process by which the evil in Phaedra has its full consequences both within herself and upon others. In Stoicism her mania is a sin, as the nurse indicates (143–44), and moral disorders are mental disorders. So Seneca dramatizes the disintegration of her personality, that is, the disintegration of her rationality. In dialogue with Phaedra, the nurse turns aside her mistress's specious excuses, as when Phaedra blames her obsession on Cupid's cosmic force. Seneca has the nurse give the Stoic rejoinder that "foul and phrenetic lust has made a god out of love and, for greater license, has honored passion with the title of a false god" (195–97). Throughout the scene, Phaedra is like the man for whom the experience of a dream has the impact of reality (*Ep.* 102.1). Her dream of relationship with Hippolytus has become a false reality, making her believe that Theseus will never return (218–21), that, if he does, he will perhaps pardon her new love (225), that the misogynous Hippolytus can be tamed by love as the Cretan bull was tamed (240). At the end of the scene, Phaedra threatens suicide as an act of shame, but the nurse diagnoses her motivation as impulsive emotion (250–56). Passion has destroyed her as a rational being.[56]

What Phaedra is dramatically and what she means philosophically are matched clearly. The character Hippolytus is ambivalent. As early as Episode I, the nurse explains that his hatred of all women is derived from his Amazonian origin (230–32) in a monosexual mania reversing the Amazons' hatred of men. So both his and Phaedra's obsessions come from the environments of their births. Even before the nurse can tell her mistress's desire,[57] Hippolytus himself expresses his hatred in a passage (559–64, 566–68) that specifically calls attention to his violation of Stoic values: "Whether it be reason or nature or raging passion (*dirus furor*, 567), I hate women and am glad I do."[58] We could not be told more clearly that in his mania Hippolytus violates reason and nature.

However, in Episode II he also voices the values that Phaedra profanes, as the nurse has done earlier in her moralistic advice to Phaedra. When the nurse reluctantly approaches Hippolytus to make trial of him, she continues to project the philosophical themes required by the dramatist, now reversing her advocacy of restraint with Phaedra by urging Hippolytus to indulge in life more freely. His reply is a set piece praising sylvan life as the closest approximation to the purity of the Golden Age, now destroyed in the greed and violence of the "present day" (483–564). In this way, Phaedra's passion is further analyzed as a latter-day corruption of the values of idealized primitive times, another Stoic theme.

A different interpretation is that Seneca has Hippolytus use language suggesting that his moral philosophy is only a pose "concealing . . . an obsessional hatred of women,"[59] but the textual evidence is doubtful, and the purity of primitive life is a common and serious theme in Seneca, not likely to be manipulated for such subtlety. We are left with two possible explanations. In the first, Seneca allows inconsistency in the portrayal of Hippolytus because he is using him to voice ideas considered essential to the thought of the play, because he wants to characterize the irrationality of Phaedra from several viewpoints. In this case, Hippolytus is faulty as a dramatic character. Or—and this explanation is preferable because it takes the text at face value—Seneca's Hippolytus is one in whom the active, ongoing conflict between passion and reason is dramatized.

Problems of dramatic analysis often occur in the opening scenes of the plays where the *exempla* are being constructed with single-minded philosophical purpose. However, once this process is completed, philosophy and drama are fused in stark and powerful demonstration of the consequences of the moral qualities conveyed in the models. The result, as in the *Phaedra*, is often exciting theater. This power seems obvious and gross to us now, but it is illuminating to remember that the dramatic excitement has a substantive source; it flows from the conception of characters who are on a psychic battleground.

In the climax of Episode II, love-crazed Phaedra and tempestuous Hippolytus meet. She swoons, recovers in his arms, and the two speak at cross-purposes, she dreaming that she can hide her sin in the respectability of marriage, he giving her words conventional meaning that she in turn distorts to suit her desires. She asks him to pity her love. Hippolytus explodes in moral indignation. Here too, Stoic ideas are being communicated through him, for he expects that a sentient universe will share his sense of outrage by changing its natural order in a storm of protest (671–84). He accuses her of being more bestial than her mother. She admits the corruption of her family[60] and her own weakness, using familiar Stoic language (*sed mei non sum potens*, 699). She tries to embrace him. Impulsively he draws his sword, but, when she welcomes death, throws it down and rushes off to the purity of nature (715–18). The nurse raises a false alarm that Phaedra is being attacked.

Anger, "the most loathsome and savage of all emotions" (*Ira* 1.1.1) is endemic in Senecan drama. Hippolytus has shown it, and it now appears in Theseus.[61] Returning from Hades, he is told by the nurse that Phaedra wants to die to save her honor. Phaedra, now suddenly determined to betray Hippolytus, claims that she has been violated and shows the abandoned sword as evidence of Hippolytus' guilt. Theseus blames the crime on his son's Amazonian heritage,[62] scathingly mocks his moral pose, and calls down the curse of death.

Seneca uses Theseus' return significantly on the theme of death and annihilation. While in Hades, he has been suspended between life and death psychologically as well as physically. The ambiguity of his status there has held him "between the evils of death and life" (841). He was alive only in his "consciousness of evil" (842–43). The change from the darkness of Hades to the light of the upper world should be beneficent, but he is welcomed home by all the sounds of death (850–53). It turns out that true death is not in Hades but in the psychic chaos of the passions in Phaedra, Hippolytus, and Theseus. Phaedra is distracted so unaccountably that Seneca can have her passionately pursuing Hippolytus in Episode II and plotting to betray him in Episode III. Hippolytus is fragmented by the conflict between anger and moral principles. Theseus' violence, which ignites the catastrophe, also has a long history. There are references to his lack of fidelity (92, to Phaedra? Ariadne?), his turpitude in helping the adulterous Pirithoüs (96–98), and his killing of Antiope, Hippolytus' mother, in a fit of anger (226, 927, and 1167 where he is said to be a destroyer of his wives[63] through either love [Phaedra] or hatred [Antiope]). The interaction of these passions causes annihilation that is absolute, beyond the imagination. The messenger's account of Hippolytus' death (1000–1114) is a spectacular piece of rhetorical narrative designed to produce the utmost horror at the shattering of the victim's body.

The full brunt of the horror now comes down on Theseus. Phaedra tells him that Hippolytus is innocent and stabs herself. Her suicide redeems nothing because it too is a function of her mania: now she can pursue Hippolytus in Hades (1179–80). Theseus' outburst of anguish (1201–43) seems to anticipate his suicide as well, but Seneca diverts him by having the chorus say that he has all eternity for lamentation. By putting the suicide theme in abeyance,[64] Seneca combines two results. The fustian of Theseus' outburst, with its complete recognition of his own guilt and Hippolytus' innocence, expresses a kind of rationality achieved too late, and Theseus survives to participate in the incredibly grisly finale of assembling the pieces of Hippolytus' body. It is no wonder that the execrable taste of the passage has been likened to the psychology of the gladiatorial contest, but the use of mythological material in metaphor is transparent here, and there could be no more emphatic way of concluding a drama about the annihilation and fragmentation of human personality.[65]

The four choral odes come as aftermaths to the preceding stages of the action, giving commentary on the significance of what has happened.[66] They are like the Argo odes of the *Medea* in being detached from the action but are not as organically related to the process of developing thought about the connotations of the dramatic model. Although very conventional in theme and language,[67] they have a cumulative effect and give a comprehensive interpretation of the play. Chorus I (274–357), coming after Phaedra's obsession has been shown, treats love as an evil that infects all of nature. Hippolytus' flight from Phaedra in disgust and the nurse's plot against him are followed by an ode (736–823) devoted entirely to Hippolytus' beauty and the vulnerability of beauty. It contains the poetic equivalent of philosophical language about physical beauty as an "indifferent" (*Anceps forma bonum mortalibus*, 761; *quis sapiens bono/confidat fragili*, 773–74). After Theseus' curse, Chorus III (959–88, used at the end of chapter 1) contrasts divine order and human chaos. Chorus IV (1123–53) reinforces III with the common literary and Stoic theme that Fortune attacks the high and mighty; it also points to the theme of death and annihilation: Theseus has found his hell on earth (1144–48).

Oedipus

As far as we know, Seneca's version of the standard story is original in orientation. It is centered on two Stoic conceptions, the destructive effect of fear and the definition of Fate as what is to be according to the plan of an orderly universe.[68] The chaos of fear is contrasted with the rationality of accepting what is to be: "All men are enslaved to fear" (*Ep.* 47.17); "Fear is slavery" (*Ep.* 66.16); "Fate is woven from a train of causes" (*Ep.* 19.6). Seneca's Oedipus moves from a psychotic fear and rejection of the truth about himself to a reconciliation with the truth of Fate. His irrationality is of a different order from Medea's or Phaedra's or Theseus' because his crimes were accidental events of the past, but he is as guilty as they insofar as he fears and does not come to terms with the necessary train of events.

The *Oedipus* is a good example of the fact that the Senecan plays begin at the *anagnorisis* and use the action to amplify the denouement.[69] This effect is accomplished by a fully developed technique of foreshadowing that assumes the hearer's familiarity with the story and works upon it to create anticipation of the denouement.[70] The dramatic technique is exactly right for Seneca's purpose, to reveal the nature of the *exemplum* immediately and continuously so that the hearer can apprehend the psychology—in the deepest sense, the state of soul—of the characters. When critics feel, for example, that the prologue shows Oedipus in a state that he will reach only later in the play,[71] they are right in terms of conventional dramaturgy but do not recognize that Seneca departed from conventional dramaturgy for reasons essential to the nature of his drama.

The prologue shows Oedipus' fear (again, the destructive force in the play) obliquely but transparently. The sequence of thought and emotion is a skillful adaptation of philosophical content to dramatic form. The dawn comes gloomily (2). Oedipus questions the rewards of royalty, which is exposed to the storms of Fortune. He was happy to leave the kingdom of father Polybus, then fell into the rule of Thebes. His fear of the double crime foretold by Delphi shook his moral self-confidence in Corinth and shakes him now in Thebes because the plague has spared him alone in the devastation of the city. His fear is so intense that it causes madness (*Q.N.* 6.29.2), and the crimes he fears become crimes he has done: "Could you hope to have a healthy kingdom among crimes so great? I have made heaven guilty" (35–36). The whole environment and social structure of Thebes are being destroyed. Begging that his fate come, he urges himself to flee from the land he has infected and go—"even to his parents" (81, which, of course, is exactly what he has done).

These last ironic words apparently are thought to usher Jocasta in, for she is suddenly there, urging him to face Fortune with the fortitude of a true Stoic (83–86). He reacts with an even more extreme form of fear, asserting with bravado his "virtue which knows no fear" (88). He would confront Mars and the Giants even as he faced the horror of the Sphinx. That this is sheer braggadocio is indicated when he says that he had his chance to die in combat with the Sphinx and that now the destroyed monster is destroying Thebes (103–8). His process of thought is obviously hysterical.

Here again, the chorus functions both inside and outside the action of the play, depending upon the dramatist's needs. Chorus I describes the horrors of the plague with emphasis upon the reversal of natural process in various forms of death, including the unnatural results when animals are sacrificed (135–41, preparation for the following divination scene). The corruption caused by Oedipus' crimes is portrayed as a total corruption of nature. It has even been suggested that the abnormality dominant in the play reflects "psycho-sexual tensions" in the psychotic Oedipus, that the actions of Laius' ghost in Episode II "are allegorical reflections of Oedipus' own guilt and fear of his father," in other words, that Seneca was aware of what we would call "the Oedipus complex."[72] But there is no hint of sexual aberration anywhere in the text. Neo-Stoic psychology is far too simplistic to admit such implications. To explain all the horror of the play, it is not necessary to go further than the factors clearly present in the text: the contagion of Oedipus' unnatural acts spreading into a sentient universe, his fear of his fate, and the conception of Fate as a necessary concatenation of causes.

So the nature of the horror is fully established in the prologue. The rest of the play is designed in a dramatic crescendo to create a mounting effect of the horror.[73] In the first scene of Episode I, Creon returns from Delphi with a report from the oracle that Thebes will be restored to health if it banishes the murderer of Laius now in Thebes, the murderer who has been known to Apollo since childhood, who will leave war to his sons, and who has foully returned to the source of his birth (233-38). All this is made even more obvious because the oracle delivered to Oedipus addresses the murderer in the second person and calls him "a fugitive stranger" (234); Oedipus has already denied that he is a fugitive (23) and has called himself "stranger" (80).[74] Such wordplay, common in Seneca, breaks the dramatic illusion and is more characteristic of rhetorical communication directly between speaker and hearer.

Wordplay becomes fully developed allegory in the following scene. Tiresias is led in by his daughter Manto, who describes the sacrifice of a bull and a heifer performed to divine the meaning of the oracle. The movement of the fire on the altar, the death of the animals, and the appearance of the heifer's entrails—all the devices of soothsaying are used in this gruesomely spectacular scene to represent the past and future of Oedipus and his family: the enmity of Eteocles and Polynices, their mutual murder, incestuous birth, Oedipus' self-inflicted blindness, the suicide of Jocasta, her two marriages, and so on.[75] The originality of the divination scene cannot be known in detail because our information is inadequate, but clearly the scene ingeniously combines divinatory lore and the dramatic material.

The divination is a good example of Senecan characteristics and criticism of them. Quite understandably, it has been faulted as undramatic because it has no effect upon the dramatic action and has even been considered a separate sketch not intended as part of a drama.[76] No doubt Seneca was attracted by the opportunity to write learnedly and showily. But the allegory by its very nature is aimed at the hearer, not the dramatic situation. It is an esoteric kind of communication which calls upon the hearer to interpret it on the basis of his knowledge of the story, to catch subtle wordplay like the use of the word *torus* (360, meaning both "elevation" and "marriage bed") to describe the fratricidal Eteocles and Polynices as "two heads of equal elevation" and at the same time to refer to the "like marriages" of Jocasta to Laius and Oedipus.[77] In other words, Seneca here is not concerned with the development of the action but with the effect of his language upon the hearer, a declamatory effect. He is declaiming the horrible truth about Oedipus, so that the hearer can anticipate the catastrophic effect of what is fated for the king and can be prepared to observe how he reacts to the truth.

Chorus II is something of a puzzle. Most of it (403–503) is a conventional encomium of Bacchus using the familiar myths. Bacchus' associations with Thebes may have prompted the theme. Yet there may be more to it. Tiresias asks the chorus to praise the god while he "is opening the barriers of the Styx" (401) to consult Laius about the identity of the murderer, a clear contrast of opposites. At the close (504–8), the adoration of Bacchus is to last as long as the beneficent functions of nature—stars, ocean, moon, dawn—continue their order. To Seneca the Stoic, Bacchus is one of the aspects of God, being the father of all things, the seminal force that maintains life (*Ben.* 4.8.1). Perhaps Bacchus is praised here not merely as a god who can save Thebes but as a symbol of the natural order standing unchanged behind the chaos of the drama.

The more Seneca calls attention to the truth, the more unbelievable Oedipus' ignorance becomes. The result is poor dramaturgy, no matter how much Seneca's purposes are recognized. This criticism is certainly true when Creon reluctantly reports the necromancy under Oedipus' threat of death. In an atmosphere of utter horror, Laius has identified the present king (642) as the cause of the plague, guilty of murder and incest. Oedipus is terrified (659–60) but clings to the illusions that his parents are safe and sound, that Laius was killed before he arrived, and that Tiresias and Creon are plotting against him. His irrationality has reached its peak when he continues to resist his fate after the evidence of his guilt has become irrefutable.[78] Creon gives the right Stoic advice, that Oedipus must now bear his lot (681), but the king's bravado and pride have mounted so high that he claims, "My soul is better known to itself than to the gods" (766–67). In Stoic thinking, such moral egotism is ultimate evil.

The denouement is the most creative part of the play, both dramatically and philosophically. After the final pieces of evidence have come out, Oedipus excoriates himself with the eloquence of desperation, in which Seneca's rhetoric is highly skilled: "Gape open, earth . . . criminal of the age, anathema to the gods, destroyer of sacred law" (868–78). He leaves the scene urging himself to do something worthy of his crimes.

The reconciliation with Fate is developed gradually. First Seneca uses the chorus to present the conventional theme that the best adjustment to Fate is to follow a middle course of moderation (*media . . . via*, 890–91). Then the messenger reports that Oedipus entered the palace bent on death but in agonized reasoning has determined that death would be inadequate atonement for his several crimes. If only there could be another reversal of nature in his case, so that the experience of birth and death would be continuous. At least he should choose "a long death" (949). His weeping suggests the self-blinding, an act portrayed as a horrible act of passion but nonetheless considered heroic. It has been noticed that Oedipus' behavior here closely parallels the situations analyzed by the philosopher making the point that "indifferents" are often rejected in impulsive passion, just as they are always rejected by Virtue (*Ep.* 76.20–21).[79] The self-blinding is not an act of Virtue, but it is admirable because Oedipus rejects the fear of pain and performs an act that Virtue would have chosen. For this reason, Oedipus can indeed say, "I have now acted justly, I have paid my debt" (976).

The specific Stoic content continues in the thought about Fate expressed in the following Chorus. Its theme is much more than the inescapability of Fate. The distaff of Lachesis holds the threads of human experience and human action that come from heaven (983–86). "God may not change things which are woven from their causes" (989–90); or, as the philosopher writes, "Fate is woven from a series of causes" (*Ep.* 19.6). Many, like Oedipus, are harmed by the very fear of Fate, "many have come to their fate while fearing Fate" (993–94). Fate is not merely inescapable. It is order (992), it is divine.

This poetic version of technical Stoicism raises logical questions. One scholar notes the apparent anomaly that, in the case of Oedipus, Fate conceived Stoically becomes a malignant force because it is fused with the persistent effect of a curse; and he also questions the words of the chorus just quoted, whether they mean that Oedipus and Jocasta would have done better to bear resignedly the crimes as fated.[80] These questions are a fair challenge to Stoicism, which has trouble with the issue of Fate and human freedom. Presumably Seneca the Stoic would reply that the workings of the mechanism of Fate are not to be questioned and that the attitudes of Oedipus and Jocasta toward Fate are more significant morally than what Fate has in store for them. However, in the play Seneca is using the Oedipus myth to dramatize only the ideas that Fate is a divine mechanism and that fear and rejection of it are evil.

Further, the blinding is not an isolated act but part of a moral process. When Oedipus appears, he is satisfied that his self-punishment is just (998–1003). When Jocasta joins him, he rejects their relationship and any communication between them, banishing one of them to a different world if another world exists (1015–18). This absolute repudiation leads Jocasta to realize that she shares his guilt and must share his punishment. She stabs herself with the sword with which he killed Laius. He recognizes that she has died for his sin (1045). Thus Oedipus has completed the process of atonement, is reconciled with the moral universe, and is able to reassure his plague-ridden city that there is hope in its future as he takes the forces of destruction with him into exile (1052–61). A very Stoic and impressive close.

The dramatic problems of the play have been noted, but by and large *Oedipus* is a successful dramatization of Stoic thought about Fate, really a companion piece of the essay *De Providentia*. The classic example of Oedipus is ideally suited to the presentation of Stoic doctrine. Fate can be represented as unqualifiedly absolute because the double crime of Oedipus is circumstantial. Fear is a natural result of his ignorance. The plague conveys the idea of corrupted nature. The original prophecy of Apollo, the later one reported by Creon, the divination scene, and even the necromancy are all in tune with the Stoic acceptance of prophecy. For all these reasons, the play is one of Seneca's more successful efforts in writing philosophical drama.

Phoenissae

Little analysis of this "play" is possible because it is fragmentary. It consists of an Oedipus-Antigone section and a section featuring Jocasta and her warring sons; it also lacks choral passages. The problem is even worse because efforts to show that the two sections belong to a single play[81] are not conclusive. The presence of Antigone with Oedipus as the inseparable guide of his wanderings in the first section is hard to reconcile with her presence in Thebes with Jocasta. The second part fits the tradition of "Phoenissae" as it is known from Euripides, but the first does not because Oedipus and Antigone are not just leaving for exile but apparently have been wandering in the vicinity of Thebes for some time. Only the themes of the separate parts can be analyzed with any confidence.

Suicide is the major theme of the first part. Oedipus, as Seneca imagines him here, is deranged by the pollution of his crimes. Contrary to the close of the *Oedipus*, he has not come to terms with his past or present state and even fears that Antigone may be the next victim of his unnatural acts (49–50). His suicidal passion is surely the *libido moriendi* condemned by the philosopher. Stoic language about the pros and cons of suicide is used when Oedipus asserts that he is free to choose life or death (103–4) and that God has wisely provided many ways to die (151–53; compare, for example, *Ep.* 70.14); and when Antigone urges her father to overcome his present troubles by recovering the courage he once had (77–79) and defines *virtus* as the opposite of Oedipus' fear of life, as the spirit to face great misfortunes (190–92). At the end of this section, Oedipus agrees to do whatever Antigone bids, even to live (319). Apparently Oedipus has arrived at the understanding that Seneca found in his own experience, deciding to live because his father could not bear his death (*Ep.* 78.2). Elsewhere (*Ep.* 104.3) the philosopher illustrates "good emotions" by the decision to continue life for the sake of loved ones. Oedipus has surmounted his cowardice.

A second theme is Oedipus' hatred of his sons, the opposite of Antigone's loving-kindness and in Stoic terms another aspect of evil (*Ep.* 106.6). His hate and condemnation of them are so absolute that he believes he has sired sons who alone can outdo his own crimes (273–74). On this point also, Antigone is an *exemplum* of Virtue, set off against the faulty attitudes of her father and the criminal passions of her brothers. She urges Oedipus to live because he alone can control the madness of his sons and restore peace in the city (288–94). Oedipus himself recognizes that only Antigone can "moderate cruel emotions and teach *pietas* in our house" (309–11). Antigone alone has the quality of *pietas*, which cannot exist without Virtue (*Ep.* 74.12).

Antigone's virtue is the only substantive link between the two parts, and it may account for the shift from her presence with Oedipus to her presence in Thebes. Since Oedipus refuses to intervene in Thebes (347–62), perhaps she goes in his stead. Jocasta refers to Antigone's *pietas* as a force of reconciliation (536–37). However, in the text as we have it, Antigone makes no appeal to her brothers, and it is obvious that the insensate passions and unprincipled ambitions of the brothers will allow no reconciliation.

Despite the limitations of the text, the philosophical thrust of both parts is clear. Seneca has converted the traditional heroism of Antigone to Stoic Virtue. He is working with the Stoic absolutes of reason and passion, using Antigone's familial goodness as a positive *exemplum* versus the psychological agonies of her father and mother and the moral nihilism of her brothers.

Thyestes

The nature of the evil in this gruesome but successful play is shown in the prologue. The Fury (*Furia*) lashes up the spirit of the ghost of Tantalus to inspire the criminal family with madness (*furiis*, 24). Here again Seneca is using the old mythology metaphorically. Tantalus is portrayed as a model of a vicious family, and when Fury supernaturally forces him to incite the loathsome actions of Atreus, anticipated in full detail (57–66), we have a powerful *exemplum* not merely of a particular kind of irrationality but of *furor* itself, the totality of human bestiality as an active force.[82]

The chorus in this play also functions both within and outside the action. In Chorus I it responds directly to the impending chaos and prays that some divinity who loves the city and its land will come to stop the everlasting hunger and thirst of the Tantalids. But Atreus' enormous villainy appears immediately in Episode I, where an attendant is used as a foil to show the complete obliteration of reason in his master.[83]

Atreus' *furor* is manifold. The aspect first presented, and apparently the primary motivation, is his lust for power. His wrong estimate of the "indifferent," political power has destroyed his rationality and made him vengeful, angry, violent, and aggressive (176–204). Images of false things drive him mad (*Tranq.* 12.5). The point is apparently very important to Seneca, perhaps because of his own political experience, and he explores it in some depth by an exchange between Atreus and the questioning attendant. Atreus defines kingship as absolutely unprincipled, self-indulgent tyranny (204–17), the antithesis of Seneca's ideals in the *De Clementia*.[84] His rejection of all moral standards (217–18) exposes his whole being and turns all his energy to evil, to passion so monstrous that he feels it as a force outside himself driving him on to something unknown (260–62).[85] The force is an agent of chaos, anti-Nature, for the ground rumbles, the clear sky thunders, the house creaks, and the household gods avert their faces (262–65). Under its influence, Atreus is moved to a vision of the children slaughtered and served up to the father (281–83). The plot to entrap Thyestes is based on Atreus' cynical calculation that the exile will be enticed to return to Argos by his own thirst for power and his sons' discontent.

Chorus II in a limited sense is part of the action because the chorus has been taken in by the apparent prospect of reconciliation between Atreus and Thyestes. But essentially the chorus is functioning externally, philosophizing about the implications of the passion for political power. The theme—the common man's view of kingship—is conventional and is developed conventionally, with many echoes of Horace. The brothers' violent rivalry for the throne is *furor* (339), "unchecked ambition" (350), whereas true kingship lies in qualities of the mind (*mens . . . bona*, 380): acceptance of Fate (367–68), an internal royalty that man can give himself (390). The chorus chooses to die in contented obscurity; the power-hungry man, known to all, dies without the most precious thing, knowledge of himself (401–3).

These ideas obviously relate to Atreus[86] but are even more central to the play. It turns out that Thyestes too, though the victim of his brother's *furor*, has not gained Stoic self-knowledge and for that reason becomes vulnerable. Seneca is interpreting the grisly story in terms of the destructive realities of political ambition that violate the cardinal Stoic value of self-knowledge.

Thyestes is a more subtle dramatic creation because, like Jason and Hippolytus, he is not of a completely negative type. He is a *proficiens* who does not reach the goal of rationality. His adjustment to exile has opened his eyes to the illusoriness of regal power (412–20) but not to the point of rational strength that can reject the delusion of others.[87] His immature son Tantalus is able to persuade him to put aside his rational misgivings (423–28), his recognition that "a great kingdom is the ability to be satisfied without kingdom" (470). His thirst for power is not completely quenched, so he succumbs to young Tantalus' opportunism and folly. The brothers have a reconciliation that is a mockery.

Atreus' every word is a deception. Thyestes crawls before him, admitting his crimes of the past and consenting only reluctantly to be crowned jointly with his brother. Atreus, who has been given charge of Thyestes' sons, "will now offer the appointed victims to the gods" (545).

In Chorus III Seneca writes an effective hyperbole that heightens the irony of the reconciliation and prepares the way for the ugly catastrophe by its bizarre manner. It is both internal and external to the action because the chorus's optimistic reaction to the reconciliation has to be reversed in meaning to catch the dramatist's commentary on the action. The irony is hinted in the opening words: "Is anyone to believe this?" (546). The brothers are reunited by the power of piety and love (549–51). Peace reigns in Mycenae like a calm sea after a violent storm. The true meaning for the hearer obviously is that the brothers' relationship is the antithesis of these redeeming qualities. In this way, Seneca is able to call attention to the values for which the brothers are negative models. At the same time, he indicates the unreality of the chorus's hopes by its initial incredulous question and in philosophical terms by its concluding thought that pleasure and power are vulnerable to the conditions of Fate and Fortune (596–622).

The two stages of the catastrophe are a crescendo of horror. These episodes, the most hideous in Senecan drama, call up the utmost dramatic power to convey the utmost degradation. First, under the questions of the chorus, the messenger reports how Atreus has butchered and cooked the three sons of Thyestes. Seneca organizes the details so that the murders are an infernal sacrifice,[88] a kind of Walpurgis Night. They are committed in a Tantalid Hades, a mysterious sanctum containing trophies of the family's crimes, a grove with trees of death, and a pool like the Styx where spirits walk and ghosts shriek (650–82). And Atreus is the priest (691), standing before the decorated altar with all the paraphernalia of a proper sacrifice, tying up the boys like animals, chanting the song of death, undisturbed by ominous portents. He kills like an animal (707–11, 732–36). Conversely, young Tantalus dies like a Stoic, self-secure, making no appeal, falling upon Atreus in lifeless condemnation (720–25). But this is a "proper" rite. The slaying of the victims is followed by divination from inspection of the entrails (755–58) and preparation for the communion feast! The ritualistic preparation of the sacrificial meat for feasting and communion with the god becomes a sickening barbecue.

Why did Seneca compose such a scene? No doubt rhetorical penchant for vivid description (*enargia*) and his time's inurement to physical violence have something to do with the answer, but every reader of his Neo-Stoicism knows the realistic description of the effects of passion found in an essay like the *De Ira*. Atreus' acts are shown so horribly because his passion is horrible. They are shown so horribly so that the hearer will feel horror and thus aversion to such nonhuman behavior.

The format of the infernal sacrifice has its own purposes. In Stoicism, Hades becomes a metaphor for moral death, for the irrationality, violence, and degradation that are the death of the human soul.[89] And a sacred rite (695) so degenerate that it terrifies the gods (704–5) is the ultimate desecration of religion.

Seneca's religion is of course not conventional religion. Stoic divinity is synonymous with the universe. So the divine reaction to Atreus' sacrilege is a colossal protest from the universe, an upheaval of Nature. The messenger has reported the coming of night at midday (776–78). Chorus IV describes a universal hurly-burly, making good use of Seneca's whole battery of mythological lore. Phoebus has disappeared. Vesper is not ready to appear. The farmer is amazed that supper time has come so soon. Why? Are the Giants again at war with Olympus? The alternations of the universe are gone (813). Sunrise and sunset are confounded. No stars, no moon. Will gods and men again be buried in shapeless chaos (831–32)? No more order. The constellations of the zodiac will fall. Finally (here the chorus clearly speaks Stoicism), is this the last day of the universe? If so, there is no cause for fear since we and the universe die together (875–84).

But Atreus is his own grotesque universe: "I walk on a level with the stars and proudly tower into the lofty sky" (885–86). In his megalomania, he dismisses the gods because he has accomplished what he prayed for (888) and relishes the darkness because it banishes any sense of shame (891–92). Yet he wishes he could force the gods to stay to see his revenge (893–95). With abominable sadism, he anticipates not merely Thyestes' pain but also the process of pain coming over his victim (907). He is god of gods and king of kings (911–12)!

The final scene is an absolute bedlam. Before Thyestes learns the truth, he is maudlin, drunkenly tries to be festive, and weeps either from fear or joy. Seneca gives Atreus lines of frightful *double entente* to the effect that Thyestes will never be separated from his sons. Thyestes is unable to drink from the ceremonial cup containing their blood. The darkness increases. His insides rumble and cry out. When the truth is out, the two scream at each other. While Atreus gloats, Thyestes calls upon the universe to crash down upon this chaos.

Seneca's *Thyestes* is the only ancient play on this theme surviving, so we do not know what other dramatists did with the subject. But surely Seneca's version is legitimate in its own right because his purpose is to show the horror of human degeneracy. To that end he powerfully exploits the potentiality of the dismal theme.

Troades

This play has been much discussed because it is one of the most popular Senecan dramas, but has a disjointed structure often criticized for its contradictions and gaps.[90] In part, the disjunction results from the way in which the rhetorical dramatist composes, in scenes concentrated upon a separate highlighted effect as in a *controversia* or a *suasoria*. This characteristic is more pronounced in the *Troades* because it has more dramatis personae. The purpose of its larger scale of characters and events is to interrelate two groups, the Trojans and the Greeks, in their experience of the fleeting and corrupting nature of military and political power. We see the Greeks acting and the Trojans suffering. The relationship between these two states constitutes the unity of the piece.[91]

The Stoic view that temporal power is illusory and "indifferent" appears immediately in Hecuba's first words of the prologue: "Whoever puts his trust in royalty and plays the mighty master in his great court, not fearing the changeful gods, but credulously believing in his prosperity, let him look to me and you, Troy. Fortune has never given stronger proofs of how crumbling the ground on which the high and mighty stand" (1–6). Hecuba is synonymous with Troy as an *exemplum* of the agony that is the price of commitment to unstable and amoral values.

The pain of the Trojan experience is projected intensely in Hecuba's prologue speech blending with the following *kommos* serving as *parodos*, truly a dirge in which Hecuba and the Trojan women alternately beat their bodies in grief for Troy, Hector, Priam, and themselves. The concentration on the portrayal of Trojan suffering effectively begins the crescendo achieved in the play as a whole.[92]

The opening introduces also a larger picture of the victors' irrationality and of rational responses to defeat. Hecuba describes the Greeks as insatiable in their plundering of the city and insecure about the reality of their victory (18–27). She recognizes that life is ending for her, just as it has ended for Troy and Priam (41–54). Priam is ultimately secure in death and should be called "happy Priam" (144, 157), having taken his dying kingdom with him (158, 162–64). Positive implications of behavior in defeat will become a major feature of the play.

In the two scenes of Episode I, the dramatist is so much interested in epideictic and apotropaic effects that he has made dramatic problems. First the herald Talthybius reports the spectacular appearance of the ghost of Achilles bursting through the barrier of death to demand the sacrifice of Polyxena on his tomb as the price of the safe departure of the Greeks from Troy. Then Achilles' son Pyrrhus and Agamemnon appear, debating the merits of Achilles' demand. After a hot argument, Agamemnon calls Calchas to decide the issue. Calchas confirms Achilles' demand. So nothing has been accomplished dramatically by the debate and the two scenes stand imperfectly related.

Obviously, Seneca is most interested in exposing the characters of the Greek princes.[93] He has used the two characters to contrast the moderation of Agamemnon and the mania of Pyrrhus. Agamemnon can be considered a *proficiens*. He regrets the violence and arrogance of his past (266–67), has learned that good fortune is transient (268–70) and that royal power is empty (271–73), and wants to save Troy from complete oblivion (277–87). Yet he allows himself to be drawn into an insulting match with Pyrrhus and, like Thyestes, is unable to follow his new principles and withstand the external pressures of traditional religion and traditional soothsaying. The ambivalence of his nature sharpens the picture of Pyrrhus' irrationality—wrathful, murderous, and absolutely addicted to the illusion that might makes right (335). The dramaturgy is faulty, but the philosophical point is strong.

Chorus II is mystifying but helps to explain Seneca's composition. It is one of the more successful Senecan choral passages, brief, uncluttered, and direct. The chorus skeptically asks if there is any truth in the myth of afterlife and develops the theme that there is no personal immortality. Does human misery continue even after death (376–77)? "After death there is nothing, and death itself is nothing, merely the last marker of a swift course" (397–98). Death destroys the soul as well as the body. "Do you ask where you are to lie after death? Where things not born lie" (407–8). The Stoic denial of personal afterlife and the doctrine of the soul's corporeality are unmistakable here. As we have seen, Seneca mainly follows these doctrines, although he has dreams going beyond them. The words of the chorus can be paralleled in his prose writings, for example: "Death . . . restores us to that place in which we lay before birth" (*Cons. Marc.* 19.5).

The passage can be taken as a consolation to the Trojans in their passion, but on the surface the denial of afterlife is out of joint with the preceding scenes concerning the return of Achilles' ghost and with the following appearance of the dead Hector to Andromache. Explaining the dislocation as the result of using traditional material in the surrounding scenes is inadequate. Other explanations are too contrived.[94] It is simpler to follow the evidence already met, showing that the Senecan chorus serves a movable function depending upon what the dramatist wants to communicate to his audience. So here the chorus, which has been an integral part of the action, is withdrawn from the action to comment on an issue that is very important in the attitude of Stoicism toward traditional religion and mythical material based on that tradition. The dramatic format is ruptured to make room for interpretation that Seneca considers essential to the philosophical purposes of his drama.

The crescendo now mounts. We have seen the Trojans and the Greeks separately. We now see them and their moralities interacting. To this end Seneca creates a scene that is his greatest dramatic success and is perhaps the most successful that can be achieved through a dramatic art limited by his moralistic purposes: the confrontation of Andromache and Ulysses. Calchas has reported that Astyanax will be executed (365–70). Andromache, warned by the ghost of Hector that their son is in danger, seeks a place to hide him. She is unable to follow her spirit and join Hector in death because of her maternal responsibility and love (418–25). She agonizingly decides to hide the boy in his father's tomb. Ulysses appears to take Astyanax to his death.

Ulysses is well drawn, the soldier doing the ugly job of eliminating a threat to Greek security. Andromache makes the correct diagnosis when she describes the victors' violence as the product of anger and fear (586). Ulysses poses as an unwilling emissary (524–28) and professes sympathy (545–50, 736, 762–65), but he himself is just as insecure as the rest of the Greeks (535, 548–50, 592–93). He ruthlessly threatens to get the truth from Andromache by torture and coolly manipulates her emotions. After lying that the boy is dead and defying the threat of torture, she is unable to conceal her anguish for the boy's life and gives in to the threat that Hector's tomb will be destroyed if Astyanax is dead, that is, to the threat that both the sanctity of the tomb and the life of the boy will be destroyed together.[95] Admittedly, Andromache's dilemma is as artificial as a situation in a declamatory exercise. Even so, Seneca has succeeded in conveying dramatically an exciting confrontation of pure natural emotion and egoistic cruelty in the name of security.

The chorus is returned to the action with a song, full of Greek geography, speculating where the Trojan women will be taken as captives. It serves little purpose except to prepare loosely for Polyxena's "marriage" to the dead Achilles.

The parallelism of the Astyanax theme and the Polyxena theme[96] provides a telling climax. The Astyanax theme has been brought to its penultimate stage, and the Polyxena theme is now brought to the same point, so that both can culminate simultaneously. Helen, sent to fetch Polyxena as Achilles' bride of death under the guise of marriage to Pyrrhus, performs much the same role as Ulysses did. The unity of the two themes is underlined by the role of Andromache in confrontation with Helen just as she has been with Ulysses.[97] In both cases, she is the voice of moral indignation raised against the victors' vicious use of power.

The *Troades* is unified also by the final fulfillment of the positive implications of behavior in defeat introduced at the opening. The last Chorus hits a bittersweet note. It follows typical Stoic reasoning that the individual's experience of grief is relative to its circumstances, as in other human conditions. "Sweet for the mourner is a people in grief, sweet the echo of a nation mourning, less stinging the pain of weeping shared in the tears of a multitude" (1009–12). As Seneca writes in a prose *consolatio*, "To share one's grief with many takes the place of consolation" (*Cons. Polyb.* 12.2). Now these common tears will be dispersed when the Greek ships take the captives to their new homes, and the departing women will look back at the only remaining sign of Troy, the smoke rising from its ruin. An adjustment to pain has been made.

The deaths of Astyanax and Polyxena are reported as truly moral victories: "The maiden is sacrificed, the boy fallen from the walls, but both died nobly" (1063–64). The full report is carefully written as a showpiece, as the finale of the Trojan passion. Astyanax is led to the walls by Ulysses. He is spirited and composed. The sightseeing crowd is moved to tears. While Ulysses recites the ritual of sacrifice, the boy voluntarily (*sponte . . . sua*, 1102) jumps from the tower and is dashed to pieces. Polyxena appears as in a wedding procession, showing the radiance of the hour when the sun gives way to the stars (1138–42).[98] She stirs the sympathy of the crowd. She goes to meet her death (*leto obvius*, 1146), facing the killing blow (*conversa ad ictum*, 1152), and falls like an attacker on the earth of Achilles' grave. In Hecuba's bitter words, "A maiden and a boy have died. The war is over" (1167–68).

These actions can be dismissed as posturings. However, the stance of equanimity and submission to what is to be is the ultimate Stoic shield against adversity. More than this, when Astyanax interrupts Ulysses' ritual and leaps, when the dying Polyxena assaults Achilles' grave, they are in effect committing legitimate Stoic suicide in the grandest manner, pitting their spirits against brute force. We are reminded of the many passages in Seneca's prose where the most extreme trials are opportunities for glorying in adversity. The behavior of Regulus shows us, "the greater the torture, the greater the glory" (*Prov.* 3.9). "Great men often rejoice in adversity like brave soldiers in war" (*Prov.* 4.4). The boy and the maiden are moral gladiators, not captives but free, not victims but victors.

Agamemnon

Not surprisingly, this drama was among the last accepted as Senecan.[99] It is probably the poorest, lacking dramatic force and concentration. It has been called a "drama of revenge"[100] but makes most sense when seen as a dramatization of Stoic insights into the moral significance of Fate and Fortune.[101]

The ghost of Thyestes—again the foulness of Hades—opens the play as a representative of the chronically criminal house of Pelops. He emphasizes his brother's and his own crimes, particularly incest with his daughter, and vengefully anticipates the murder of Agamemnon in detail (39–48). Justifying himself, he attributes his crimes to Fortune (28) and Fate (33). This simplistic excuse making immediately raises the central issue of the play, the relationship between human behavior and the workings of these forces conventionally thought of as external agencies. It will be recalled that Fortune and Fate are virtually synonymous in Stoicism since they both denote reality. They are different only in that they are views of reality from different perspectives, Fortune being the flux of the world and Fate its system.

The relationship between the instability of Fortune and human guilt emerges in Chorus I, functioning as the voice of the philosopher-dramatist. Very common poetic themes are associated so as to express his meaning. (1) Fortune confers kingship deceptively, placing the high and mighty in danger and insecurity. (2) Royal courts are full of crime, interfamily strife (Aegisthus), and marital infidelity (Clytemnestra, Agamemnon). (3) Even without violence and crime, "great things sink under their own weight, and Fortune too heavy with itself gives way" (87–89). (4) Only the modest life is secure. The passage fuses Fortune and immorality and treats Fortune not as an agency external to human life but as a moral condition, a state of excess causing its own downfall.

In terms of this thought, Clytemnestra and Aegisthus are agents of Fortune who will cause Agamemnon's downfall. But they are also victims of insecurity caused by their own criminality. In Episode I, dramatically the most successful part of the play, Clytemnestra expresses in rhetorical style her second thoughts about commitment to Aegisthus and his plan for revenge. She is fully aware of her own and her partner's immorality but is tossed in a storm of conflict (138–40) between her better instincts and the passions of desire for Aegisthus (134–35) and of anger caused by Agamemnon's crimes: the treacherous sacrifice of Iphigenia (158–59, 162–67) and his adulterous affairs with Chryseïs, Briseïs, and now Cassandra (175–91). Her inner debate and exchanges with the nurse and Aegisthus pour out language of fear, doubt, hesitation, and distraction. In the end, she realizes that she has gone too far to turn back and commits herself to the irrational course of following chance (144). Aegisthus too dreads the moment when he will have to act (226–27). His threat of suicide (304–5) brings Clytemnestra around to support him.

This network of ideas began when the ghost of Thyestes blamed his crimes on Fortune and Fate as external causes. Chorus I gives the counterview that Fortune, if not controlled Stoically by the moderate life, brings exposure to insecurity and crime and an excess that destroys itself. Clytemnestra and Aegisthus are themselves such criminals and are exposed to the most radical kind of insecurity. But their motives, or at least Clytemnestra's motives, are substantially a response to Agamemnon's crimes. So Agamemnon is a victim of violence mostly because he is guilty of the self-destructive excess of Fortune.

The treatment of criminal behavior in Seneca prompts a glance at Aeschylus' version, not because of any specific debt to Aeschylus but because of a significant contrast. In the *Oresteia*, suprahuman power and human behavior are interlocked so tightly that there is no escape from the network of evil perpetuating itself. Evil is an aspect of the way things are (see chapter 1). Resolution of the issue requires a purification of both divine governance and human affairs. This view would make no sense to Seneca. The order of the universe is beyond challenge. Any evil resulting from any of its characteristics, such as the flux of Fortune, is due to human failure to live in harmony with Nature.

Seneca's moralistic interpretation of the basic plot in the first third of the play means that we can follow the play as directed by the interpretation but also that dramatic development is minimal. Chorus II, a thanksgiving to the gods who watch over Mycenae and have assisted the Greek victory at Troy, has a small ironic effect because the chorus welcomes "the return of peace" (326), and loosely prepares for the messenger Eurybates returning from Troy. In his conversation with Clytemnestra, the queen counterfeits normal emotions. Eurybates' report of the storm is a showpiece of vivid narrative, inexcusably long.

However, the theme of Fortune continues in a parallelism drawn between the experience of Troy in defeat and the experience of the Greeks in victory.[102] Fortune levels victors and victims, and brings both sides to the same test of morality. The roles of victor and victim are reversed morally, for the Trojans make a rational adjustment to misfortune and the Greeks commit excesses in good fortune. "Those are wrong who think that Fortune gives us any good or any evil. It gives us the stuff of good and evil, the source of things which within us will turn out to be evil or good" (*Ep.* 98.2).

The parallelism begins with the idea that the victorious Agamemnon is a captive of his own eroticism. Clytemnestra calls him "captive in the love of a captive" (Chryseïs, 175) and "husband of a captive" (Cassandra, 191). He is "conquered without any enemy" (183). Eurybates describes him as returning from the storm "a victor like one vanquished" (412). The storm is an atonement to Troy (577).

To bring out the Trojan side of the issue, Seneca shifts from the chorus of Greek women to a chorus of Trojan captive women. For their thoughts, what Seneca writes in prose might be substituted: "He who has learned to die has learned not to be a slave [*servire*]. . . . What have prison and guards and bars to do with him? He has an open door. The only chain which holds us in bonds is love of life [*amor vitae*]" (*Ep.* 26.10). In the poetic version, excessive attachment to life (*vitae dirus amor*, 590) is the only barrier to the peaceful harbor of death, which gives refuge from misery, all the storms of life, Fortune, civil uprising (Aegisthus? Clytemnestra?), violence of a victor (Agamemnon?), storms at sea, and war (589–604). A man not afraid of death will break through every kind of slavery (*servitium*, 605). The Trojan women recall the last desperate night of Troy. The murder of Priam (referred to earlier by Eurybates, 448) caps the account of Greek excesses.

Significantly, Seneca does not make this attitude of resignation merely passive. He uses a spirited Cassandra to make it morally aggressive. She will not let the women speak for her grief. She will be a match for her own troubles (663). The chorus meekly takes refuge, like the chorus of the *Troades*, in the consolation that it does not weep alone. It aptly describes Cassandra as "an unyielding, enduring heroine" (668).

She is truly another Stoic heroine. In moral self-dramatization, flaunting her spirit in the face of adversity, as the trance of clairvoyance comes over her she cries that the gods and Fortune have no more power over her (696–98). Trojan troubles have transcended fear. Nothing is left. The women see her walking taller (716–17) as she struggles against the power of Apollo. Her vision of the murders of Agamemnon and herself is set in the larger context of the theme of Fortune and its significance in the case of the Greeks and the Trojans. She sees a double Mycenae but also the woods of Ida where Paris made his fatal judgment of the goddesses. The lion (Agamemnon) is savaged by the lioness. Cassandra imagines that she is called to death by her dead kindred. Let the curtain be lifted so that the dead Trojans may see what is happening in Mycenae: "The fates are reversed" (758). Tantalus leaves off his thirst to grieve for his great-grandson Agamemnon, but Hector's great-grandfather Dardanus rejoices and walks in dignity (769–74). For Mycenae, death is shame; for the Trojans, honor and victory.

Agamemnon enters, boasting that long-mighty Troy has fallen. He has Clytemnestra revived from her trance and urges her to welcome a day of celebration, as if the two were harmonious life-mates. Their conversation reinforces the parallelism. This day of celebration is like Troy's celebration of apparent victory: Agamemnon = Priam, Mycenae = Troy, Clytemnestra = Helen, and the security that Agamemnon offers Cassandra is the security of death (791–99).

The rest of the play is not successful either dramatically or thematically. The chorus, now of Greek women again, gives a very ordinary encomium of the Labors of Hercules. The only visible connection with the play is that Hercules is a hero of Argos (808–15) who long ago conquered Troy with the arrows used by Philoctetes to conquer latter-day Troy (863–66). Hercules is, of course, a Stoic hero of great interest to Seneca, but nothing substantive is made of this status here. If the passage is to be related to its context, the effect would have to be ironic in the light of the Trojan moral victory, but finding irony is a weak substitute for finding a more organic function.

The murder of Agamemnon, clairvoyantly described by Cassandra, is proclaimed as the final victory of Troy. The roles of conqueror and conquered are reversed (868–71). The banquet in Mycenae is parallel to the last banquet in Troy: the couches are covered with Trojan purple, the wine is drunk from Trojan cups, Agamemnon wears booty taken from Priam (875–80).[103]

The ending is cluttered and flat. Electra sends the young Orestes away in the safekeeping of Strophius. She is prepared to die and joins Cassandra, who has taken refuge at an altar. We might have had a meaningful association of the two. Instead, Electra has a heated exchange first with Clytemnestra and then with Aegisthus; she is taken off to be imprisoned and tortured to reveal where Orestes is hidden. Cassandra marches off to her death still sounding the note of Trojan victory (1005–9).

The *Agamemnon* is dramatically weak because Seneca has not been able to fuse his moralism and the action of the drama. There is no character like Andromache in the *Troades* serving both dramatic interest and moral interpretation. Rather, Seneca has imposed his commentary upon the events of the action. The failure of the play has been taken as evidence that it is a youthful, immature work, the pessimism as perhaps an indication that it is a late play reflecting the disillusionment of Seneca's career.[104] All such speculation aside, the play is what it is because Stoicism has priority over drama.

Hercules Furens and Hercules Oetaeus

The Hercules in both plays is a Neo-Stoic version of the traditional Stoic hero. He is not what he was for the Cynic Antisthenes and the early Stoics, a naturally good, not very intelligent, self-sufficient servant of humanity. The characteristic of "naturally good" would not well suit Neo-Stoic thought with its concentration on the conflict between good and evil in human nature.

In the prose writings, Hercules is not very prominent. He is still the selfless benefactor of the world (*Ben.* 1.13.3). But he is depreciated because he belongs to an outmoded primitive world; Cato, by comparison, is a stronger exemplar of the *sapiens* because he fought against political ambition and for freedom (*Const.* 2.1–3). Similarly, Hercules, Regulus, and Cato are cited as equivalent examples of those who overcame pain to become eternal (*Tranq.* 16.4). The human dimension of Hercules dominates the *Furens* and the first part of the *Oetaeus*. No longer does he combat only external evils. He is vulnerable to pain and human frailties.[105]

The interpretation of the *Furens* sketched above (pp. 24–25) will be expanded here.[106] A sentence in the *De Clementia* approximates the theme that Seneca draws from the material: "Even if there is someone who has purified his mind so well that nothing can disturb and deceive him any more, still he has reached purity by sinning" (1.6.4).

The play begins with Juno's tirade. She has left Jupiter and Olympus, enraged because she has been supplanted by Jupiter's favorites. Her latest anger is against Alcmena and Hercules. Against them she will wage eternal warfare (28–29). But what warfare (30)? Hercules has surmounted all the trials set for him and turned them to his own glory. "This violent youth" (43–44) has made a mockery of Juno's enmity and is now hailed as a god throughout the world. He has even broken through natural barriers and despoiled Hades of Cerberus. Next he will smash his way to heaven, dethrone Jupiter, and rule the ravaged universe. "He has learned that he can conquer the sky by his might" (69–70).

She will personally destroy him by enlisting his only equal match—himself. "Now let him wage war with himself" (85). The nature of this conflict with self is indicated when Juno threatens to bring against Hercules the forces of death—that is, moral death—on earth (90–91): discord, sin, impiety, error, and madness (93–98). The metaphor equating Hades with moral death continues when Juno summons the Furies to inspire both Hercules and herself with irrational fury (107–12). Let Hercules return from Hades to find his sons unharmed, and let him return with mighty hand. "May he conquer himself and want to die" (116).

Obviously, this evil Juno is a gross example of the anthropomorphic religion and mythology rejected by the Stoics. Dramatically she is much more. Her passion as a destructive goddess prepares us for the audacity and violence of the destructive hero.[107] She puts us into the world of megalomania to which Hercules has succumbed. Her plan to invoke evil forces to set Hercules against himself is a clear sign that the dramatist is interpreting the theme of madness in terms of psychic conflict within Hercules. Thus the prologue informs us immediately that the title *Furens*, one of the terms used most heavily by the philosopher to denote irrationality, means that the catastrophe is caused by the human weakness of the hero.

The process of showing Hercules' vulnerability to excess begins allusively in Chorus I, a well-written lyric on the activities of the new day breaking. It contrasts innocent, carefree pursuits in the purity of nature with ambitious, fearful activities in the social and political life of the city. The passage is one of those in which the dramatist seems to fuse the time of his own Rome and the mythic time of his material. He expects us to make the leap from the urban context to the case of Hercules, from the wasting of precious time in the ambitious rush to death to Hercules' audacious invasion of Hades (186). The connection between going to Hades physically and going to Hades morally is implied when the chorus rejects the excessive renown of one who is raised to the level of the sky and the stars (194–95), which is the level of Hercules' ambition. "Bold courage has a long fall" (201).

The foreshadowing of Hercules' fall continues unobtrusively in the well-dramatized confrontation of Amphitryon and Megara with Lycus. Here, as well as anywhere in his dramas, Seneca has differentiated individual characters and put them in a lifelike interrelationship. Amphitryon appeals to Jupiter as governor and judge of the universe (205) for an end to their troubles, calling attention to the fact that whenever his son returns from a Labor, another enemy is awaiting him because of Juno's hostility. Now the world has lost its "maker of peace" (250), and Thebes is the victim of the criminal Lycus. Megara calls upon Hercules to break through the barriers of Hades, just as he has previously moved mountains by his enormous physical strength. "Burst through the boundaries of nature" (290, *rerum terminos*, familiar Stoic language for the orderly arrangement of the universe). Amphitryon reassures Megara that Hercules will overcome the physical problem of returning to earth as he has overcome similar problems before (319–24).

Lycus, who now enters, is a particularly loathsome tyrant, bent on his own survival to the point of proposing dynastic marriage to Megara and threatening to take her by force if she refuses. Their heated argument produces some important implications for the case of Hercules. Lycus justifies his murderous violence as "glorious courage" (*clara virtus*, 340). When he attacks Hercules as a failure, Megara boasts that Hercules has gone to Hades in order to reach Olympus (423), for "there is no easy road from earth to the stars" (437). Amphitryon defends his son against Lycus' charges of effeminacy and womanizing, and predicts that Lycus too will be a victim of Hercules' violence (480–89). Lycus orders the burning of Megara and her sons in the shrine where they have taken refuge.

The scene is successful dramatically and as an appraisal of Hercules the hero. He is a mighty "maker of peace," but through physical conquest. When Lycus calls his own violence *virtus*, claims being made for Hercules' *virtus* come into question. He has shown flaws before and now is trying to force his way to Olympus and divinity. He is vulnerable to the moral enemies that Juno is raising against him. Seneca is building the recognition that *virtus* requires inner supremacy, victory over self.

Amphitryon hears Hercules approaching with a crash: the shrine totters, the earth rumbles from its depths (520–23). But before he appears, the chorus comments on the injustice of Fortune. Hercules has overcome all these trials and now has boldly invaded Hades. Juno has said that she will show Hercules hell on earth (*hic tibi ostendam inferos*, 91). Now he has plunged into hell (*ad inferos*, 547). The chorus can only hope that he will overcome the laws of Hades (558–59), rupture Fate (566), and conquer with his might the kingdom that Orpheus overcame with song (590–91). Physical hell and moral hell are becoming identical.

Hercules' mania and recovery from it are powerfully dramatized. The beginning is normal, even pious. Hercules appeals to the gods to avoid defilement at the sight of the monster Cerberus. Yet his audacity quickly asserts itself. He might have become king of Hades if he wished (610). Now that he has seen and shown Hades (*vidi et ostendi inferos*, 613), he challenges Juno to present the next trial of his strength (614–15). Amphitryon can hardly believe that his son has returned but recognizes him by his bulging muscles (624–25). Hercules goes off "to draw the blood of Lycus as his last foe" (635–36), although Theseus tells us immediately that Lycus has already been dispatched!

During Hercules' absence, Amphitryon wants to hear from Theseus the sequence of his son's exploits in Hades (*virtutum ordinem*, 647). The account is much longer than it needs to be, presumably because Seneca cannot forgo the opportunity for the writing of spectacle. The barrenness and motionlessness of Hades are well expressed. Also, the account includes details suggesting a connection between the sins punished in Hades and the evils that are about to overcome Hercules and destroy his family. Theseus explains that punishment is meted out to sinners on the principle that the punishment matches the crime. "Each man suffers what he has done" (735). Bloody rulers are punished with prison and beatings by their subjects. On the contrary, beneficent rulers who use their power sparingly and without violence are rewarded and "reach the skies" (743). Where Hercules stands on this scale is clearly indicated when Theseus describes how he manhandled Charon (773–75) and clubbed Cerberus into submission (800–802). Hercules' violence is about to be inflicted upon his own.

The violence of the madness, it must be emphasized, is not an isolated characteristic nor is it caused externally as in Euripides. It is a symptom of inner delusion, of egocentricity, audacity, and pride. This moral disease now appears clearly in Hercules' behavior. Preparing to offer sacrifice in thanksgiving for victory over Lycus and his company, he calls upon the gods, including whatever brother of his lives in the sky (907). Amphitryon tells him first to purify his hands stained by the slaughter. He asserts that the blood of Lycus would be a libation welcome to the gods (920–24). Amphitryon continues, "Pray for an end to your Labors." Hercules declares that he will offer prayers "worthy of Jupiter and myself" (926–27) and then prays Jove-like that the universe be at peace. If there is any wicked monster still to come, "let it be mine" (*meum sit*, 939), a very obvious wordplay.

The loss of reason and its recovery interest Seneca deeply, of course, and in dramatizing the process of movement into and out of madness he succeeds both dramatically and philosophically. The mental phenomena are mirrored in physical phenomena. The midday is darkened. Hercules begins to hallucinate, seeing the constellation Leo, his first Labor, glowing furiously, ready to attack the Bull. Amphitryon's cries of consternation punctuate the growing wildness. Now, instead of viewing the sky crazedly, Hercules imagines that he is making his way into the sky. All of the universe except the sky has been mastered. Even if father Jupiter does not keep his promise of godhood, Hercules will have it, either being welcomed by the gods or by breaking his way in. He can lead another assault of the Titans on Olympus (965–73). The hellish Furies threaten him and block his path. Hallucinatory heaven and hallucinatory hell are confounded.

In this mental chaos, identities are transferable. Hercules identifies his children as those of Lycus, and Megara as Juno. As Amphitryon in the reality of horror describes what is happening, the whole family is slaughtered in a bloody and wild scene conveying the fury of the madness. Amphitryon offers himself as the final victim, but Hercules falls into exhaustion and sleeps.

The horror is moderated by Chorus IV, probably the most artistic of all Senecan choral lyrics as poetry, emotion, and thought. Let the whole universe mourn for Hercules' misery, and may Sleep, the great comforter, restore him to his former self. The world will resound to his lamentation as his sons follow the path that their father took to Hades. Most substantively, the chorus prays that Hercules will regain his *pietas* and *virtus* (1093–94), the moral qualities opposite to those Juno enlisted against him. That is, his recovery will be the recovery not merely of his wits but of the moral integrity he has lost. In Stoic terms, the recovery of reason can mean nothing else.

The process of recovery is more complicated than the onset of the madness. Hercules has farther to go to reason than he had to go to passion. Several levels of cognition take him all the way from learning where he is physically to knowing what he must be morally. His initial disorientation gives way to the recognition that he has returned from Hades (1143). The sight of the corpses makes him wonder if he is still seeing infernal phantoms (1144–46), a telling point since he is emerging from the hell of his own violence. He is afraid. Where are his father, his wife and sons, his shield and bow? Someone must have conquered him.

He now recognizes the dead bodies and challenges the unknown murderer. The next stage is to become aware of the behavior of those around him. Amphitryon and Theseus evade his questions and weep. Hercules' own logic now begins to work: the bloody arrows are from the bow that only he can draw.

The final stage is how he will cope morally with his misery and shame. Amphitryon tries to persuade him that Juno is responsible and that his actions have been innocent "error" rather than "sin" (1201, 1237). But he rejects this reasoning, declaring that error may be the equivalent of sin (1238). In saying this, he is identifying two of the moral enemies raised against him by Juno (93–98) and is expressing the dramatist's view that the violence against his family, though unintentional, is the result of moral weakness.

So Hercules takes full responsibility for his acts. In a torrent of self-accusation, he calls the wrath of the universe down on himself and imagines torments of the magnitude he deserves (including the pyre of his final trial in the *Oetaeus* [1216–17]). Amphitryon urges him to be "Hercules" and endure (1239), but his shame is so deep that he demands his weapons and prepares to execute himself. Amphitryon pleads with him to act with *virtus*, apparently to no avail, and finally in despair threatens to take his own life. The father's desolation brings Hercules to new insights. His suicide will cause the added crime of Amphitryon's death. He must surmount his own guilt. It is the part of *virtus* to yield to his father's love and live (1314–17).

Thus Hercules moves from audacity, violence, madness, and egoism to rationality and altruism, from moral death to moral life. Although the process is simplistic and sensational, the *Furens* is competent philosophical drama because Seneca fuses the psychological delineation of the central character with the Neo-Stoic conception of a faulted hero who achieves *virtus*.

As in the *Furens*, Hercules of the *Oetaeus* is subject to human weakness and the experience of pain,[108] and the rhythm of this play is much like that of the *Furens*, from degradation to fulfillment. However, its scale is far grander. Fulfillment here is apotheosis. Hercules reaches the status of being regarded by the Stoics as an aspect of Jupiter because "his might is unconquered and . . . will pass away into [creative] fire" (*Ben.* 4.8.1).

The prologue, spoken by Hercules, tells us immediately that the play will examine the culmination of the life of the hero. We are also led to expect that the course to godhood will be tortuous, for the Hercules of the prologue is not morally suited to such glorification. He is an aggressive, braggart hero, demanding admission to the sky as the reward of his glory. How he has brought peace to the world is recounted at great length. "Is the sky still denied to me, father" (7–8)? "Are you afraid of me" (11)? His father and the stars should be restored to him as his natural right (31–32). All of nature has given way to him (46). Now that all monsters have fallen before him, he is becoming the only monster left (55–56, a significant touch). The gods are threatened by the beasts he slew, now changed into constellations, while he the victor looks up at them from the earth. "At least let me protect the gods, Jupiter" (87). He instructs Lichas to carry home the news of his latest "triumphs" over the kingdom of Eurytus (99–101). The enormous incongruity of this vainglory cannot be explained adequately as rhetorical mannerism. It must mean that the braggadocio has to be transformed to a different kind of spirit.

In Chorus I the implications of these "triumphs" are explored through the feelings of the captive women and the princess Iole. The women hope for a quick death as they view the desolation of their land. Hercules cannot be the son of Jupiter and Alcmena but—like Dido's description of Aeneas in Virgil—must be the product of raw nature, rough, impervious to weapons, and above all wrathful. Their misery is to have seen Hercules *angry* (172). Their view of the hero might be discounted if it were not for the fact that it is consistent with what he has just revealed about his present state. Iole gives a more personal and even more damaging picture. She wants to weep as mythical figures weep, eternally. She has seen her father smashed by Hercules' club and her mother and brother killed—all because Hercules was attracted by her beauty and was refused by her father in fear of him (219–23). Her words prepare us for what will be said later about Hercules' erotic behavior.

Seneca is creating a moral situation in which the tribulation of the hero is caused by a nexus of his own and Deianira's passions. The latter is shown overpoweringly as the scene shifts to Trachin. In Episodes I and II the dramatist writes his most explosive and thorough version of the theme "Heaven has no rage like love to hatred turned, Nor hell a fury like. . . ." He outdoes even his portrayal of Medea in writing a poetic version of the Stoic recognition that "anger is born as much from love as from hate" (*Ep*. 18.15).

The nurse speaks of the *furor* caused when concubine and wife live in one house (233–34).[109] The sight of Iole's beauty (we are to assume that she has reached Trachin in the meantime) has made Deianira react like a threatened animal or a maddened maenad, rushing about the house in distraction, showing all the physical signs of inner turmoil (247–53). Deianira is already at fever pitch when she first speaks. If Juno still hates Hercules, let her send the worst imaginable beast against him to satisfy Deianira's rage. Failing that, "change my spirit into any evil I can become" (264–65). "In my heart you will find every beast to terrify Hercules" (269–70). The nurse tries to calm her, but she rages on. "The pain of an angered wife is something worse than Hydra" (284–85). "The last day of our marriage will be the last day of your life" (305–6). The language about beasts is transparent metaphor for the bestial nature of Deianira's passion.

Seneca composes this dialogue with more care and skill than usually go into his scenes of this type. The nurse reasons with her mistress ingeniously, warning that all the world will rise against anyone who harms Hercules, reassuring her that Hercules was interested in Iole only because of her royal status, now ended, and that his many liaisons have been brief. His affections have wandered even as he has wandered (365). Deianira is wildly adamant. If she dies, she wants to die as Hercules' wife. If Iole is to have a child by Hercules, she will tear it out (345–47).

On the other hand, quite exceptionally in this case, Seneca creates genuine sympathy for her. She speaks movingly about the erosion of her beauty caused by time and motherhood and about her pride in the fame of being the wife of Hercules (380–406). Then in her next breath she caustically calls the hero a philanderer, whose wanderings have been a search not for glory but for maidens, giving the name of *virtus* to his excesses (410–27). The long conversation continues. Deianira is prepared to die (443–44). She still loves Hercules deeply and recognizes that her great passion is caused by her great love (450–52). After much discussion and explanation, the robe smeared with the poisonous love charm is sent off to Hercules.

The empathy with Deianira must have a special significance for it is not Seneca's usual technique. Certainly he does not make us sympathize with Medea, despite the case that might be made for her. Probably the reason is that Deianira's passion is not considered a chronic state. Her only fault is excessive love, and essentially she is the victim of Hercules' excesses. Probably Seneca thinks of her moral state as the equivalent of temporary insanity.

Sensitivity to Deianira is maintained in Chorus II, spoken by her fellow countrywomen. First they lament her insecure marriage (*dubios . . . toros*, 585) and recall their life together as children. The rest of the lyric sounds like a satirist's view of imperial Rome, but it contains hints indicating that the dramatist has in mind the insecurity of a powerful and renowned life like that of Hercules, including the life of a woman married to such a figure.

The women claim that loyalty such as theirs to Deianira is rare (602–3). It is not found in the life of kings, surrounded with those seeking wealth and power. The doors of kings, guarded by the Fury (moral death), are opened to admit treachery and violence (609–12). "Let someone else," the chorus prays, "be hailed as fortunate and great. May no crowd call me powerful" (692–93). The royal wife pursued by the Fury (671) is contrasted with the wife in modest circumstances, whose marriage is secure (*non dubios . . . toros*, 670, a recall of 585).

Clearly, the vulnerability of Hercules and Deianira to the perils of grandeur is being referred to, although the picture of imperial immorality does not entirely fit their cases. This kind of dramatic anomaly will be used later as presumptive evidence that Seneca is projecting his own experience of the Roman court onto the dramatic situation.

Deianira's irrationality, though understandable and not habitual, is fully destructive, causing the physical deaths of both Hercules and herself. Stoically, irrationality is vice, no matter what its nature. When Deianira discovers that the love charm is corrosive fire, she is filled with fear that the felicity and grandeur of her marriage have called down compensatory disaster (713–14). When son Hyllus reports that Hercules is being consumed with fire, she plunges into a torrent of self-accusation, invoking the wrath of the universe to punish her. She must be destroyed as a beast worse than the monsters destroyed by Hercules (851–52). Like Hercules in the *Furens*, she rejects Hyllus' argument that her action was "error," not "sin"; in Stoic rhetoric she replies that to use Fate as an excuse of wrongdoing is to deserve "error" (884–88, 900–902).

The parallel between Hercules in the *Furens* and Deianira in the *Oetaeus* is a significant part of the dramatist's conception. Hyllus pleads with Deianira that Hercules was able to surmount his violence and find purification (903–9). But although Deianira recognizes that she is spiritually innocent (964–65), her anguish allows no adjustment to the reality of suffering. At great length she rages against herself, as Hercules has done, demanding the most hideous punishment that Hades can provide. Her purification will come from the tortures of the damned (934–37). Or should she wait to be destroyed by Hercules (971–82)? Finally, the Furies appear in her hallucinations, the universe advances against her, and she leaves the scene. Hyllus follows to prevent the "real crime" (1030) of her suicide.

Seneca continues to use the chorus effectively for his purposes, in a role that falls between the action and the interpretation of the action. Chorus III sets up the significance of Hercules' trial. With allowances for the excessive mythological detail, it efficiently uses the poetic theme of Orpheus in Hades to establish the idea that "nothing is made to be eternal" (1035). The success of the theme lies in the fact that Orpheus' music has a universal effect upon nature, so that when Orpheus concludes that everything is subject to the divine law of death (1093–99), the application of this law has been extended to the entire universe. In this context, the chorus takes the case of Hercules as evidence of Orpheus' view and anticipates that the universe will soon suffer destruction (1100–1127). Some form of death and chaos (1115) will be the end of everything. When the din of Hercules' approach is heard (1128–30), the audience is prepared for an event of universal proportions.

One of the reasons for the great length of the *Oetaeus* is the emphasis on Hercules' vulnerability to pain, which the modern reader finds unbearably excessive. The excess cannot be excused dramatically, but there are legitimate philosophical reasons for it. Hercules becomes a symbol of the mortal Neo-Stoic struggle between the vice of susceptibility to passion and the virtue of victory over this susceptibility.[110] Deianira is unable to achieve this victory and escapes from her anguish by suicide. The magnitude of Hercules' victory is conveyed by exaggerating the intensity of his physical and mental pain.

The effects of the pain devastate him. Hyllus reports that at the attack of the poison "we saw Hercules weep" (806). In delirium he grabs Lichas and hurls him into the sea. He tears at his own flesh. When he arrives in Trachin, he wildly asks Jupiter to reduce the universe to chaos and bury him in its ruin (1134–50). In long speeches, he agonizes that, after all the threats to his life he has overcome, he is dying at the hands of a woman ingloriously; laments the destruction of his mighty body by the unknown pest within him; and now for the first time asks Jupiter for help and a quick death.

Consistently with the Neo-Stoic view of Hercules as a *human* hero, the impetus that carries him from delirium to composure begins in a human source. In love for her son, Alcmena urges him to overcome his pain and be victor once again (1374–76), and so performs a function like that of Amphitryon in the *Furens*. When Hercules falls into an exhausted sleep, Alcmena prays that he may recover his strength. He is still delirious when he wakes, but his imaginings are no longer bound to earthly pain. He imagines that Jupiter and Juno, now reconciled to him, are receiving him in the sky (1432–40). Even when he realizes that he is still on earth, he refuses to admit that he is overcome by pain (1446–47). Complete composure and imperturbability come when Hyllus announces Deianira's suicide—she has suffered more pain than she caused (1464)—and explains how she was deceived by Nessus. Hercules recognizes the truth of the oracle predicting that one of his victims will cause his death and prepares to die worthily (1481–82). He consoles Alcmena with the thought that she has borne a son worthy of Jupiter. He goes to Hades still a victor (1516–17).

The use of the chorus to introduce the philosophical meaning of the dramatic events is now clearly visible. Hercules, at last calm in his strength, expects to die like a mortal. The chorus is put into the position of not knowing what to expect. In two approximately equal parts of its song (1518–63, 1564–1606), it speculates about the death and then the apotheosis of the hero, as mutually exclusive alternatives. The Sun is asked to carry the news of the death of Hercules, the benefactor of the world. He will go to Hades a wasted shade (1554–55) and become one of the judges, still prosecuting tyranny as he has in life. But "his *virtus* has a place among the stars" (1564). Where will his place in the sky be? His power and glory will endure as long as the orderly processes of the universe continue (1576–86). Mysteriously the universe rings out (*mundus sonat*, 1595). Philoctetes enters (if this is the correct assignment of lines), clearly bearing good news.

The issue is so important to the dramatist that he follows good dramatic principles to create excitement and expectation. He portrays Hercules in an optimistic yet realistic mood and manipulates this mood against the uncertainty of the chorus, which expands the possible prospects of his death. By this dramatic technique, we are prepared for the philosophical significance of the event, that the alternatives do not exclude each other, that the hero will both die as a mortal and live as a star-god.

Another reason for the length of the play is the detailed, deliberate development of the Neo-Stoic climax, taking almost one-fifth of the entire text. Philoctetes gives a long account of the building of the immense pyre on Oeta and Hercules' behavior at the end. He has added fire to the list of his Labors (1614–16). Mounting the pyre with the look of one seeking the stars (1645), he has calmed Alcmena's weeping as unworthy, appealed to Jupiter for admission to the sky, and subjected himself to the fire, confident that Jupiter will hear him. Victorious over the fire, he gathers it around himself and is consumed.

The grotesque horror of the scene is offensive to normal standards. The scene probably would be much more successful if less realistic. However, it deals with the most basic and universal fear, fear of pain, and for the rhetorical moralist the strongest picture of victory over pain requires the most graphic picture of pain. Indeed, the scene is repulsive partly because it exposes the hearer to his own phobia, which is the essential prerequisite for the Stoic therapy intended by the dramatist. An obvious parallel in the prose is Mucius Scaevola thrusting his hand into the fire to punish himself for failing to kill an enemy (*Ep.* 24.5).

Hercules on Oeta is a powerful *exemplum*, how to turn to glory the experience of the "indifferent" pain. (*Ep.* 82. 10–11).

The nature of the glory now appears. Alcmena, left alone to face a world full of her son's enemies, laments inconsolably despite Hyllus' view that Hercules is not to be mourned because his *virtus* has stopped the course of Fate (1834), that is, his *virtus* has crowned the sequence of events that was to be his life. "But," she cries, "he is dead and buried as a mortal" (1911–12). The voice of Hercules is heard from the sky. No more tears. "My *virtus* has carried me to the stars and the company of the gods" (1942–43). "My mortality inherited from you is gone in the fire surmounted [by my spirit]. My father's part of me is committed to the sky, your part to the fire" (1966–68). In astonishment Alcmena accepts the divinity of her son (1980–81). The chorus concludes that *virtus* never dies but reaches the sky when mortal life ends. May Hercules' spirit continue to protect the world, if necessary crushing any new evil "with three-forked thunderbolts cast with more might than your own father's" (1994–96). Hercules has achieved a kind of identity with Jupiter.

The double state of Hercules may seem to be mere mythologizing about a hero of mixed parentage, but it is significant in the light of Seneca's Neo-Stoic thinking about death and the nature of the soul. The dramatic lines echo passages in the prose affirming that the purified soul rises to the company of the gods. Also, the distinction between the survival of Hercules' soul and the death of his body fits the Senecan tendency to differentiate sharply between soul and body and to stretch the traditional Stoic tenet that the soul also is material. The *Oetaeus* conveys the same dream.

Both plays show Hercules progressing from imperfections and irrationalities to a level of purification. In the *Furens* the mythical tradition of Juno's hostility to Hercules is changed to the Neo-Stoic idea of an internal struggle between the irrational and rational faculties of the soul. Hercules passes from complete preoccupation with self—the feats of *his* physical strength, the shame of *his* madness, the degradation of *his* murders—to a recognition of what his self-destructive urge means to someone who loves him. The defect of self-love (*Ep.* 109.16) is purified by submission to unselfish love.

Purification in the *Oetaeus* goes far beyond the level of human relationships. The impurities are not unlike those in the *Furens*, although more complicated: Hercules' demand for the extraordinary reward of his physical feats, his angry and violent destruction of Oechalia, eroticism, Deianira's love-crazed passion, the insecurity of power. The purging of these evils is truly in the crucible of fire. Put on the right track by Alcmena's loving counsel and compliant with his fate, Hercules is able to withstand the torturing pain of the fire, which burns away mortality and leaves him pure soul. By victory over the irrational self, he has earned the apotheosis he claimed.

The *Oetaeus* may be overdone, but it is the culmination of Senecan drama. Poetically, the variety and scope of the subject matter call forth full and heavy use of all his systems of figurative language.[111] For example, the metaphor of fire is used profusely to express both the negative and the positive implications of the theme. It describes the erotic fury of Deianira and Hercules' womanizing. But the destructive fire of irrationality dies with the pyre, giving way to the creative fire of Hercules' purified spirit. This major image in Seneca's dramatic poetry culminates in the Stoic belief that Hercules is an aspect of Jupiter because his invincible might becomes creative fire (*Ben.* 4.8.1).

The scope of the play has been explained variously. We can no longer accept the old view that it is a pastiche of the genuine Senecan plays. The most stimulating theory is that the play shows Seneca consciously resuming themes appearing in the other plays and bringing them to a final solution in Hercules' psychic victory.[112] Many cross-relations between the other plays and the *Oetaeus* are thus explained. It becomes the end and the climax of the progressive series of all the plays.

It is impossible to be sure that the cross-relations are to be explained precisely in this way because such parallels crisscross all the plays, and in Seneca's view all forms of irrationality are interrelated and ultimately the same evil. But the *Furens* and the *Oetaeus* together, and particularly the *Oetaeus* separately, are the climax of Neo-Stoicism in the dramas. They are written as an allegory of human life in the full range from its deepest depths to its highest heights. The Neo-Stoic conception of Hercules is used to dramatize the imperfections and trials of existence surmounted humanly in the *Furens* and transcendentally in the *Oetaeus*.

Summary

Since Seneca's main purpose is to dramatize positive and negative *exempla* of a philosophy in which Virtue and Vice are absolutely opposed, the dramas are full of moral extremes. The negative models include the chronic manias of Medea's wrath, Phaedra's lust, Hippolytus' hatred, Theseus' anger, and Atreus' cruelty. Other destructive passions are the brothers' ambitions in the *Phoenissae*, Pyrrhus' addiction to power, Ulysses' cruelty in the name of security, Clytemnestra's infidelity, and Agamemnon's infidelity and arrogance. Positive models are seen in Antigone's *pietas*, young Tantalus dying like a Stoic in the *Thyestes*, Andromache's pure love, Astyanax and Polyxena affirming their spirits against brute force, and Cassandra's morally aggressive heroism.

Such chiaroscuro gives the impression that "characters are white or black, right against wrong, and not one mixture of right and wrong against another mixture of right and wrong, as in Greek tragedy."[113] Actually, Seneca's material is more varied than this. There are mixtures of right and wrong, although in the moralistic formulation the mixture has to be within the character, and it is not a true mixture because Vice and Virtue exclude each other. Oedipus' psychotic fear finally gives way to recuperative reconciliation with the truth of Fate. In the *Phoenissae* he renounces his suicidal passion. Hercules *furens* rises above his megalomania and recovers *pietas* and *virtus*. In the *Oetaeus* he wins a transcendental victory over his own and Deianira's passions.

Other characters do not fall in the black-white category. Jason, who has good qualities, becomes a victim partially because he chooses the "indifferent" security. In a drama about the annihilation of human personality, Hippolytus is fragmented in a conflict between reason and passion. Thyestes is a victim not only of Atreus' bestiality but also of his own weakness. Agamemnon in the *Troades* is, like Thyestes, a *proficiens*. Deianira suffers more pain than she causes.

The dramatic quality has to be appraised in terms of what Seneca undertook to write. In his drama, philosophy has priority over dramaturgy, and the normal nature of drama is changed. The dramatic world that he creates is not autonomous but a system of moral communication between the dramatist and the audience. As a result, there are radical "faults" by normal standards. Moral paradigms are so important to him that the specific motives of characters are sometimes not clear, and individual scenes are not organic to the structure. Few characters are individualized personages rather than models. A most conspicuous "fault" is rupture of the dramatic illusion to keep the hearer informed about the nature and significance of the *exempla* through constant specific foreshadowing and pervasive imagery.

The use of the chorus is significant. Although the Senecan chorus sometimes has a clear individuality (as when Hecuba and the Trojan women lament in Chorus I of the *Troades*) and sometimes participates in the action (as when it delivers the marriage song of Jason and Creusa in Chorus I of the *Medea*), its most frequent and important function is exegetical.

Choruses II and III of the *Medea* develop the Argo theme into an interpretation of Medea's cosmically destructive nature. The four Choruses of the *Phaedra* move from the infectious nature of Phaedra's lust to the vulnerability of Hippolytus' beauty, to a contrast between divine order and human chaos, and to the theme of death and annihilation. The theme of Fate is developed Stoically in III and IV of the *Oedipus*. Choruses II–IV of the *Thyestes* treat the ideal of true kingship, the destructive relationship between the brothers, and the protest of the universe to Atreus' sacrilege. In the *Troades*, II comments Stoically on the question of afterlife, and IV presents Stoic reasoning about the experience of grief. Choruses I and III of the *Agamemnon* present the negative and positive implications of human behavior in relation to Fortune. The moral dangers threatening Hercules *furens* and his recovery from them appear in I, II, and IV. In the *Oetaeus*, I and II create sympathy for Iole and Deianira as victims of Hercules' violence, eroticism, and grandeur, and III and IV set up the apotheosis of the hero. In each play at least one-half of the Choruses develop the Stoic meaning intended by the dramatist.

Within this kind of drama, there are degrees of success and failure. Success is greatest, that is, philosophy and drama are most organically related, when the material allows concentration on a dominant character such as Medea, Phaedra, Oedipus, Atreus, or Hercules. The *Troades* and the *Agamemnon* are particularly revealing. Although they both dramatize a contrast between Greeks and Trojans on a similar theme, the *Troades* achieves greater unity through the concentration on Andromache as the voice of moral indignation.

Seneca's distinctive achievement is to dramatize philosophical *exempla* powerfully. Medea's fury, fed by Creon's tyranny and Jason's faded heroism, mounts to infernal mania of universal proportions. Phaedra's lust, Hippolytus' male monomania, and Theseus' anger are interlocked in frightful fragmentation of human personality both psychically and physically. The unnatural relationship between Oedipus and Jocasta is finally purified by reconciliation with moral order. Antigone's *virtus* is set in antithesis to the chaos of distraction and hatred in her family. Thyestes' incomplete mastery of himself makes him vulnerable to Atreus' degeneracy. In the *Troades* the Greeks are morally defeated by victory and the Trojans are morally victorious over defeat. Similarly, in the *Agamemnon* the Greeks use the gifts of Fortune corruptly while Cassandra exemplifies the Trojans' courageous and spirited adjustment to misfortune. The myths about Hercules make it possible to convey the Neo-Stoic image of the human soul subject to the ravages of moral faults but able to surmount them in altruism and ultimate purity. All these effects are grandiose and limited by their moralism. However, they are the insights of a potent moral philosophy into the vast consequences of human behavior in an orderly and sentient universe.

5. DECLAMATION

We have analyzed the plays individually in terms of Neo-Stoicism because the philosophy is the main substance of Seneca's interpretation of the dramatic themes. So it is the only basis on which to differentiate the plays as different aspects of Seneca's overall purpose of dramatizing the traditional stories Neo-Stoically. In so doing, we run the risk of seeming to underestimate the importance of other elements that permeate all the plays and may not be as specifically identifiable as the philosophical ideas. The most notable other element is declamatory rhetoric.

Years after the family moved from Corduba to Rome around A.D. 4, the younger Lucius consoled his mother for his exile on Corsica with a series of arguments about the relativity of home and exile. At one point he analyzes the motives for which people were flooding to Rome "from their towns and colonies, indeed from the whole world. . . . Some were brought by ambition, others by the requirement of public office, others by an envoy's duty. Still others, seeking a place which offers a rich opportunity for vices, were brought by wantonness, others by a desire for higher education [*liberalium studiorum cupiditas*], others by the public games" (*Cons. Helv.* 6.2).

There is no evidence that Seneca senior held public or imperial office in either Corduba or Rome, nor that he was occupied as an attorney or teacher of rhetoric, although his education and experience in rhetoric pointed in these directions. As an old man, probably in his late eighties, he writes interestingly about his three sons in relation to public careers (*Contr.* 2. pref. 3–4). Mela, the youngest, he praises extravagantly as averse to "public office" and "every ambition," dedicated to rhetoric, and the most talented of his sons. He urges him to follow his inclination, *content with the father's equestrian rank*, but also points out that rhetoric is a path to all the arts. He disavows any intention of influencing Mela to devote himself entirely to rhetorical interests. "I am not blocking any honorable purpose." He continues: follow the model of Fabianus, who, while a student of the philosopher Sextius, practiced declamation as if he were preparing himself for that career and not another. In contrast, the older sons Novatus and Seneca are concerned with ambitious aims in the forum and public offices, a precarious course that the father himself had been eager to follow.[1] He fully supports their active life provided that it is honorable.

These attitudes increase our understanding of the motivation of the younger Seneca's career. The father's appraisal of his sons' activities is a little strange. Why, in a work dedicated to all three, does he rate Mela's talents above those of Novatus and Seneca, and at the same time indicate that Mela's rhetorical interests may be only a means to another end and that he thoroughly approves of the older sons' political ambitions? He was a staunch supporter of the republican tradition, a patriot for whom phrases like "forum and offices" still had a galvanizing ring. He had married late and was already affluent and well known in influential Roman circles when near the age of sixty he brought the young family to the city. Perhaps he had relinquished political hopes of his own under the pressure of other affairs. His words about the sons sound as if he is taking care not to offend Mela, putting the best appearance upon Mela's studious interests but showing his belief that political activity is still the highest ambition. Perhaps the developing careers of Novatus and Seneca were surrogate for his own desire to rise above equestrian rank.[2] It is likely that the younger Seneca was goaded by his father's motives.

Near the end of his memoirs, Seneca the elder seems not only to affect weariness at the completion of his long chore but to be melancholy about his lifelong interest in rhetoric when he says, "Now I am ashamed, as though for a long time I have done nothing serious" (*Contr.* 10. pref. 1). We know that the "higher education" mentioned by his son as an incentive for coming to Rome—meaning the study of rhetoric and attendance at declamations—had brought the father to the city two or three times before, as a student and later. They continued to be an intellectual avocation of intense interest to him. No doubt financial interests were time-consuming. Also, considerable evidence shows that he was deeply involved in the education of Novatus, Seneca, and Mela.

Lucius senior is one of those important minor figures in the history of Roman culture, an interesting man of substantial intellectual talents.[3] It is unnecessary to emphasize his financial acumen, except to add that at his death around A.D. 39 the sons received patrimonies that apparently were substantial (*Cons. Helv.* 14.3). His values and attitudes were those of one who believed that the Republic was a political, cultural, and moral zenith. Growing up in Corduba during the civil war, he may have been exposed to the republican sympathies of towns in the Baetis valley that remembered Pompey's support and the violence of Caesar's officers. Seneca comes through to us clearly as a reasonable and equitable person, but political and moral issues quicken his spirit. The intensity of his commitment to the old political and oratorical tradition appears in what he writes about his "saints": the elder Cato, holy prophet of the moral foundation of oratory (*Contr.* 1. pref. 9); and Cicero, identified with the greatest achievement in Roman oratory, "the only genius comparable to the status of Rome as a power" (*Contr.* 1. pref. 6, 11).

He seems to have made his adjustment to the regime of Augustus, whose clemency and preservation of freedom are noted (*Contr.* 2.4.13, 4. pref. 5), and to have disfavored the stubborn opposition of the talented but violent T. Labienus (nicknamed Rabienus, "madcap"), who abused freedom and clung to his republican sympathies in a time of great peace (*Contr.* 10. pref. 5). However, near the end of Augustus' rule, the burning of the books of Labienus ordered by the senate shocked him deeply and stirred an eloquently indignant protest: "A new kind of punishment was dreamed up . . . to punish a man's writings! It was a good thing for the public, by god, that cruelty against thought was invented after Cicero's time! . . . You lunatics, what is this incredible madness that drives you? . . . Thanks be to the gods that persecution of talent began at a time when there ceased to be talent!" (*Contr.* 10. pref. 5–7).

Equally intense is his reaction to the decline of public and private morality during a lifetime that extended through the regime of Tiberius to the early years of Caligula (*Contr.* 1. pref. 7–10). Oratory has deteriorated because of luxury, or the shift of competition from the honorable arena of politics to materialistic purposes, or a kind of fate that brings everything down to the bottom more quickly than it has risen to the top. On this topic he is not merely vehement but contemptuous. "Go, try to find orators among those smooth-plucked youths who are virile only in sexuality."

Seneca is often cast as a conservative rich man. His son's words are used to characterize him as a person of *antiquus rigor* who was not willing that his wife Helvia pursue her interest in philosophy beyond the rudiments (*Cons. Helv.* 17.3–4), and who in fact "hated" philosophy

(*Ep.* 108.22). Actually, the attitude toward Helvia's unusual interests would have been commonplace in a Roman family. His "hatred of philosophy" has been exaggerated and distorted. It is mentioned in a letter where Seneca the younger recalls how zealously he responded as a youth in his early twenties to the teaching of the Sextian philosopher Sotion and how he followed the vegetarian principles advocated by that group. His father asked him to stop this because at that time Egyptian and Jewish rites had been outlawed, and abstinence from certain meats was considered evidence of membership in these cults. "So, at the request of my father who was not afraid of false accusation, but hated (the) philosophy, I returned to my original ways. He had no difficulty persuading me that I should begin to have better dinners." In other words, "It was more a matter of hating (the) philosophy than of fearing prosecution"; or, "He used fear of prosecution as a cloak for hating the philosophy." In any case, Seneca senior admires the "noble and strong" principles of Fabianus, the Stoicizing Sextian (*Contr.* 2. pref. 1), and speaks highly of his son's other teacher of philosophy, Attalus the Stoic (*Suas.* 2.12). He may well have had something to do with the selection of these two as his son's teachers, even as he discouraged what he considered the harmful influence of Sotion.

Today we would probably call the elder Seneca "an old-fashioned liberal." His values were attached to the past, but a past in which responsible and articulate participation in the activity of politics was the hallmark of a true Roman. The flashes of passion we have seen in what he wrote as an old man reveal, not conservatism in a negative sense, but a lively political and moral conscience, which must have ignited more often when he was younger. The intensity of his republicanism and moralistic concern will reappear in the son's career, though in different forms.

However, the father's most apparent influence lay in sharing with Novatus, Seneca, and Mela his keen interest in rhetoric and his phenomenal knowledge of orators and rhetoricians over a period of some sixty years, from the later years of the Republic through the days of Augustus into the time of Tiberius. Details such as the exact ages of the sons are not known, but the three were about of an age and in their middle teens would have been ready for instruction in rhetoric as the traditional training for legal, political, or governmental careers. From the father's memoirs we learn that father and sons attended declamations together (*Contr.* 10. pref. 2, 9). Their activity obviously went beyond mere educational requirements, and the Senecan home must have buzzed with conversation and argument about styles, logic, originality, laws, digressions, characterization, equity, persuasion, voice, gestures, correct Latinity, and so forth.

In educated circles, the public declamation was a popular intellectual exercise and a curious exhibitionistic fad, a hothouse product of the Greco-Roman oratorical tradition. Roman political oratory, which had been the loud voice of the Republic, faded during the relatively stable principate of Augustus when the republican political forms and offices were used to concentrate continuous power in the person of the *princeps*. The energy and heat of the forum and senate house waned, even though the senate continued to meet, debate, and act. Active pleading still continued in the courts, and indeed legal business seems to have increased, but this function was more professional than civic. However, Rome was part of "a culture taught to regard speech as the noblest human art,"[4] and any decline in the opportunities for public address was compensated by other outlets. C. Asinius Pollio invited the public to readings of his literary work (*Contr.* 4. pref. 2), and thus began the literary *recitatio*, which became a standard procedure for the introduction of new compositions. For several centuries *declamatio* had been the traditional exercise to train Greek and Roman students in the rhetorical schools and was only occasionally done by adults, privately or in semi-privacy for practice and recreation. During the Augustan period, declamation continued to take place in the schools for the most part, but it was an activity not restricted to students and teachers. It became a public, intellectual, and even social function for students, their teachers, guests, other teachers, experienced amateurs like the elder Seneca, and others indulging in a fashionable pastime.

The nature of the declamation had changed somewhat over the long period of its use, but in the early empire there were two types of set exercises, the deliberative *suasoria* and the judicial *controversia*. Declamation in general and the *suasoria* and *controversia* in particular were essentially histrionic and theatrical.[5] In the *suasoria* the speaker assumes the role of being, or being the confidant of, historic persons confronted with a "dramatic" choice in a real or, more often, imaginary situation. The speaker can be or can advise Agamemnon deliberating whether to sacrifice Iphigenia. The speaker can be or can advise Cicero deciding whether he should burn his writings to save his life on the supposed option given by Antony.[6]

The *controversia* was considered the harder exercise. Its role playing is more intricate because more principals are involved in the dispute, and the conditions of speech making are freer. It is assumed that a given "case" is under a certain law—Roman, Greek, or fictitious. Law: "An assaulted woman may choose either the execution of her ravisher or marriage to him without dowry" (*Contr.* 1.5). The circumstances of the criminal or civil charge are fabricated so as to allow a variety of viewpoints on both sides and are often sensational and fantastic. Circumstances: "A man has raped two women in one night; one victim wants execution, the other, marriage." The speaker may take the part of either litigant or of an advocate for either side.

Before exploring the dramatic nature of declamation more closely, we must introduce the writings of Lucius senior. Practically nothing survives of his history of Roman affairs, covering the period "from the beginning of the civil wars, when truth first withdrew, almost up to the day of his death" as we learn from a fragment of the younger Lucius' biography of his father (Haase, frag. 98–99). From this small fragment some inferences about the son's attitudes and conflicts can be drawn. He has withheld publication of the writings that his father wanted published, presumably because at the beginning of Caligula's regime it was thought dangerous to expose publicly the father's republican interpretation of recent events, dangerous, we assume, for the political careers of Novatus and Seneca, who would then have been in the early stages of senatorial careers. If the language "when truth first withdrew" is not a direct quotation from the history, it is at least a signpost of politically loaded criticism.

Other language in the fragment supports the suggestion made earlier that the elder Seneca was unable to achieve his ambition to rise politically and socially, to raise his family to the status of becoming *nobilis* through a tradition of holding curule office and, particularly, the consulship. If his writings had been published, the son writes with seeming regret, "he would be considered one of those who by their talents have *earned* the rank of nobility with honorific inscriptions which are unstained as well as illustrious." Any reader of his history "would have thought it precious to know of what parents he was born." Filial loyalty, also mentioned in the fragment, may have led the younger Seneca to exaggerate—as he says, this would be "an honorable mistake"—but from his own words he is clearly conscious of the distance between the achievements of a colonial like his father and social acceptance in the very traditional Roman society where "noble" families continued to dominate the scene. Understandably, such sensitivity would make the son very careful politically and competitive to surmount the obstacles that had blocked the older Cordovan.

The elder Seneca's surviving work takes the reader right into the rhetorical world where the son's mental and linguistic habits were formed. What we have called "memoirs" were apparently titled *Oratorum et Rhetorum Sententiae, Divisiones, Colores*; that is, *Remarkable Expressions, Logical Analyses, and Circumstantial Interpretations Used by Orators and Rhetoricians*. Since the themes of the *suasoria* and the *controversia* were a stereotyped, limited repertory, the interest was in the originality of conception, argument, and, particularly, language achieved by the speaker. For the education and interest of the three sons and for the preservation of past achievement, Seneca reproduces by memory examples of coups of imagination and language devised by well over a hundred speakers whom he had heard during more than a half-century, arranged according to the declamatory themes. The work is a display of extraordinary memory—he boasts disarmingly that as a schoolboy he could repeat two thousand names in the original order and could recite from the last back to the first over two hundred verses given one at a time by his mates (*Contr.* 1. pref. 2)—and a unique record of Roman oratory and education in the closing years of the Republic and the beginning of the first imperial century.

The intellectual qualities shown in the work are well worth pausing over as an aspect of the potential heredity and of the environment affecting the son. The father's discernment and honesty appear in his attitudes toward declamation itself. As we have seen, he understands the political reason for the decline of real-life oratory and is under no illusion about the artificiality of the public exhibitions. In one of the surviving seven prefaces of the books of *controversiae*, he recalls asking Votienus Montanus, a successful orator, why he never declaimed. The answer: so as not to get bad habits from a kind of prostitution, aiming to charm rather than to convince, tricked out with seductive ornaments, self-indulgent, irresponsible, artificially stimulated, undisciplined (*Contr.* 9. pref. 1–2). Other salty comments by Cassius Severus: "In declamations everything is useless since they themselves are useless"; they are like "working in your sleep"; "judging an orator in this puerile exercise is like judging a pilot on a fishpond" (*Contr.* 3. pref. 12, 14).

However, it is significant that these caustic remarks are quoted from others. Seneca himself would not have expended so much of his declining energy on the undertaking if he had not believed in the value of "training in the fairest of the arts" (*pulcherrimae disciplinae*, *Contr.* 2. pref. 5). This art is, of course, *eloquentia*. His immediate purpose is to meet the sons' wish to have models of eloquence from the previous generation as well as from their own. At the same time, he sees the value of having multiple models in order to differentiate the qualities of originality and imitation or, in his judgment, to note the contemporary decline from Ciceronian standards (*Contr.* 1. pref. 6). His material provides a variety of good and bad models, which can develop sensitivity to language, form taste, and be judged independently. Despite the obvious faults of declamation, it did have its values, not the least being the creation of many articulate speakers and writers as well as a sophisticated audience for the reception of them.

Within the limits set by *declamatio*, the elder Seneca shows an acute feeling for language, styles, and their effects. The memoirs are a kind of verbal laboratory or a field of live criticism in which the raw data of his direct quotations from the different speakers are subjected to sympathetic but discriminating appraisal. For the most part, his criticisms follow from the quotations convincingly. For example, various kinds and degrees of praise are borne out by citations from his "first team of four" most illustrious declaimers: M. Porcius Latro, Arellius Fuscus, C. Albucius Silus, and L. Junius Gallio (*Contr.* 10. pref. 13). Latro is praised for his force when he argues the case of the father renouncing a heroic son who wants to return to war illegally; the father will lay his own dead body on the threshold so that the son will have to tread him underfoot to reach the enemy (*Contr.* 1.8.15). Arguing against a depraved Fagin who starves children and forces them to beg for his profit, Latro describes them bent over and crawling, and exclaims: "Good god! Is a healthy man fed by them?" (*Contr.* 10.4.21). Seneca notes that Fuscus, of the Asianist school, concentrates all his essentially poetic talent on imaginative, elegant descriptions: for example, a graphic word-picture of the menacing Tarpeian rocks from which the vestal virgin will be thrown and a lengthy account of the variety of nature in a Stoic-like scientific tone, which Fuscus ties in rather improbably to the question of sacrificing Iphigenia (*Contr.* 2. pref. 1, 1.3.3; *Suas.* 3.1). Albucius is treated more ambivalently owing to the strong and weak performances apparent in the quotations, but he is rated among the best because he combines brilliance and clarity, and is an honest man. Gallio, a close friend of the family and perhaps unduly favored in Seneca's judgment for that reason,[7] is capable of a variety of styles and can be very eloquent on humanitarian grounds, as when he speaks in defense of a son who has disobeyed his adoptive uncle and supported his needy father: "Will you forbid me to weep when I have seen a man in trouble? . . . Our emotions are not in our power to control [*Adfectus nostri in nostra potestate non sunt*]. Some laws are not written, but are more decisive than any written law. . . . I have the right to give a mite to a beggar and to bury a corpse. It is wrong not to give a hand to the fallen. This right is common to the whole human race" (*Contr.* 10. pref. 13, 1.1.14). Here we may anticipate a point to be expanded later, that the philosophical tradition, especially Stoicism, has pervaded *declamatio*: Gallio uses Stoic language in the Latin sentence given above and throughout his argument is expressing this school's notion of universal equity.

Seneca is not an indulgent critic. Licinius Nepos, he says bluntly, goes as far as madness can go in speaking against the painter Parrhasius, who tortured an aged prisoner of war and in this condition used him as a model for a picture of the tormented Prometheus: "If you want to give Parrhasius what he deserves, have him do a self-portrait" (*Contr.* 10.5.24). Antonius Atticus earns the palm for silliness in portraying Othryades, the mortally wounded sole survivor of a battle between Sparta and Argos: "Victor almost from the tomb Othryades pressed his wounds with his fingers, to inscribe the name of Sparta on the trophy. The ink was worthy of a Spartan: surely he was a hero who even wrote in blood."[8] In the same *suasoria*, where the three hundred Spartans deliberate whether to flee from Thermopylae, a Seneca unknown to us is ridiculed:

> Seneca, whose name perchance has reached your ears, had a
> disorderly and uncontrolled talent. He always tried to talk in a
> lofty style, and at last this desire became a disease and made him a
> laughing-stock; . . . Believe me, I am not jesting, his madness
> came to such a pass that he had his shoes made too large for him
> . . . and took a giantess for a mistress. . . . Once in my young
> days when he had stated in this suasoria the objection: "But, you
> will say, all the troops sent by Greece have fled," raising his hands,
> standing on tiptoe . . . to look taller, he calls out: "I rejoice, I
> rejoice!" As we marvelled what great good luck had befallen him,
> he added: "Xerxes will be entirely mine." He said also: [Xerxes]

"has stolen the seas with his fleet, he has narrowed the lands, he
has enlarged the deep, and commanded nature to take a new
shape: let him set his camp against heaven, I shall have the gods as
my comrades-in-arms."[9]

It is hard to follow some of these judgments. In such artificial and
highly charged material, the line of discrimination between success and
failure is not always clear. But the "bad" things are clearly bad, and
critical standards can be seen at work. Seneca comes closest to summarizing his ideal in a statement about Cassius Severus. "Thus he had all
the qualities which equipped him to declaim well: a diction not vulgar
or low, but choice; a delivery not negligent or weak, but fiery and
animated. His explications were not labored or empty, but had more
meanings than words, and were carefully prepared" (*Contr.* 3. pref. 7).
Surely the memoirs show a highly literate environment for the development of the son as a writer.

These examples take us into the melodramatic world of *declamatio*:
the corpse on the threshold blocking a son's return to war; children
starved into beggarhood; the Tarpeian rocks; the complexity of nature;
rich uncle versus destitute father; emotional reaction to the unwritten
universal principle of equity; a tortured model for a picture; red ink
pressed from wounds; Xerxes altering nature and opposed by the
speaker and his allies, the gods. On the surface, connections between
this overstimulated, sensational, nightmarish soap opera and Senecan
drama can be drawn easily enough. However, analysis of these connections will go deeper if we see that the characteristics of declamation
result from a rhetoric operating in a dramatic mode with its own cir-
cumscribed sense of reality. Comparable conditions, we may anticipate, are present in Senecan drama.

Parallels between oratory and drama are obvious and commonly
noted in the literature on rhetoric. In the *De Oratore*, for example,
Cicero often compares oratorical delivery with histrionic technique,
stressing in both the importance of bodily motion, gesture, facial expression, modulation of voice, and mimicry.[10] However, Cicero and his
colleagues were engrossed in the serious, public and private business of
live oratory and were condescending toward drama: performance in
oratory is more severely judged than in the insignificant craft of actors,
a mere imitation of reality.[11] At one point, impersonation in oratory is
mentioned where Cicero has Antonius describe how he practices the
three different roles of himself, his legal opponent, and the judge in
preparing for a case; but the idea is not developed (*De Or.* 2. 102–3).

Actually, to use Cicero's description of actors as *imitatores veritatis*, for truly dramatic elements in rhetoric we have to look to another "imitation of reality," namely, declamation.

The artificiality and inventiveness of the role playing in declamation can be shown by an abbreviated summary of the first *controversia* in the seventh book. Here, as usual, Seneca is recording for a given theme the approaches used by a variety of speakers and thus gives us a conspectus of the attempts at originality characteristic of the exercise. Our model is on the theme of "The Father Released by his Pirate-Chief Son." The circumstances:

> After the death of his wife, who had borne him two sons, a man married again. On the accusation of the stepmother, the father in a domestic trial condemned one of the sons on the charge of parricide, and turned him over to the other son for punishment.
> The other son put his brother on board a bare boat. The brother was carried to pirates and became their chief. Later the father on a trip abroad was captured by the pirate son and released to go home. The father disinherits the other son.

The *sententiae* begin with those of Albucius Silus speaking in the person of the other son, obviously the more challenging, novel, imaginative—and therefore popular—side of the issue. Albucius speaks as a young person in emotional and mental turmoil at the time of the domestic crisis: "overwhelmed by the storm of events," "racked by fortune," unable to see or judge clearly, not knowing whether his father turned the brother over to him free or bound for punishment, not remembering whether father or stepmother entrusted him with this responsibility or how it was intended.

> You order me to sew up my brother in the sack? Father, I cannot. You do not excuse or believe me? I swear, neither could you bring yourself to it if a tyrant had said, "Come, sew up your son with your own hands." . . . Can you bear to hear the cries of your son in the sack? If you can, I fear that you have condemned an innocent. If you cannot, my father is witness of what a brother could not do to a brother.

The other son continues in a more rational strain: it was fate or fortune (*Contr.* 7.1.2–3) that defeated his intention to substitute a more humane kind of execution. For there was no hope of survival on the bare boat: no rudder, oars, companion, sail, or yards; no equipment, no prop of hope. More animatedly: "Am I to seek pardon from my father or my brother?" The excerpts from Albucius peak in a final theatrical justification expressed in the imagined "last words" of the pirate to his brother:

> I must die. Father has ordered it. I do not beg you for life, and you must do what has been ordered. Caught between your angry father and condemned brother, make the choice required by your love for both. Let Father have my blood, but save me from the sack. I am willing to die if only your hand is pure. I shall carry to the underworld the gift of your love.

Asinius Pollio, speaking next as the other son, apparently conceived of the two brothers as following a higher morality than the one prevailing in the household. At least this is the impression given by the brief *sententiae* quoted. "I will make you see that even he who has been condemned must be acquitted." Of the moment when the father confronted the other son with the truth: "Your brother is alive." "I don't believe it." "He has saved me." "Now I believe you." *Sententia* 3: "In this house in which parricide was easily believed, I could not kill my brother, nor he his father."

The selections from Q. Haterius indicate another psychological dimension, the sensitivity of the defendant, shown in graphic descriptions of the hurly-burly awaiting the parricide on the sea, blotting out the light of day, and of the poor condition of the boat. "The brother was already shipwrecked when he left the shore."

The elder Seneca's indefatigable interest in this material is hard to share, so only unusual variations will now be noted. Blandus vividly imagines the state of shock into which the other son is thrown when ordered to punish his brother. "Suddenly, without my realizing it, I dropped both my sword and my senses. My hands are numb. Some kind of disorder pours darkness before my stunned eyes. I understand how difficult it is to commit parricide even when a father orders it." Such passages are close to the psychological world of Senecan drama, where disturbed psychology and physical manifestations of intense emotion are essential components.

Cestius Pius takes the occasion to indulge in philosophical commonplace. "Nature has opened many roads to death. Our destinies hasten down many paths. The saddest human condition is that we are born in only one way, but die in many: hanging, the sword, a precipice, poison, shipwreck—a thousand other deaths lie in wait for our poor life." Also, Cestius imagines that the exile's innocence causes a miracle: "Look, the boat is rigged by the gods. All at once sails appear, the boat rises into position." The craft is protected from the storm. "The seas are more just than sentences, the windblasts more gentle than a father."

Musa's other son, to justify his clemency, delivers a kind of set piece on the variety of human psychology. "You accuse me of being too gentle. One man is softer than he should be, another is crueler than he need be, another is of moderate disposition [*mediis . . . adfectibus*], avoids both extremes [*inter utrumque positus*], and is complete master of himself [*totus in sua potestate*]. Some can accuse, condemn, and execute. Others are so mild that they cannot even testify on a capital charge. I cannot execute a man, a failing which is found even among pirates." Equally various are attitudes toward public service, marriage, warfare. "When the diversity of characters is so great, how very little is the fault I ask you to pardon. . . . I am compassionate. I cannot kill a man. . . . This fault I inherited from you." Again, the Latin phrases are given to show the fusion of such rhetorical psychologizing and Stoic concepts. Musa's passage is practically indistinguishable from the younger Seneca writing in a philosophical essay or epistle.

After a few snatches of argument on the other side by the father, the section of *divisiones* begins. These logical analyses of the issue are the more intellectual part of the *controversia*, even though they too become stereotyped. In this instance, as often, Seneca gives prominence to the *divisio* of Porcius Latro, who for the case of the other son draws his favorite distinction between "what he is allowed to do" and "what he ought to do," between legality and equity. On the legal side, the duty to obey a father's command is set aside by the nonlegality of a domestic trial. Also, if the other son executes, he is in a legal quandary: he might be acquitted in a domestic court but would have no defense in a public court. On the side of equity, even if his brother is guilty, he is bound by the sacred laws of nature, respected even by pirates. Once these distinctions and alternatives are established, they become a warp for weaving a network of contrasts and parallels such as we have seen in the *sententiae*.

Finally, Seneca gives selected *colores*, particular interpretations "of events or motivation which [the declaimers] adopted as the basis of prosecution or defense."[12] They show very clearly the freedom of the speaker to invent from his uncontrolled imagination. Cestius has the two brothers pass by the tomb of their mother after the trial, and the condemned brother invokes her spirit. The other brother is moved and delivers a *color* that Seneca finds "childish": "What was I to do? Execution was ordered by my father, forbidden by my mother." Evidently, the antithesis was more important to Cestius than sense.

Passienus uses the *color* of assuming that the father did not want his son executed and acted out of compassion in trying him at home and entrusting the execution to his brother. In Asinius Pollio's argument against the stepmother, he has the son reason that the parricide should be punished not by him but by the public prosecutors, the court, and the executioner. In the version of Varius Geminus, the stepmother has divided her hatred between the two stepsons, accusing one of parricide and imposing parricide upon the other. The other son cross-questions his brother and elicits the fact that he has not been tried by due process. Triarius composes for the son a fervent appeal for help in judging his brother, addressed to "whatever power commands the earth, rules the deep, and looks upon human affairs from above."

The apparently unpopular case of the father is represented by three excerpts. According to Cestius, the pirate son released his father because this action would be a more grievous punishment than death. Of the same act, Varius Geminus says that the pirate was hedging against the charge that he had contemplated parricide earlier. Porcius Latro coins the pathetic question, "Who is more wretched than I, who owe my life to a parricide?"

This summary of *Controversia* 7.1 has been tedious, like declamation itself, but it is essential to demonstrate in some detail an activity that formed the mental processes and language of the younger Seneca. Its importance went deeper than normal in his case because in the Senecan family rhetoric was not merely an aspect of traditional education, nor even merely a major intellectual trait of the time, but virtually a way of life. Our study will show that the drama is derived from declamation in a number of ways. The transfer is natural and substantial because declamation has much of drama in it.

The *controversia* and *suasoria* are embryonic drama. The speaker plays his role in a scene set by the traditional mold of the theme. This reality assumed by him is an unnatural reality, as we have seen, consisting of moot situations that are free from the limitations of ordinary experience and therefore stimulate a great variety of imaginable constructions.

The declaimer is not speaking to a court or an assembly but is seeking approval and applause from an audience of sophisticates who have presumably heard the theme before and are looking for novelty and ingenuity in the performance.[13] From the roles allowed by the theme, he chooses one, prepares the part as quasi-dramatist, and delivers it as quasi-actor.[14] He chooses the particular role presumably because it gives the greatest play to his imagination, the greatest outlet for original or unusual interpretations and, above all else, impressive verbal effects. Whatever new dimension he can invent, whatever standard dimension he can vary, however he can elaborate or intensify, his overriding purpose is to interest, impress, move, startle, shock with language. This is rhetoric, and what matters is the word.

Declamatory Latin, though covering a variety of individual styles, is generically a passionate and pictorial language. It draws its verbal force from two major sources: psychological disorder and moral thought.

Its most obtrusive theme is the delineation of human nature under stress. The purposes of rhetorical training and display were served best by having speakers perform the roles of historical or imaginary characters put into tense and sensational situations. Such situations forced the speakers to take strong positions, shred emotions, and in general make loud noises.

In the memoirs we have already encountered the father deliberating whether to sacrifice the daughter, the statesman deciding whether to relinquish his writings to save his life, the son torn between the claims of natural father and adoptive uncle, and the tangled relationships among pirate son, the other son, father, and stepmother. Other bizarre and pathetic scenes could be cited: for example, the real-life situation of the orator Q. Haterius, who melodramatically poured his tears over the death of his son into a *controversia* involving a suit brought against a rioter who had forced a father to abandon the grave of his three children; incidentally, Seneca senior here shows a revealing attitude about the relationship between rhetorical performance and emotional state when he remarks about the incident, "We see how much true pain contributes to talent" (*Contr.* 4. pref. 6). The son of a disabled soldier and a woman caught in adultery faces the choice between matricide and disloyalty to his father (*Contr.* 1.4). On occasion, the material of the memoirs parallels situations in Senecan drama: two brothers, warring like Polynices and Eteocles in the *Phoenissae*, are urged to make peace; their hatred is compared to that between Atreus and Thyestes (*Contr.* 1.1.6, 21, 23).

From all these *suasoriae* and *controversiae* taken together, we gain a massive picture of essentially psychological interpretation engaged in by hundreds of speakers over a long period of time. The performers project themselves into a great variety of public and domestic problems. They assume the personalities of persons from many walks of life, slave and free, in highly varied *ethopoeia*. They devise and declaim the words giving reality to the thoughts and emotions of crisis and conflict. It is no wonder that interest in the portrayal of subjective experience and psychological disorder, which long before had become a literary phenomenon among Roman writers influenced by Hellenistic literature, reached its peak in declamatory rhetoric and strongly marked the literature of the early imperial centuries.

The rhetorically fertile states of excitement and distraction leave little room for anything else, but a more rational milieu can be found when the memoirs are scrutinized. This environment appears occasionally rather than systematically, of course, in the words of a number of speakers. It consists of legal, social, and political concepts and echoes of philosophy, specifically Stoicism.

A number of the Stoic echoes have already been noted. The presence of this philosophy is not surprising, for its spirit and general principles had entered the Greco-Roman oratorical tradition. Cicero in his *Brutus* has Atticus and Brutus discuss some of their older Stoic contemporaries: they are thought better at reasoning than at public speaking but are given a place of distinction in public affairs and oratory (113–20). Of the bits of philosophy in the speeches recalled by Seneca, some are probably Stoic, such as the rejection of the Epicurean view that pleasure is the summum bonum[15] or the question whether the vestal virgin has survived execution from the Tarpeian rocks by Providence or Chance.[16]

Other pieces are quite clearly Stoic. In the characteristic Stoic monism, Nature is both passive matter and active energy, being both physical creation and the spirit that activates the universe. In the *suasoria* advising Alexander the Great whether to venture across Ocean, Nature is a system that sets physical limits to everything except Ocean, where its creative energy ends and there are no light and stars. Hercules gained his immortality in the world defined by these limits. Since the universe is finite physically, it "follows" that morally Alexander's aspiration and prosperity must be finite, must be limited by self-control. Ocean, poured around the world by Nature, is inviolable (*Suas.* 1.1, 3, 4, 9–11). Even when a speaker simply says, "I was moved by nature, filial loyalty, and the vicissitudes of life" (*Contr.* 1.1.16), it is implied that Nature determines the qualities and conditions of human experience. The moral laws of Nature are so powerful that they are respected even by pirates (*Contr.* 7.1.17)! When these laws are over-turned, Nature is called upon to protest and reverse its normal system: let rivers flow backward and the sun reverse its course (*Contr.* 1.5.2), as in a melodramatic hurly-burly. Nature is sovereign over human life and determines its fortunes (*Contr.* 1.6.3).

Since man is closest to the gods, his destructive behavior in war is all the worse (*Contr.* 2.1.10). The practice of reason (*ratio*) is the highest function because it transcends the sanction of law (*Contr.* 2.1.19). A Stoic would find no inconsistency between the ideas that human life is on the one side directed by Providence (*Contr.* 2.2.1) and on the other buffeted by Fortune (*Contr.* 2.1.1, 4. pref. 6). Fortune's gifts are super-ficial: "No one is free or slave by Nature; these terms are put on individuals by Fortune" (*Contr.* 7.6.18). In matters of honor and purity, death is a noble exit (*Contr.* 1.2.3, 1.8.3; *Suas.* 2.2).

Of the eleven speakers who use these fragments of Stoic thought, only Fabianus Papirius is identifiable as a Stoicizing philosopher. In declamation, as in other fields like oratory, literature, and law, the popular philosophy has spilled over into nonphilosophical thought and become a lingua franca for moralistic and optimistic feeling. The use of Stoic elements in declamation is understandable quite apart from the wide currency of the philosophy in educated circles, for Stoicism has a rhetoric of its own—paradoxes, apothegms, rational analysis, emo-tional intensity—from which declamatory language drew the strong and contrastive effects desired.

Other kinds of thought coalesce with the Stoicism into a generalized, humanitarian atmosphere.[17] We have already found such topics as a speaker's concern for beggar children, the son who justified sympathy for his estranged father in terms of universal equity, indignation over the mistreatment of an enemy, the choice of a humane kind of execu-tion, love for both angry father and condemned brother, unwillingness to execute a man, the transcendence of equity over law, the absence of due process, the necessity of peace between warring brothers, and so forth. Obviously these social and legal insights are simplistic and sen-sational, but they express the ideals of compassion and equity in the face of the disturbed and violent "realities" appearing in declamation.

Also, they have a political counterpart in republican and antityrannical sympathies.[18] In Roman declamation, tyrants are without exception fair game. A woman is unsuccessfully tortured by a tyrant for evidence against her tyrannicidal husband. The husband kills the tyrant. Later he divorces the wife on the charge of sterility. She prosecutes him for ingratitude (*Contr.* 2.5). A tyrant catches a man in the act of adultery. The adulterer seizes the tyrant's sword, kills him, and claims a reward (*Contr.* 4.7). The theme was traditional, but some Roman republicans considered even Augustus a tyrant. While declaiming, a man could be a tyrannicide vicariously and safely. The tenacity and vehemence of republicanism appear most clearly in the sixth and seventh *Suasoriae*, where Cicero is considering whether to beg Antony for his life and whether he should burn his writings in exchange for his life. In the former, one speaker raises Cicero to Herculean herohood as the Stoics would describe it: "All that will pass away is the frail, perishable body, subject to disease, liable to mischances, exposed to proscription: but the soul, of birth divine, which knows neither age nor death, freed from the heavy bonds of the flesh, will hasten to its familiar home among the stars."[19] The declamation hall gave some outlet for protest against creeping absolutism, the prime political issue of the time.

Declamation is truly a world-in-language. The nature of the "world" is surely now clear. It is a very restricted sphere, consisting in the histrionic exploitation of stereotyped, essentially unreal situations. Formally these situations are legal or deliberative, but declamatory rhetoric turns them into analysis and verbalization of emotional turmoil. So the prevailing tone is of psychological disorder. However, this tone is modulated by a set of humane, philosophizing ideas gathered from social thought—much of it Stoicizing—and from Stoicism itself. These ideas cumulatively have the effect of a normative system. As a result, the selections from declamation recorded in the memoirs show a polarity of disruptive and constructive elements, of torn emotions and aspiring thoughts. The interplay of contraries is a product of rhetorical themes and rhetorical purposes, but potentially it contains the ingredients of melodrama. The quasi-dramatic model of declamation was to have a deep formative effect upon the son's dramatic writing.

6. RHETORICAL DRAMA

Probably the most famous statement about this drama is T. S. Eliot's: "In the plays of Seneca, the drama is all in the word, and the word has no further reality behind it. His characters all seem to speak with the same voice, and at the top of it; they recite in turn. . . . the centre of value is shifted from what the personage says to the way in which he says it."[1] Without detracting from this acute criticism, we can be more exact than Eliot's explanation that Seneca's recitation-drama was caused ultimately by "the Latin sensibility which is expressed by the Latin language." A much more demonstrable explanation lies in the specific reasons why Seneca made his characters abstract, removed from the concrete actuality of normal drama, including Greek tragedy.

The main reason has been presented in detail. He saw the tradition of tragic drama, like all poetry, as significant in what it revealed about human experience when this experience was examined in the light of Stoic morality. As Eliot says, his characters have virtually no private life. The reason that they do not speak as living personages is that they are not constructed as individuals. Their characteristics are restricted to what Seneca wanted to show morally. He would say that there *is* a reality behind the words of his characters, the reality of human degradation and nobility—not Eliot's kind of dramatic statement, of course, but the statement of a moralist. Another dramatist might convey such morality in live drama, but the result would be less directly hortatory than Seneca's purpose. "Hortatory purpose" brings us to rhetoric.

In passing from the philosophy to the rhetoric, one point must be repeated categorically. Since the Neo-Stoicism and the rhetoric are inseparable, precision in assigning many dramatic features exclusively to one source or the other is simply not possible. The use of *exempla*, the vivid description of the physical signs of inner turmoil, the convulsion of nature reacting in protest to evil, the conception of a world of tearing and torn emotions—such features can be explained in terms of both philosophical analysis and rhetorical technique. This fusion is natural

Senecaism. He was trained in a rhetorical tradition that used Stoic ideas and values. In his philosophy, extreme positions of despair and exhilaration reflect both substantive content and rhetorical intensification. The spiritual power of his philosophy—and the drama is an extension of this power—stems from his command of rhetoric.[2]

The moral tensions dominating the plays (chapter 4) had their predecessor and presumably their origin in the psychological tensions of declamation. Clearly, the moral nature of the Senecan dramatic world, the mechanism of the human soul in good and evil, and human behavior under moral stress were determined by his philosophy, but before he was ready to dramatize such moral insights, he had been exposed to the psychological drama of declamation (chapter 5). For rhetorical training and display, declaimers speak and perform the roles of diverse characters placed in conditions of stress. These conditions evoke conflict, quandary, and pathos, emotions that the speaker must verbalize, intensify, and dramatize, exploiting the whole range of human feeling from distraction to aspiration. The psychological world of declamation was the seed of the drama.

The truth of this explanation is supported by other signs of declamation in the drama.[3] Scenes with the advising nurse or attendant (*Med.* 150–76, 380–430; *Phaedr.* 129–273, 435–582; *Thyest.* 204–335; *Troad.* 426–518; *Herc. Oet.* 233–540) are essentially poetized *suasoriae*. Confrontations of dramatic characters bear the imprint of *controversiae* pro and con: Medea and Creon discuss their cases in terms of tyranny and kingship (*Med.* 203–71); Pyrrhus and Agamemnon debate the morality of Achilles' demand (*Troad.* 203–352); Helen and Andromache clash about Polyxena's "marriage" to Pyrrhus (*Troad.* 861–1008). In the *Phoenissae* Jocasta's arguments to reconcile her sons twist and turn with the complexity of a double-issue *controversia*.

One scholar has found not less than ten ways in which passages in the drama are "written with a view to giving the actor or declaimer suitable material for energetic declamation." For example: "parts involving sudden transitions, in which the countenance and voice of the declaimer change quickly with change of feeling"; lines "portraying the emotion of persons represented as perceiving a vision"; and "passages showing in a striking way various features of a declamatory style, such as exclamation, interrogation, entreaty, apostrophe, sudden transition."[4] Such techniques were more likely the result of ingrained manner than of conscious purpose.

This relationship can be seen more deeply when we think of declamation as creating a distinctive form of personality, thought, and expression. Its rhetorical purposes produce characters who are states and stances, not individualities. They are at peaks of excitement and distress. Their emotions, generated by domestic strife, violence, blood, or sex, are on the surface and are poured forth with all the passion and diagnosis that verbal technique can contrive.

Parallels show that these characters of declamation are the forebears of the dramatic characters. The arguments for and against the suicide in *Controversia* 8.4 sound like the exchange between Oedipus and Antigone in the *Phoenissae*. The same inflated talk is found when Alexander is advised against breaking the bounds of nature by sailing across Ocean (*Suas.* 1) and when Hercules in both plays challenges the whole universe; one declaimer is reported to have warned Alexander by examples of kings (*exempla regum*) who have fallen from their eminence (*Suas.* 1.9), even as the chorus says of Hercules, "Bold courage has a long fall" (*Herc. Fur.* 201). The indefatigable Spartan Othryades shows the same kind of braggadocio (*Suas.* 2.16–17) as Oedipus prepared to face Mars and the Giants (*Oedip.* 89–91) and Hercules ready to lead another assault of the Titans on Olympus (*Herc. Fur.* 965–73).

The dramatic characters have a declamatory personality. They are not delineated as living individuals but are created as voices of attitudes and emotions that serve the dramatist's purposes. Like the declaimer, Seneca creates personifications that produce the effects and points he wishes to make. Medea, Hercules, and Pyrrhus—all are such voices. They do not differ as living characters differ but in what they represent.

Various consequences result.[5] On the negative side, the emotions of characters operate in categories, so that any enraged character or any fearful character will speak in the same way. Also, there is little differentiation of characters and situations. Whether Medea is voicing her fury against Jason, or Phaedra her passion for Hippolytus, or Hippolytus his hatred of women, they use the same language and the same themes. The technique is monotonous and lifeless, very serious faults in any poetry and particularly in drama. Further, the concentration on verbal effect makes the dramatist always strive for the extra power, for the extra vividness, often resulting in bombast and incredibility.

The other side is not inconsiderable. Declamation gave Seneca a technique for analyzing motives and diagnosing emotions. The inner struggles, the moral failures and victories analyzed in chapter 4 are only a step, though a large step, from the agonies of the "other son" in the *controversia* summarized in chapter 5. He too soliloquizes about human nature, loses his senses, has visions, suffers emotional and mental turmoil. Even the ranting derived from declamation has its merit; the history of post-Senecan drama shows that "heroic character was enriched . . . by the faculty of ranting."[6]

Still, the step from declamation to drama was indeed large. Most of the characters in declamation are in legal crises of a personal or domestic nature. These crises are used to generate excitement, tension, and verbal power as the characters seethe and boil. But the issues are limited and pedantic in comparison with the issues of the drama. When the verbal power of declamation is turned into poetry, applied to the bigger-than-life figures of the dramatic tradition, and converted to Neo-Stoic analysis of the issues, the result, far from rhetorical exercise, is powerful melodrama.

We seem to have spoken of the dramatic characters as if they were marionettes. They have been called this,[7] and it is true in the sense that they are voices of the ideas intended by the dramatist. However, these ideas involve human passions, values, and virtues, and therefore mirror life, even if in very extreme forms. In the plays we do not see human persons, but we do see the motives and consequences of human behavior. Seneca himself speaks of "this drama [*mimus*] of human life in which we are to play our assigned roles badly" (*Ep.* 80.7). Badly or nobly played parts in life—this is the serious business of Senecan drama, and no puppet show. "Life" in the drama is interpretation of life.

Other specific marks of declamation have been found. Years ago Leo used language parallels between the drama and declamation as reported by the elder Seneca to prove that the son wrote a new type of tragedy, "rhetorical tragedy," empty of characterization but full of passion, declamations composed in dramatic form.[8] The parallels are no surprise as the product of this rhetorical family. More than this, it is a commonplace that rhetoric was the main new ingredient of the so-called Silver Latin, and its appearances are natural in both the prose and poetry of the time. It is impossible to tell the difference between significant parallels and common features of the new style. We must add that today's criticism of the drama finds Leo's view very oversimplified. As rhetorical as the drama is, it is far more than declamation in dramatic form. Seneca would be completely mystified by the interpretation that the prevalence of passion in his drama excludes characterization.

The most important rhetorical feature is the poetic language, obtrusive to anyone who has read a Senecan play in Latin. Description of his poetic style in chapter 2 emphasized its strongest characteristic, a closely packed, highly figured expression so pervasive that figures and images appear in just about every line. The style, well called "athletic,"[9] incessantly punches, thrusts, and parries, mounting climaxes, shifting attacks, always trying for a verbal knockout. It is a potent instrument for high emotion. We know that Seneca thought of the power of poetry as muscular: "When meter is added and its regularity compresses a great thought, the same idea is hurled with more muscle" (*Ep.* 108.10).

Declamation manufactures emotion by putting its characters into critical situations. In the drama the case is similar, for here philosophical themes occasion high emotion, whether of mania or nobility. Philosophy and rhetoric reinforce each other. The former creates opportunities for the rhetorical style. It uses models of rage, lust, hatred, fear, suicidal passion, piety, cruelty, tyranny, courage, purity, and the rest. These polarized absolutes of Stoicism require a language capable of extreme effects to match the extreme states. Conversely, as in the prose writings, the intense style sharpens the philosophical positions, deepening the horror of passion and elevating the nobility of reason.

Seneca's poetic style was influenced mainly by the increasingly rhetorical tradition of Virgil and Ovid[10] but goes far beyond its forebears in rhetorical nature. Four samples from the plays will be used to show the power of the style to communicate a variety of psychic states, although the full effect of the rhetoric can be felt only in the entirety of the Latin. In the following analyses, commentary will be italicized.

Clytemnestra

In the first scene of Episode I of the Agamemnon *(108–225), Clytemnestra, with the nurse, agonizes about her moral quandary.* "Why am I so slow and cautious? The better road is closed already. Time past, you might have safeguarded your bed and throne—husband gone—with chaste faith. Now faith is gone, along with character, honor, and the rest. Gone, too, is purity which, once it has left, does not know the way back" (*et qui redire cum perit nescit pudor*, 113).[11]

"So give free rein, lean forward to whip up evil to the full. It is always through crime that crime finds a safe path" (*per scelera semper sceleribus tutum est iter*, 115).[12] "Unfold from within yourself a woman's treachery, do whatever a faithless, lust-blinded wife has dared, or a stepmother's hands, or the maiden hot with passion as she leaves home in Jason's ship. Sword, poison. Or you must steal from your home with your mate aboard. But why this timid talk of stealth, exile, and flight? This is what your sister did. Greater crime suits you."

To create this initial picture of the force of Clytemnestra's passions, Seneca follows a simple but effective metaphor. The passage is full of physical movement along various "roads": Clytemnestra's cautious movement, the closed better road, the departure of virtue, the nonreturn of purity, Clytemnestra as chario-teer, a safe course for crime, Medea's flight, possible exile for Clytemnestra, Helen's flight. These are outer signs of inner force and turbulence. When they are expressed in aphoristic language and intensified with easily identifiable mytho-logical parallels, the result is a fast projection of a destructive, anguished per-sonality.

This portrayal is internalized more and more. The second stage of the orches-trated process of crescendo—the Latin rhetorical term is gradatio—*begins when the nurse notices in Clytemnestra's appearance the external signs of internal pain:* "Every bit of your pain shows on your face" (*totus in vultu est dolor*, 128).[13] *The nurse's diagnosis of the queen's irrationality is so certain that the only possible remedy is delay (130).*

So Seneca has positioned us to see within Clytemnestra. Her ferment and torment—pain, fear, jealousy, lust—are conveyed by the favorite metaphors, raging fire and stormy water. "I am carried by shifting surges, as when the sea is driven from this side by the wind, from that by the tide, and the water can not decide to which force to give way. So I have let the rudder loose and will go wherever anger, pain, hope take me. Let the waves take my boat. When mind goes astray, it is best by far to follow chance" (138–44). *The road that she will now travel is crooked and blind.*

The emotions of the two characters are now raised in the quick exchanges of stichomythia. (Nurse) To follow the lead of chance is rash; (Clytemnestra) in a desperate crisis, why fear its uncertainty? (N) Your guilt can be hidden; (C) not in a palace. (N) Are you ashamed of your first crime of adultery, yet planning a second one of murder (*Piget prioris et novum crimen struis*, 149);[14] (C) yes, because moderation in evil is silly. (N) Heaping crime on crime increases the penalty you fear; (C) cutting and burning often replace medicine. (N) No one tries last things first (*Ex-trema primo nemo temptavit loco*, 153);[15] (C) when in trouble, you have to plunge down steep paths.[16] (N) Turn back before the sacred name of marriage; (C) should I, deserted for ten years, have any thought for husband? (N) At least you should remember your offspring from him; (C) indeed I do remember, remember my daughter's wedding and Achilles as son-in-law—what a betrayal of the mother!

The nurse's reply that Iphigenia's death freed the Greek fleet (160–61) brings the climax of the exchange. Clytemnestra explodes in a tirade about Agamemnon's betrayal of their marriage. Into it Seneca pours the force of the extreme emotions caused by the broken relationship. Clytemnestra's first words are: "What shame, what pain!" (162). She is haughtily indignant that she, of divine family, bore a life to be sacrificed for the Greek fleet (like an animal). She has a hideous memory of "the father of the bride" praying at the altar.[17] She is contemptuous of the Greek mission against Troy. She ridicules Agamemnon's sexuality, itemizing his amours with captive women: Chryseïs, Briseïs, Cassandra; he is a slave of slaves three times over, worn out with lovemaking (183) but always seeking a new mate for his bed (184–85). The great enemy of Paris comes home as Priam's son-in-law (191).

Finally, Clytemnestra aggressively considers how to protect Argos and her remaining children against Agamemnon and his new Trojan "allies." Her last resort: "If this is the only way, drive the sword through yourself into him and dispatch two at once. Mix your blood and his. In your death kill your husband. Death is not wretched when you die along with the one you choose" *(mors misera non est commori cum quo velis, 202).*

It is obvious that Clytemnestra here speaks like a character in declamation. Registering the intensity of emotion via the intensity of language is so important to the rhetorical writer that he is driven to sensationalism close to absurdity. Suicide and murder at one thrust! The rhetorical turn is designed to impress the hearer with an ingenious and memorable effect (such as the elder Seneca would remember).

Like most Senecan scenes, this one is concentrated on a separate highlighted effect, the portrayal of Clytemnestra's aggressive violence. It is not part of a process by which her psychology develops but a static moment. The truth of this is shown by the following scene (226–309), where Clytemnestra and Aegisthus appear in torment. The queen's psychological state is quite different here, for now she is struggling against the impulse to remain loyal to Agamemnon and capitulates to Aegisthus only when he threatens suicide and she realizes that she has gone too far to recant. So here Seneca draws the complementary picture of Clytemnestra's insecurity. The result is as if the dramatist juxtaposes two rhetorical exercises—Clytemnestra violent, Clytemnestra insecure—not to relate the two states dramatically, but to show both the criminality and the anxiety caused

*by the betrayal of marriage and parenthood and so to double the emotional
content of his dramatization. These scenes are rhetorical both in style and in
structure.*

*Such scenes appear to create abstracts because they are focused on a particular
entity or state, in this case Clytemnestra violent and Clytemnestra insecure.
This procedure may be effective rhetorically, but it does not suit the needs of
drama where continuity and cohesion are essential.*

Atreus and Thyestes

*The connection between declamatory rhetoric and literary interest in the por-
trayal of psychological disorder is well illustrated by the final scene of
the* Thyestes *(885–1112). Atreus comes to the banquet room where Thyestes
has eaten his sons' flesh. Seneca shows the villain at the peak of megalomania.
Indeed, Atreus is his own grotesque universe.* "I walk on a level with the
stars and proudly tower into the lofty sky" *(885–86). Since the gods have
fled, taking daylight with them, he will himself become a perverse source of light
and remove from Thyestes the darkness of not knowing his misery (896–97). So,
like an evil demon manipulating and enjoying human agony, he can see his
brother in the process of becoming wretched. Only a rhetorical poet would have
written the chiastic line:* miserum videre nolo, sed dum fit miser, 907 ("I
want to see him *become* miserable, not just *be* miserable"). *The banquet
room is now opened. Seeing Thyestes surfeited and sodden at the royal table, he
considers himself* "loftiest of the gods, king of kings" *(911–12).*

*The horror of this sadistic mania is increased by a strong statement of Thyestes'
insecurity. This is accomplished skillfully in a lyric soliloquy (anapests) in which
Thyestes tries to put aside the unhappy memories of his past but is unable to feel
secure. The festive garland slips from his head, his hair bristles, and tears stream
without apparent cause (947–51).*

*In this situation, the states of violence and insecurity are being used differently
from what was just seen in the* Agamemnon. *Here they serve to differentiate
the two characters. Atreus is viciousness personified. Thyestes is no longer the
person whose weakness contributes to his downfall but the absolute victim, about
to be plunged into unspeakable catastrophe. The stage is set for an explosion of
evil and suffering.*

*A crescendo of terror is effected by a verbal technique of intimation and
double entente moving along stage by stage. Atreus welcomes the occasion on
which his rule will be* "confirmed" *(970–72). Thyestes wants to share his good
fortune with his sons. He is assured,* "Your sons are here in their father's

embrace[18] and always will be. No part of them will be taken from you. . . . I will fill the father entirely with his brood" (976–79). *Promising to summon the sons, Atreus offers Thyestes a cup of wine, but the language seems to suggest another meaning:* poculum infuso cape/gentile Baccho (982–83). Gentile *describes the cup as an ancestral object, but the phrase "a cup of the family" allows another, grisly meaning.*

Vivid physical details increase the grossness of the scene. The cup of the sons' blood and wine mixed is heavy for Thyestes' hand. The blood-wine avoids his lips and smears his open jaws (987–88). It is as if nausea affects the universe: the sky is empty of constellations, the darkness deepens, every star is gone. With intolerable irony, Thyestes prays that this chaos will spare his sons and Atreus, and break like a storm upon himself. "Now give me back my sons" (997). *Senecan rhetoric is producing its utmost sensationalism.*

Seneca prolongs the horror in two stages: Atreus has killed the sons; Thyestes has eaten their flesh. Thyestes hears groans within himself that are not his groans. Atreus brings in the identifiable remains of the children. "Do you recognize your sons?" "I recognize my brother."

Thyestes' first reaction to the murders is one of Seneca's grandiose loud cries of suffering and indignation. "Earth, can you bear so great an evil" (1006–7)? Break, sink, sweep away everything: the king, palace, Mycenae, us. Put us below the underworld, in an abyss below the abyss of the damned. "But the earth lies inert, unmoved, the gods have fled" (1020–21).

In the rhetorical mode, emotional peaks call for peaks of verbal technique. Thyestes, wanting to bury his sons: "Give me back what you are to see cremated at once. I ask you for nothing expecting to have it, but to lose it" (*redde quod cernas statim/uri; nihil te genitor habiturus rogo,/sed perditurus*, 1028–30). *Atreus, in the technique of the repeated word (*iteratio*) used throughout this scene, picks up the* habiturus *and turns it to* habes *and the meaning,* "You have here what is left of your sons, and you already have what is not left" (*Quidquid e natis tuis/superest habes, quodcumque non superest habes*, 1030–31). "Are they fodder for birds and beasts?" "You have eaten them."

Thyestes' second reaction is of course wilder and also more religious than the first. Now he understands why the sky has darkened. What can he say? He sees the remains before him and feels the remains within him trying to escape. He wants to release his sons with the sword that has slain them or else crush his breast with blows, but—the attempt at rhetorical cleverness cannot be avoided—he must spare the spirits of the corpses inside. "Is there any limit of crime"

(1051)? *No limit, replies Atreus (again repeating), when wrong is being paid back. He regrets not being able to pour the blood hot down the father's throat. He recalls for Thyestes' benefit how he prepared the flesh for cooking. The nonrational condition of Atreus reaches so far that antilogically he wishes all the horror had been perpetrated by the father on the sons and that they all had been conscious of what was happening (1065–68).*

Thyestes can only call upon the universe to hear Atreus' crimes. He asks the supreme ruler of the sky to unleash the powers of nature in protest: clouds, winds, thunder, lightning. Strike down both of us in our evil or at least me, cremating my sons inside. *Seneca is ringing all the changes on the theme to increase the impact of the horror.*

The ending is ugly without relief. Atreus, referring to the seduction of his wife by Thyestes, enjoys Thyestes' suffering especially because it proves that the children murdered were his. Otherwise Thyestes would have prepared a similar banquet for Atreus. The final exchange is vicious. Thyestes consigns Atreus to the gods for punishment (his puniendum vota te tradunt mea, 1111). *And Atreus? He consigns Thyestes to his children for punishment* (Te puniendum liberis trado tuis, 1112). *The thought is unspeakable.*

Oedipus and Jocasta

The style is equally potent in moments of moral affirmation. When Oedipus appears after the self-blinding, he considers his act a complete satisfaction for his crimes (iusta persolvi, 998). *Seneca sharpens the moral point by reversing the usual connotations of light and darkness and equating darkness (blindness) with purification. So Oedipus delights in his darkness and counts it a blessing from some god who has pardoned him (999–1001). We are being prepared for a confrontation between a purified Oedipus and a Jocasta still to be purified.*

According to the chorus, she enters like Agave when she realized that she had decapitated her son (1005–7), probably the most shocking and revolting story of mother and son. The parallel is driven home by Jocasta's agonized, repetitive words: "Should I call you 'son'? No? You are my son. Ashamed of 'son'? Though unwilling, speak, son" (1009–11).

The sound of her voice—"my mother's voice, yes, my mother's" (1013) *—intrudes upon Oedipus' world of purifying darkness. The reality of her presence brings him back into reality, in a figurative sense restores his sight* (quis reddit oculos, 1013). *They must never meet again, even if one of them has to be taken to another world.*

Jocasta decides that she must share Oedipus' punishment even as she shares his guilt. She must purify herself, she must drive out her evil spirit that has confounded and destroyed the glory of human law (1025–27). How? In a dreadful moment, she asks Oedipus to complete his role as parricide, but immediately she seizes the sword with which he killed his father and thrusts it within herself. The blood drives out the sword.

The affirmative close comes abruptly. Because of Seneca's concern for morality, his Oedipus is far more completely a scapegoat than Sophocles' Oedipus. Taking responsibility for the deaths of both father and mother, he reassures his Corinthians and rejoices that he is taking the forces of corruption and death with him into exile.

Cassandra

Cassandra, under the spell of Apollo, foresees the crimes of Clytemnestra (Agam. 720–74):

"Sacred ridges of Parnassus, why do you stir me with goads of madness again, why sweep me off out of my wits? Go away, Phoebus, no longer am I yours. Put out the fires set in my breast. For whom now do I plunge and race about, for whom rant and rave? Troy has now fallen—what am I, prophetess believed false, to do?

"Where am I? The kindly light is gone, deep night covers my eyes, the sky is hiding in the darkness. But look! The day breaks brightly with twin suns, and a doubled Argos raises two palaces.

"I see the groves of Ida, fateful judgment seat of the shepherd before mighty goddesses. Kings, I warn you, fear the stealthy son; this child of the field will overturn your house.[19]

"Why does that mad woman hold out the weapon drawn in her hand? What hero does she attack? She is dressed like a Spartan, but carries an Amazonian axe.

"What is that other sight which catches my eye? An African lion, towering king of the beasts, lies under the base jaws of his bold mate, suffering her bloody bites.

"Shades of my people, why do you call me, sole survivor of my house? I follow you, father, as witness of Troy's burial. Brother, bulwark of the Phrygians and terror of the Greeks, I do not see your old-time glory or your hands scorched from the fire of the ships, but torn legs and those famous arms wounded from heavy fetters. I follow you,

Troilus, who met Achilles too soon. Your face, Deiphobus, is blurred. Your new wife gave you this.

"What a delight to walk by these Stygian pools, to see the savage dog of Tartarus and the kingdoms of greedy Dis! Today this boat of black Phlegethon will carry royal souls, captive woman and captor. I pray you, shades, and the river by which the gods swear, open up a little the surface of the black world, so that the spirit-throng of Phrygians may look off at Mycenae. See, poor spirits: the fates are reversing them- selves.

> "The foul sisters pursue,
>   swinging their bloody whips,
>   in left hand torches half-burned,
>   pale cheeks are bloated
>   and robe of black death
>   girds moldering groins.
>   Fears in the night rustle.
>   Bones of a giant body
>   rotted by long decay
>   lie in a swamp all mud.
>   See, the tired old man
>   no longer chases thirstily
>   the water mocking his lips,
>   sad at the death to come.
>   But father Dardanus
>   exults and walks grandly."

These examples could be multiplied many times over but are enough to show the hyperbole created by Seneca's rhetorical poetry for a va- riety of emotional and moral states. Intensification through exaggera- tion: queen in violence and anguish, monstrous viciousness and suffer- ing of brothers, son and mother achieving an agonized purity, princess in prophetic spell taking us into the spirit life of Hades and exposing the ugliness of physical death.

Another outstanding feature is Seneca's highly developed "pictorial imagination."[20] We are told that the many impressive and theatrical effects are to be credited to "his painter's eyes, his . . . visual imagina- tion and fantasy":[21] the appearance of Hecate in the *Medea*, the shatter- ing of Hippolytus, the upheaval of nature in the *Thyestes*, the moving scene of Astyanax' and Polyxena's deaths, Hercules' sons on the road to

Hades. Particularly graphic are the cases where moral and mental states
—Medea's anger, Hercules' insanity—are visualized and described as if
they were physical realities. The same principle underlies the imagery:
good things are bright and clean, evil things are dark and foul; human
violence and distraction are transmitted to physical nature—mountains
heave, seas boil, constellations flee. The identification of psychic and
physical states (consistent, as we have seen, with the Stoic view that
virtues and vices are corporeal) provides a battery of descriptive devices
applicable to any kind of phenomenon.

Seneca's own virtuosity is beyond question, but this visual capacity
must be considered another aspect of rhetoric. A declaimer was admired principally for novelty achieved by power of imagination, for the
faculty of seeing everything alive before his eyes.[22] Here again our
"other son" can demonstrate this primary motive. He visualizes the
storm that will wreck his brother's boat. His consternation is described
in physical terms of numbness and darkness. He imagines how the
gods miraculously rig the boat. Seneca's great talent for visualization
must have been the product of rhetorical purposes and training.

Finally, in more comprehensive terms, the whole purpose of the
drama is rhetorical in nature. Long before the time of Seneca, rhetoricians recognized the value of creating an imaginative collaboration between the speaker and the hearer, so that the hearer became engaged in
making inferences from the words of the speaker.[23] Augustan literature
and particularly Silver Age literature were increasingly influenced "by
the idea of orator and audience,"[24] by concern about the effect of the
writing upon the minds of the audience. So theory and the practice of it
implied a view of rhetoric not merely as the technical art of persuasion
but as "the art of all who aim at some kind of attitude change on the
part of their audience or readers."[25]

Analysis (chapter 4) has shown that the dramatic art is designed to
make the audience collaborate with the dramatist in apprehending the
significance of the dramatic content. Prologues immediately project the
destructive forces and the themes on which the plays are focused: the
fears of Oedipus, the vicious family of Tantalus in the *Thyestes*, the
theme of Fortune and Fate in the *Agamemnon*, Hercules' internal moral
enemies introduced in Juno's tirade. Foreshadowing, wordplay, allegory, and imagery call upon the hearer to recognize the moral themes
and to experience them continuously. Evil and noble emotions of characters are fully exposed in declamatory style. Most of the choral pas-

sages develop the issues that the dramatist is drawing from his material: the Argo theme showing the cosmic proportions of Medea's passion, Fate as divine order in Chorus IV of the *Oedipus*, the moral interpretation of Fortune in I of the *Agamemnon*, the violence of Hercules in I of the *Oetaeus*. Characterization, some of it very skillful, allows the hearer to see the ignition of explosive passion: how the natures of Creon and Jason contribute to Medea's mania, how Thyestes' weakness promotes Atreus' villainy. The whole dramatic system enables Seneca to engage his audience in the moral suasion that is his prime purpose.

For all these reasons, Senecan drama is rhetorical, not merely in Leo's sense, but far more deeply and comprehensively. The world of rhetoric—its psychological tensions, argumentation, mannerisms, personalities, stances, self-dramatization, analysis, language, visual power, and persuasion—is converted to a world of moral drama. Since rhetoric contributed such major ingredients, the form of rhetoric is really prior to the dramatic form. Rhetoric is the substratum of the drama.

7. REALITY AND THE DRAMA

The period in which Seneca rose to become probably the most distinguished and influential man in the empire was chaotically eventful. It saw the change from the more or less constitutional principate established by Augustus to various degrees of tyrannical monarchy. During the thirty years between Seneca's return from Egypt in A.D. 31 and his ultimate retirement from the court, his career developed under four emperors.[1] The principate of the competent but insecure Tiberius was winding down in a reign of terror conducted from seclusion on Capri at the time when Aunt Helvia used her influence to help Lucius secure the quaestorship and consequently senatorial rank. Under Tiberius, Seneca recalls, the mania for accusations of treason "destroyed the citizenry worse than any civil war" (*Ben.* 3.26.1). During the brief, power-maddened autocracy of Caligula, Seneca apparently became prominent as an orator in the senate, for we have the story that the jealous emperor criticized his style and spared him from a worse fate only because he was considered a dying man. Seneca probably has this principate in mind when he writes that anger "is the only passion which is contracted by a whole society" (*Ira* 3.2.2).

This mild example of the fact that in imperial Rome success was often measurable by the trouble one got into was followed by a serious political setback under Claudius. In A.D. 41—a miserable year for Seneca because then he also lost his only child, a son, and his wife (probably his first)—he was accused of adultery with Julia Livilla, one of Caligula's sisters, judged guilty by the senate, and condemned to death, but was finally allowed the remission of a moderate kind of exile on Corsica. The remission may have resulted from the influence of another sister, Julia Agrippina.[2] The charge was probably instigated by Valeria Messalina, Claudius' very young wife. Details are not known, but it is very likely that Seneca was caught in the Machiavellian politics of the imperial women, whose influence mounted under Caligula and Claudius, especially in matters affecting succession to the principate or threats to its stability. The sisters of Caligula, potentially dangerous as descendants of Augustus, had been politically active, and Messalina might well fear their rivalry to her position or at least their influence upon Claudius, her husband and their uncle. In fact, the sequel showed that Messalina gauged her competition very accurately, for the series of her own amours ended in a politically threatening liaison with C. Silius that caused her execution, and Claudius' new wife was no other than Julia Agrippina, in incest as defined by Roman law. Whatever the facts, charges of adultery and the like were a common maneuver in imperial politics, and Seneca's career suffered no moral damage, only interruption. Apparently Claudius was willing that Messalina get rid of Livilla, and there must have been signs of a growing affiliation between Agrippina and the rising Seneca that involved Seneca in Messalina's charge and made it desirable in Claudius' eyes that the relationship be checked. If these guesses are correct, Seneca was making political choices for the future and doing it very clairvoyantly.

After almost eight years, his chance to return to Rome came finally in 49, when Agrippina was able and ready to manage it. Having now added the power of marriage with Uncle Claudius in 48, she could pursue her fierce drives for power and wealth and place her son, L. Domitius Ahenobarbus (Nero), in succession to Claudius. Through her influence, Seneca was recalled, made praetor-designate, and appointed tutor to the boy Nero. Two years later, Afranius Burrus was made praetorian prefect.

Agrippina's incredibly melodramatic plan continued. She succeeded in having Nero adopted by Claudius as the guardian of his own younger son Britannicus and in marrying Nero to the emperor's daughter Octavia. Then she murdered the emperor with poisoned mushrooms (and the help of a physician). In October 54, the sixteen-year-old Nero became the new *princeps*, under the shadow of the imperial mother, Burrus the soldier-statesman, and Seneca, the most influential "friend of the emperor" (*amicus principis*). And Senecan drama is violent and chaotic!

The tale of Seneca's public life is not easily told. A modern historian of the period puts the problem well: "Since the drama of Nero's court is above all one of character, we must admit our inability to penetrate the innermost workings of the heart of the chief actors: no one can pretend to understand Nero, Agrippina, or even Seneca fully."[3] Also, our sources are either transparently untrustworthy or opaque. Of the three primary sources surviving, Suetonius and Cassius Dio cannot be trusted by themselves, Suetonius because he is a biographer more interested in scandal and color than in fact, Cassius Dio because he is inconsistent, biased in favor of absolutism in government, and prone to use sources hostile to philosophers and therefore to Seneca.[4] Tacitus is a notable historian but is so dedicated to his purpose of showing how the freedom and morality of the Republic have been eroded by imperial tyranny, so skeptical, subtle, devious, and creative, that the interpreter must try to penetrate his mind and art as much as the events he records. Consequently, there is room for disagreement in interpretation. However, he is by all odds the best we have, a responsible historian whose findings are rarely reversed by modern research. Our procedure will be to follow Tacitus as interpreted by the best authorities.[5]

We know precious little about the personality and talents that brought Seneca to political eminence. His family life, we have seen, was full of intellectual activity involving command of language; knowledge of history, politics, and law; and study of the philosophical tradition. His continuing education was remarkably broad and must have been the search of a contemplative mind. The older Seneca's unrealized political aspirations fed the son's. Years of exposure to the intricacies of Galerius' prefecture in Alexandria showed him the problems of rule in a vast empire. The complications caused by his growing prominence as speaker and politician must have taught him something about the art of survival in high circles by maneuver, influence, and compromise. In his early forties he was tested by bereavement and exile, and actually in years was more mature than most at his level of advancement. Tacitus explains that Agrippina had him recalled from exile to make her activities appear respectable, to gain popularity by advancing the career of a man famous for his literary works, to have the young Domitius trained by a good teacher, and to benefit from his advice in the pursuit of the principate—an interesting combination of good reputation, intellectual prestige, skill as a mentor, and political adroitness (*Ann.* 12.8.3). He influenced Nero, Tacitus tells us, "by his teaching of eloquence and honorable courtliness" (*praeceptis eloquentiae et comitate honesta*), in tandem with Burrus' soldierliness and severity (*Ann.* 13.2.2). These hints suggest the charm and thoughtful projection of himself to others seen in Seneca's own writings, particularly the more personal *Epistulae Morales*, where frequently the advice he gives his friend is an objectification of struggles within himself.[6] The Seneca who entered the maelstrom of the Neronian court was articulate, well-educated, contemplative, experienced, and able to mix ideals and political reality.[7]

Burrus, truly Seneca's partner in the leadership for almost two-thirds of Nero's rule, had less brilliant but substantial qualities. He was a disciplined soldier and a trusted familiar in the court since the days of Augustus, having served Livia (Agrippina's great-grandmother), Tiberius, and Claudius as procurator of their affairs. Like Seneca, he was a provincial, from Narbonensian Gaul. Although a sharp distinction between the roles of the two is not visible, and probably did not exist, Burrus as prefect of the praetorian cohorts obviously represented military force in the activities of the court, and Seneca was more the statesman and administrator. It is disappointing that we know practically nothing about the personal relationship between the two, except that their relationship was remarkably stable and creative.

Their first problem was to secure and maintain the position of being Nero's ministers. They were obligated to Agrippina for their position but could not give her allegiance. The imperious mother must have been startled when the ministers began to show their muscle. Quite on her own, she first contrived the murder of a provincial governor who was a potential source of trouble because he was the brother of an earlier victim and directly descended from Augustus. She also caused the suicide of her old enemy Narcissus, one of Claudius' freedmen-secretaries. At this point, Seneca and Burrus called a halt to her murderous purpose of eliminating real or imagined rivals to her own and her son's position.

How they managed this, by what combination of persuasion, force, threat, and influence they stopped her and began to restrict her power, is a serious gap in our knowledge. There is an unreality about the whole scene that cannot be penetrated: the emperor an adolescent; the fierce, apparently psychotic Agrippina; the severe Burrus; an enterprising Seneca who tried to make high principles work; the imperial court materially cultured but a moral jungle; the competition, suspicion, violence, intrigue. Burrus and Seneca were surely well-meaning men, but they could gain influence and hold it only by negotiation and concession. The narrative of their policies and actions will show that at several crises they had to pay a high moral price to keep their position. These crises have often been used as evidence of Seneca's weakness and self-compromise, but the fact is that Tacitus presents the two men acting in concert and together making tough decisions in political exigency.

One of Seneca's duties was to write Nero's speeches. The first reported is the oration on the occasion of Claudius' funeral, an elegant speech in the author's popular style. It contained conventional praise of the dead emperor's qualities, which made hearers snicker. Apparently the occasion caused little real grief, certainly not in the feelings of one who had spent eight years on Corsica for dubious reasons connected with Claudius. Seneca vented his antagonism in a satire of mixed prose and poetry, the *Apocolocyntosis*, or "How Claudius Was Apotheosized as a Pumpkin." Critics have worried about its taste and Seneca's ambidexterity in his writings about Claudius' death, but a less pretentious view of the piece is that it expresses "healthy, permissible irreverence directed at the imperial institution of deification and at an emperor who hardly qualified as a god."[8]

After the eulogy, Nero went into the senate house to give the usual statement of policy, presumably also Seneca's work. The older senators must have thought that they had heard it before, but the strategy is impressive. According to Tacitus' summary, Nero began by referring to the authority of the senate and the loyalty of the soldiers—a strong hand in a soft glove—and to the advice and precedents that he would follow for the auspicious beginning of his rule. He had grown up in civil peace and familial harmony (!), and was entering the principate without hostility or vindictiveness. His statement of policy was aimed at the problems that had made Claudius unpopular: he would not preempt and abuse justice as an in-camera function of his power; the palace was to be uncorrupted and kept separate from the state. The senate was to keep its traditional powers. Italy and the provinces controlled by the senate were to be ruled by civil law. The armies stationed in the imperial provinces were his responsibility.

If Tacitus' summary is close to the actual speech, the statement was conciliatory in assuring the senate that its traditional authority would be honored but, at the opening and the end, firm in calling attention to the emperor's military power. To our hindsight, the speech transparently outlines the policies that were the key of his ministers' success and even refers obliquely to their role as advisers (*Ann.* 13.4.1). Tacitus himself, the partisan of a free senate, comments that the promise to the senate was kept and cites two actions taken freely by the senate. He is of course aware that Seneca and Burrus were trying to make Nero the creature of their own ideas without causing an open break with Agrippina. On one occasion, she started to join Nero as coregent on the platform where he was hearing a foreign delegation, but Seneca quickly suggested that the emperor step down to greet her, turning the official crisis into a domestic scene.

The individual role of Seneca sometimes emerges from the opaque curtain of official anonymity. Tacitus reports acts of Nero showing restraint and clemency. He refused special honors. Using his constitutional power of tribunician veto in the senate, he quashed the prosecution of a senator accused by a slave and of one Julius Densus who was under attack for the political reason that he supported Britannicus (a rival to Nero himself!). When the consuls for 55 (Nero himself was one of them) were being sworn in, the emperor kept his colleague from pledging allegiance to his own imperial acts, thus making the colleagueship appear genuine. According to Tacitus, Nero "promised his clemency frequently in speeches which Seneca put on the lips of the *princeps* either to demonstrate the morality of his teaching or to show his talent" (*Ann.* 13.11.2). There is no reason to question the historian's cynicism about Seneca's motives—certainly his eulogy of Claudius was a showpiece—but his teachings about clemency are real enough and are preserved in his essay *De Clementia*, written at about this time and probably related to the substance of Nero's speeches. The essay is important as the best direct evidence we have of the political morality that Seneca and Burrus tried to develop and of the positive values espoused by Seneca.

The treatise is written in a form that shows Nero his supreme power and his responsibility to use it moderately "in a kind of mirror" (1.1.1); so it is "essentially the first Latin 'mirror of a prince.'"9 It is also tantalizing because less than half is preserved. Seneca announces the three books of the essay: the first will treat clemency in the sense of leniency in dispensing justice; "the second part will show the nature and aspect of clemency"; in the third, he will investigate "how the mind is led to acquire this virtue, how it is established and absorbed into one's nature" (1.3.1). Extant are the first book and perhaps a quarter of the second. We must thus get along without much of the significant moral theory in the second book and all of the third book, where Seneca's training of Nero would have been prominent.

In the first book, he faces the reality that the *princeps* has tremendous power and can be either a king (that is, a good king) or a tyrant, depending on his use of it.10 The opening words explain that Seneca will perform the function of a mirror in revealing Nero to himself "as one who will achieve the greatest pleasure of all." This metaphor indicates that Seneca is following the tradition of late Greek "royal mirror" literature, theoretical writing concerning monarchy inspired by the stability of the Hellenistic kingdoms.[11] However, as usual he has used his learning in his own way and for his own purposes: in the Hellenistic pieces, the mirror is used to project a general, theoretical image of kingship anonymously, but in the *De Clementia* the relationship between mirror and image is personalized, becoming the real-life, as well as idealized, relationship between Seneca and Nero.[12]

The good king is portrayed primarily as judge, but with the additional attributes of father, protector, and physician. His status in relation to law and justice varies radically, however, in the two surviving parts, as Seneca eclectically follows two different trends in the Hellenistic literature: in one, the king is a quasi-divine savior sent from above; in the second, he is a human creature bound to earthly conditions.[13] In the first book, the *princeps* by virtue of his office is essentially the former. His power is so great that he stands above the law. Clemency is his own voluntary benevolent action and is therefore itself a demonstration of his supralegal position (1.1.2). His relationship to his subjects is "a noble slavery" (another Hellenistic idea) like the relationship of gods to men, for in each case the superior being beneficently moderates its supreme power and bends to the needs and weaknesses of the inferior, without, of course, relinquishing its eminence (1.8.3).[14] The prince should be guided by the principle of treating his citizens as he would have the gods treat him (1.7.1). This view of the *princeps* as godlike is found in the Hellenistic treatises of Neo-Pythagorean origin[15] and may be another product of Seneca's contact with Sextianism.

He is reaching for a theory of the principate that will reconcile some old republican principles, such as his father espoused, and certain Stoic values.[16] For example, he uses an old republican *topos* when he calls Nero's principate "the most propitious form of republic [*rei publicae*] which for absolute freedom lacks nothing but destructive license" (1.1.8). The old principle that *libertas* is a civic right acquired by the Romans is converted to the Stoic notion that it is a human right by natural law.[17] The good king says: "Every man . . . enjoys my favor because he bears the name of man"; "in treating a slave, everything is allowable by law, but the common right of living beings forbids certain actions against a human being" (1.1.3, 1.18.2). The republican overtones were of course designed to influence Nero and may have pleased conservative ears, but the meaning is radically different. *Libertas* is the gift of the *princeps* (1.1.2).

The view of kingship being developed here shows the power of Seneca as a statesman, his fusion of idealistic political theory and a realistic grasp of Roman politics and history. Philosophically, kingship is according to nature, which has established its strong and benevolent system among bees and other creatures (1.19.2). But Seneca also seems to be the first on record to state publicly that political conditions in Rome and the far-flung Roman system require single rule and would disintegrate without it. The *princeps* "is the bond [*vinculum*] by which the state is held together" (1.4.1).

The fragmentary second book gives the impression that Seneca has shifted from writing a royal mirror for Nero to a philosophical discussion of virtues and vices.[18] Indeed, at the outset he visualizes for the immediate future under Nero a moral regeneration returning Rome to the Golden Age (2.1.3–4). Most of what we have discusses moral distinctions, such as achieving the virtue of clemency without falling into the vice of pity. In fact, the whole orientation has moved from considering clemency as voluntary action to the question of the moral absolutes that should direct the clement ruler. Cruelty and pity are equally vices because they both fail to achieve "truth" by the Stoic standard that Virtue is absolute (2.4.4). "Mercy joins reason" (2.5.1); the good ruler thus makes judgments not by legal formula but by equity and virtue (*aequo et bono*), and aims at absolute justice (*iustissimum*) (2.7.3). Since a statesman of Stoic convictions is writing about absolute standards to be followed by the king, it is natural that the emperor following these standards is conceived as *sapiens*, "Stoic sage," more often than as *princeps* and *Caesar*. This idea appears later in letter 90, where Seneca follows Posidonius to the extent of believing that in the beginnings of society the *sapiens* was king and the originator of law (*Ep.* 90.4–6). In other words, Seneca has enlarged the ideal of the benevolent king in the first book to the ideal of the philosopher-king in the second. He is following the old tradition of this dream and centering the dream in his relationship as mentor to Nero as learner.

It has been argued that the conception of *clementia* in the two books is contradictory because Seneca cannot have both a *princeps* achieving clemency by voluntary action and a *princeps* subordinated to the norm of absolute justice.[19] But an educational technique is clearly visible in the sequence of the argument. Seneca has moved subtly from the personality of the new *princeps* to the morality of the new principate. The initial assumption is that the personal nature of the good king will lead him to use his extraordinary power in a merciful discretion that is responsive to the natural rights of men. Mention of these natural rights puts principle as well as personality into the relationship between ruler and subjects, and in Seneca's mind would certainly imply a question about the total ethics of the relationship. What norms is the *princeps* to follow? The second book starts to answer this question, then is broken off, but Seneca has made his intention clear by saying that he wants Nero's natural inclination to become a matter of principle (2.2.2). The *De Clementia* reflects a pedagogical method: Seneca begins with the premise that Nero has a potentiality for enlightened rule and goes on to indicate the norms by which the potentiality can be achieved.

The whole attempt to develop a theory converting despotism to monarchy puts Seneca in the long tradition of Stoic political philosophy. His view that "the best condition of a state is under a just king" (*Ben.* 2.20.2) is the main traditional view. The moral absolutism of Stoicism made political absolutism acceptable, provided that morality and politics coalesced, and even desirable since the virtuous king can be a powerful spiritual director and model. But the tradition was not rigid because the philosophy was more concerned about the morality of a political system than about its structure,[20] and at times the theory was adjusted to political realities. The Old Stoa inclined toward monarchy, whereas the Middle Stoics, at least Panaetius, favored the mixed constitution of kingship, aristocracy, and democracy.[21] So Seneca's theory of the principate is legitimate in his philosophical tradition as well as tuned to political actuality.

It is easy to mock Seneca's theory. It is easy to call it pretentious, timeserving, self-serving, and preposterously impractical. Is he only writing propaganda for the new regime? Isn't he just being carried away by his own rhetoric? Isn't he merely building his own prestige and power in the court? If, as he says (2.2.1), he really hoped for a moral regeneration under Nero, how could a mature educated man well versed in Roman politics seriously entertain such a millenarian dream? If Seneca used to tell his friends that the young Nero was a savage lion whose inborn savagery would return if once he tasted the blood of a man (sch. to Juv. 5.109), what reason for confidence did he have?

The truth is, our information does not permit sure answers to such questions and doubts, and only probabilities can be reached. The hindsight that Seneca's theory and policy were doomed to failure is all too facile and does not signify concerning his motives and purposes. The closest we can come to a contemporary knowledge of the situation is to lean on Tacitus, who was born around the time of Nero's succession and had access to primary sources. Although an honest and trenchant critic of the principate, he considers Seneca a man of principle despite compromises noted by the historian. His judgment is the best basis of our judgment.

It is most likely that the *De Clementia* was written for a number of purposes: indoctrination of Nero, who was the only hope Seneca and Burrus could have; propaganda to project the new regime as a fresh start; demonstration of the author's role as the principal idea man in the court; and publication of a theory that would advance a nondespotic monarchy. The theory was not so far out of reach. It is well to remember that a hundred years later Rome would have the Antonine emperors who came close to Seneca's ideal.[22]

The essential stability of the regime would last a number of years, but its vulnerability appeared almost immediately. The advisers' power and influence were very conditional. Burrus had a formal office, but his influence as adviser exceeded the functions of his office. Seneca most of the time (he was suffect consul in A.D. 56) was a minister without portfolio. The story of their success and failure is the story of their efforts to gain some room for the pursuit of their policies by leashing two unbelievably wild and destructive personalities. Their first choice was, and had to be, to prevent Agrippina from sharing the power of the principate, to breach the relationship between her and Nero, and to make him independent of her and more dependent upon them. In allowing Nero to have his head, as long as his activities were only peccadilloes and did not discredit or weaken the principate, Burrus and Seneca became involved in utterly undignified and even rather comical subterfuge, like characters in a Roman comedy who help the dissolute youth flout convention and get the girl.

The seventeen-year-old became infatuated with a freedwoman named Acte.[23] At first the liaison was concealed by the device of having Annaeus Serenus, a close friend of Seneca, masquerade as the lover, even to the extent of putting his name on Nero's gifts to the girl. "Even the older friends of the emperor," no doubt including Seneca and Burrus, were at least tolerant of the arrangement as a control of Nero's sexual appetite (*Ann.* 13.12.2). When Agrippina found out, her reaction was spectacular. The affair threatened her position, her domination of Nero, and all the dynastic conditions she had contrived. She first tried vitriolic attack on Acte, which only increased Nero's infatuation, then complete permissiveness to the extent of offering her bedroom as a love nest for the pair. The result, which may well have been foreseen, if not calculated, was that Nero was alienated from Agrippina and became more dependent on Seneca.

The imperial melodrama continued with a quarrel between mother and son about the ownership of certain articles of dress in the palace. Tempers heated even hotter. Pallas, a powerful figure held over from the days of Claudius and long Agrippina's "man," was removed from his position as freedman in charge of the imperial accounts. Nero's advisers must have been relieved to see him go. Agrippina exploded and threatened Nero, apparently in private (*Ann.* 13.14.3). Britannicus, she said, was coming of age (he would soon be fourteen and wear the man's toga) and was the true successor of Claudius. Nero owed his illegitimate position to her crimes. Let the whole scandal come out: her incestuous marriage, her poisoning of Claudius. She would defend her status against the advisers who demanded rule of the human race, Burrus with his maimed hand and the exile Seneca with his schoolmaster's tongue.

Britannicus was Nero's first victim. Tacitus here inserts an anecdote showing how Nero tried to embarrass his stepbrother, who reacted spiritedly and turned the tables on his tormenter by referring to the loss of his rightful position. There follows one of the historian's brilliant and shocking scenes. In the palace, Britannicus and other young nobles dine at a side table in the sight of their relatives. The intimates of Britannicus have been suborned. A member of the praetorian guard and the notorious poisoner Locusta are ordered to prepare a poison. It is given to Britannicus by his own teachers. It causes diarrhea, and the boy passes the drug because it either was too weak or had been diluted to conceal the act by postponing the effect of the poison. Nero is enraged. The poisoners promise quicker results. Near Nero's bedroom, they prepare a second dose of poisons that from pretesting are known to act quickly. The security provided by the servant who tastes the prince's food and drink beforehand is circumvented by preparing a drink that is harmless, when tasted, but too hot for Britannicus to drink. Cold water—and the poison—are added. The fatal effect is instantaneous.

Of the young nobles at the table, some scatter, and others, being suspicious, keep their places with eyes fixed on Nero. He coolly comments that the prince will gradually recover from his fit of epilepsy, which he has had since infancy. Agrippina tries to control her face, but a momentary flash of panic and consternation shows that she is flabbergasted. She knows that the murder is a precedent for parricide. Octavia, a pathetic young figure, has learned to conceal all her emotions. After a brief silence, the festivity of the meal continues. The ashes of Britannicus are buried the same night.

To a modern reader, the scene seems incredible. It is, of course, the product of Tacitus' powerful imagination and very graphic dramatic art. Yet there is no reason to doubt the essential truth of his account. How do we comprehend such a monstrous crime? Maybe both Agrippina and Nero were psychotic, although we do not know this to be true. How could the murder be absorbed and accommodated in Nero's ongoing regime? Tacitus is sensitive to this question and gives a partial answer (though the text is shaky): "Most men condoned the crime, calculating the ancient enmities of brothers and the indivisibility of kingship" (*Ann.* 13.17.2). Truly, dynastic violence was commonplace in ancient society, and familiarity bred callousness. Also, although the society of early imperial Rome was highly developed in many material and nonmaterial ways, explosive volatility lay just beneath its surface. Any Roman, certainly one in high, powerful places, must have felt personally close to the experience of violence.

In his account of the murder itself, Tacitus does not mention or refer to Burrus or Seneca. If he had had any reliable evidence of their involvement, it is unbelievable that he would not have indicated this at least by his powerful art of innuendo. However, having stressed the pathos of Britannicus' death, he does highlight with satiric effect the official edict (again, presumably Senecan) defending the haste of the burial as traditional in cases of premature death. The edict went on to say that the *princeps*, "having lost the support of his brother" (*Ann.* 13.17.5), now put all his hopes in the state and was to be cherished by the senate and the people all the more because he was the only survivor of the Claudian family. Tacitus also reports that, when Nero enriched "his most powerful friends" immediately after the crime, "there were those who accused men professing austerity because they had distributed homes and villas like booty" (*Ann.* 13.18.1).

As to the edict, if Seneca wrote most of the official proclamations, he must have become very tired of this kind of window dressing and face-saving on serious matters. But a regime, his hopes for it, and his place in it were at stake. A fragment of his lost *Exhortationes* contains a revealing statement: "The *sapiens* will even do things he will not approve of, in order to find a transition to even greater things. He will not forsake morality, but will adjust it to the occasion, and what others use for renown or pleasure, he will use for accomplishing a purpose" (Haase, frag. 19). As a public figure, he had to make many concessions, and his words show that he was uncomfortably sensitive to the problem and had to make his own adjustment to it.

In the distribution of Britannicus' property, the anonymous charge against Nero's "most powerful friends" and "men professing austerity" is not entirely clear but apparently involved both receiving and distributing the property. The historian's technique of interpretation is constantly at work, and it is significant that at this point he cites unnamed sources making accusations couched in language that puts Seneca and Burrus in mind. Characteristically, Tacitus keeps a formal distance from his subject, but his posture of reserve and impartiality intensifies the passion of his narration. He has previously portrayed the violence of Agrippina and has now shown unforgettably the evil of which Nero is capable. Tacitus is revolted and shocks his reader. Nero is vicious and odious. But the historian is aware that the circle of guilt widens. The intentions of a Burrus or a Seneca may be good, but they are now stained indelibly. By Tacitus' sense of evidence, he cannot name them and call them guilty of having profited from the death of Britannicus, but he feels bound to record that there were those who believed the advisers guilty of this offense. He is scrupulous about evidence but knows the importance of insights that may not be based on more than hearsay, and records them when they support his comprehensive judgment of events.

Agrippina continued to act aggressively, keeping a close relationship with Octavia, friends, military officers, and nobility, and gathering a reserve fund of money, "as if she was looking for a leader and a supporting party" (*Ann.* 13.18.3). Nero's reaction was to eliminate her retinue and isolate her in a separate house, visited only by a few women. One of them was Junia Silana, formerly her close friend but now a bitter enemy, who stirred up the next trouble. Silana—using two of her cronies, who in turn used a freedman of Nero's aunt Domitia (another enemy of Agrippina), who in turn used a fellow freedman, Paris the actor and intimate of Nero—had it reported to the *princeps* that Agrippina planned to marry Rubellius Plautus and raise him to the principate as coregent with herself.

Paris put on his act as messenger of danger late one night, when Nero was tippling. Evidently Paris was convincing in the role, for the terrified Nero "decided" to kill Agrippina and Plautus and to remove Burrus from office because he was paying off his old debt to Agrippina. Here for the first time Tacitus indicates a chink in the structure of the regime; if the advisers were encouraging Nero to treat his mother as a political enemy, they too became vulnerable to this kind of suspicion. The historian is careful about his evidence on the matter. He points out that Fabius Rusticus, who reports in his history of Nero's principate that Burrus' position had been reassigned to another but was left unchanged through Seneca's influence, is inclined to favor Seneca, his patron (*Ann.* 13.20.3).

Tacitus in this case shows how the advisers succeeded in controlling Nero's panic by a quasi-legal approach. Nero was so upset and bent on immediate violence that Burrus had to promise the execution of Agrippina if she was convicted of guilt. He argued: everyone should be given the right of defense, most of all a parent, and the circumstances of the accusation were very dubious. A hearing was held at Agrippina's house. Burrus conducted it in the presence of Seneca and of freedmen who could report the proceedings to Nero. Burrus revealed the charges and the accusers, and pressed Agrippina for her answer. Her answer was a tirade against the whole lot of her accusers and the shocking but effective argument that all her misdeeds had been for Nero's benefit and that she stood to lose the most if a successor to Nero was to judge her actions. A private talk between her and Nero followed.

The result was to punish her enemies and reward her friends. Obviously, her power was still something to be reckoned with, but Nero was apparently satisfied that this particular accusation against her was the product of personal feuds, and the advisers were willing to make some concessions for the sake of at least temporary peace. However, there was a limit to the concessions. Tacitus tells us that one of Agrippina's intimates was designated to be governor of Syria but was thwarted by being kept in Rome on various pretexts (*Ann.* 13.22.2).

There was no end to the intrigue surrounding the court, Seneca and Burrus must have thought. It was alleged that Pallas and Burrus had conspired to raise Cornelius Sulla, son-in-law of Claudius, to the principate. Not only were Pallas and Burrus very unlikely co-conspirators, but Tacitus quickly disposes of the accuser as an unscrupulous rascal and the charge as false. Why was Burrus the one to be involved in such suspicions and allegations? Probably his military authority was the focus of fear and rivalry, and Seneca's position may have seemed less assailable. In any event, the pages of Tacitus show that Nero's ministers were subjected to continual tension and pressure as they tried to develop and maintain a political order against the constant threat of political chaos.

Certainly Nero's development was wild. The account of A.D. 56 begins with the tabloidlike tale of his riotous escapades in the streets, brothels, and taverns of the city: the *princeps* disguised as a slave, his gang pilfering from the shops and assaulting anybody in its path, his face showing bruises from the brawling; other gangs pretending to be Nero's; Julius Montanus of senatorial rank, who had defended himself when attacked by Nero in the darkness, driven to suicide; wrangling actors and their claques in the theater fomented by the *princeps* to such violence that total anarchy in the city was feared and theatrical players were ejected from Italy. The tale loses nothing when told in Tacitus' compressed and graphic Latin, but there must have been deep concern in high places about the destruction of public order caused by these "youthful pranks." The young lion was tasting blood.

Libertas in all its aspects is a major theme in Tacitus, and what he writes about its preservation, reinforcement, and erosion under Nero allows us to see some aspects of the public policy being followed. At the end of the year 55, the praetorian cohort posted to keep public order at the games in the theater was withdrawn to reduce surveillance but had to be restored in the next year because of the disturbances just mentioned. The senate was in favor of granting patrons the right of rescinding manumission to protect themselves against the offenses of their freedmen but referred the matter to the *princeps*, who apparently (the text is mangled) found his "few" advisers in disagreement and decided to favor the view that the rights of freedmen should not be abridged. He so instructed the senate. "Even so," Tacitus writes, "some likeness of the Republic still remained" (*Ann.* 13.28.1).

The senate, in its role as watchdog of constitutional powers, acted to protect the prerogatives of the praetor from encroachment by the plebeian tribune and otherwise to restrict the powers of the tribune and the aediles, all of this to prevent the abuse of power. The *princeps* transferred control of the public treasury from the quaestors to prefects, following the precedent of Augustus, but with the difference that the prefects were to be selected by the *princeps* from those who had had the experience of serving as praetors.

These technical matters show the operation of a policy that has been stated as follows: Seneca and Burrus "aimed steadily at enhancing the prestige of imperial authority but they wished this prestige to be based upon the securing of justice and economic prosperity for the Empire."[24] A case in point is the change in the control of the public treasury. Putting complete financial control in the hands of the *princeps* was not new, for Claudius had assumed this power and assigned the administration of the public treasury to quaestors chosen by him. But his control must have been less than fully effective because quaestors were young officials holding their first major magistracy. The change under Nero consolidated imperial control of finances by putting the administration in the hands of more experienced and responsible officers. The financial stability of the centralized control is shown by Tacitus' report that 40 million sesterces (several million dollars) were transferred in 57 from the imperial to the public treasury to maintain public credit (*Ann.* 13.31.2).

It would be fascinating to know what rhetoric Nero's advisers used privately to describe what they were doing. The precedents derived from Augustus, the limited but significant freedom of the senate to maintain the health of the magistracies and enforce the lawful conduct of officials responsible to it, the concentration of financial authority in the office of the *princeps*, the attention to public order (despite Nero!), and the appointment of trustworthy civil and military officers—all of these point to a conservative "law and order" policy in which a Seneca could find the ideal of a limited kingship, a principate of great power used to achieve the goals of public morality and financial security. This power was shared with other agencies of government only to the end of achieving these goals.

The vulnerability of Seneca now appeared. His enemy was P. Suillius, a notorious informer who had had a variegated career of high office, exile, and legal troublemaking for his own profit. He was prosecuted under legislation against those who undertook legal cases at a price. How proceedings against him were initiated is not known. They might have come from the senate since Suillius under Claudius had been governor of Asia, a senatorial province, and the charges against him included malfeasance as governor. However, the office of the *princeps* must have been involved, for Nero was present at the trial, and Suillius responded to the prosecution with a slashing attack on Seneca (*Ann.* 13.42.3–8). This "prosperous upstart," Tacitus has him say, was the enemy of Claudius' friends, thoroughly deserved his exile, and was such an impractical schoolmaster that he envied those who used their eloquence to defend citizens. Besides, he was an adulterer in the house of Germanicus, Agrippina's father; and Suillius wants to know by what philosophical principles he has acquired 300 million sesterces in four years of being "friend of the emperor." He has trapped legacies from the childless rich and has drained Italy and the provinces by usury.

The acrimonious trial resulted in the banishment of Suillius to the Balearics, but in the process Seneca's reputation was damaged. Although the historian condemns Suillius and some of the allegations against Seneca are obviously trite, such as his impracticality and fortune hunting, Seneca's wealth was indeed a handy weapon for his enemies. No doubt his private accumulated fortune was greatly increased by benefits received from Nero, and papyrus documents refer to Senecan holdings in Egypt.[25] But it is not at all clear how free Seneca would be to refuse Nero, and the holdings in Egypt could have started years before when his aunt and he himself were there. It is interesting that later in his narrative, when writing about the revolt of the East Anglian queen Boudicca, Tacitus makes no mention of the story found in Cassius Dio, that Seneca was one of the causes of the revolt because he suddenly called in his huge loan to the Britons and pressed them to repay.[26]

The first clear sign that Nero was asserting his own nature and becoming independent of his advisers as well as Agrippina was his relationship with Poppaea Sabina. Tacitus has prepared his reader for the worst by prefacing a lurid tale of passion and violence featuring a plebeian tribune mad with love for a worthless woman, assignation at night, a hidden dagger, intercourse followed by murder, a wounded maidservant, a loyal freedman—all the stuff for sensational headlines. Tacitus calls Nero's new relationship "equally notorious shamelessness and the beginning of great evils for the state." He comments about Poppaea, "She had everything except chastity" (*Ann.* 13.45.1–2). She used all of it, including the absence of chastity, to snare Nero in a liaison that was not merely a love affair but her plan for power. Acte had to go. Poppaea's husband was packed off to Lusitania as governor. Far more serious repercussions were to follow. In the meantime, Tacitus indicates, Nero began to use his power more brazenly.

However, the orderly mechanism of government went on, and indeed the advisers continued to work on their policy, venturing into economic innovation. For it was most likely the advisers acting in the name of the *princeps* who proposed for consideration the idea of eliminating indirect taxation in the empire.[27] The farming out of indirect taxes for collection by companies of businessmen (the "publicans" of "publicans and sinners") had long been a source of complaint about excessive taxation and exploitation, and undoubtedly caused economic stagnation in the huge system. Apparently the new idea was that the removal of these taxes, especially the customs collected at the frontiers and locally, would so increase the movement of trade that the lost revenues would be outweighed by the increase in revenue from direct taxes on expanded trade. Individual senators raised the obvious objections to tampering with the traditional system, and "Nero" had to be satisfied with modest changes ensuring greater equity and more efficient prosecution of unfair practices.

Tacitus chooses to begin the next book of the *Annals* with the events of 59. For five years now, Nero's principate had moved along the lines of stable policies, and the effect of the system was to persist for several years more. But Nero's plot for the murder of Agrippina marked a new dimension, to which the historian devotes close attention in the first fifth of book 14. The psychological impact of the new atrocity has been foreshadowed in the murder of Britannicus, but only mildly, because Nero's behavior now even exceeded the limits of crime and passed into fantasy and absurdity.

The following summary gives the basic sequence of developments in Tacitus' account. Nero has been brewing the plot for a long time. He is bolder now because he has been in power five years, his passion for Poppaea grows hotter, and she badgers him to the effect that Agrippina must be removed and Octavia divorced. He cannot resist. Everyone wants to see the end of Agrippina's power; no one believes that the son's hatred will go as far as murder. According to the consensus of sources used by Tacitus, Agrippina tries to seduce Nero. Seneca calls in Acte to divert Nero and to inform him that the incest is common gossip and that Agrippina boasts of it.

The son withdraws from contact with the mother and considers methods (Tacitus imagines). Poison? Too much like Britannicus. Dagger? Too detectable. The bright idea comes from Nero's freedman Anicetus, commander of the fleet at Misenum (and therefore "naval expert") and bitter enemy of Agrippina: a boat can be constructed so as to collapse in open water. Ingenious idea. It is arranged that Agrippina join Nero on the Campanian coast. At dinner the mother is honored and treated affectionately, then escorted to the boat for the trip to her own villa. She is attended by Crepereius Gallus and Acerronia. At a signal, the roof over them, weighted with lead, collapses, killing Crepereius instantly, but the two women are protected by the high sides of the couch where Agrippina is reclining. The general confusion prevents the acts that would have broken up the rest of the boat. The crewmen party to the plot try to capsize the vessel by leaning on one side, but others compensate on the opposite side. The boat fills slowly. Acerronia panics and calls for help in the name of the emperor's mother. She is bludgeoned to death. Agrippina is wounded in the shoulder but swims until some fishing smacks pick her up and take her to the villa.

Realizing the truth, she decides to dissemble and sends the freedman Agerinus to inform Nero of her heaven-sent survival of the accident, pleading that she needs time by herself for recuperation. Nero has already learned of her escape in conditions that have revealed the plot. Half-dead with fear, he has sent for Burrus and Seneca (a textual crux at this point will be treated below). When they arrive and learn the circumstances, both fall into a long silence because either they do not want to oppose Nero unsuccessfully or they are convinced that the choice is between the death of Agrippina and the death of Nero. Finally, Seneca takes the initiative to the extent that he looks at Burrus and asks if the order of murder should be given to the praetorian soldiers. Burrus, their commander, replies that his soldiers are too loyal to the imperial house and the family of Germanicus; Anicetus must live up to his promises. They have made their decision.

When Agerinus arrives with Agrippina's message, Nero throws a sword down at his feet and has him chained as an assassin, thus staging his own version that Agrippina contrived his murder and took her own life when her agent was caught in the act. In the meantime, people in the neighborhood of Agrippina's villa, excited and confused about the "accident," hear that she is safe and go to congratulate her, but scatter when an armed band is seen approaching. Anicetus and his men surround the villa and clear out the servants. He and two others enter the bedroom. They club and slash. Tacitus does not spare us the detail that Agrippina offers her womb for the fatal blow and cries, "Strike my belly" (*Ann.* 14.8.6).

Nero's culpability in this grotesque nightmare is one thing, his advisers' involvement quite another, and it must have been traumatic.

Even if their sense of complicity was reduced by the lower moral sensitivity to violence in another culture and another society, especially concerning dynastic matters, or by the consideration that Nero had gone too far to be willing—or able—to turn back, or that Agrippina was a clear threat to political order, or that the whole regime and their accomplishments and hopes and power would go down with Nero,[28] Seneca and Burrus were moral men. We have seen Seneca in his Neo-Stoicism despairing about the moral problems of his time. Surely the horrible moment of final decision about Agrippina would cause an emotional shock of lasting psychic effect.

Did Burrus and Seneca know of the plot beforehand? The textual crux referred to above occurs at the place where Nero summons them. The standard text says, "He had awakened and summoned them immediately; perhaps they knew of the plot even before" (*incertum an et ante gnaros, Ann.* 14.7.2). Actually, the manuscript reading reports that they did *not* know (*ignaros*), but other trouble with the context has produced the emendation. The problem has not been solved satisfactorily, and the following text may be taken to mean that the advisers were just now learning of the plot,[29] but the passage as it stands indicates the possibility of previous knowledge. The possibility is usually rejected as most unlikely.[30]

The complicated process of tidying up the mess smirched Seneca's name more certainly. The senate and the people had to have an official explanation of the death. Nero sent a letter to the senate reporting the detection of Agerinus and Agrippina's guilty suicide. These barefaced lies were supported with a safer and partially truthful attack on her political past and the Claudian regime. The public reaction to the letter was hostile, not against Nero, whose savagery was beyond complaint, but against Seneca, who in the letter had written what amounted to a confession.[31] The letter is "of all the recorded actions of Seneca the least defensible."[32] It, like the advisers' decision not to oppose the murder of Agrippina, cannot be defended but only explained as a choice for political stability. The alternative was probably death for the government.

To say that Nero's personality was deeply disturbed is obviously a monumental understatement. It is tempting to indulge at least once in a little amateur psychoanalysis. His acceptance of Anicetus' wild scheme seems to indicate a strange mixture of reality and unreality in his mind, as if he were daydreaming under the pressure of deeply felt psychological problems like the dominance of Agrippina and the erotic tension in his relationship with Poppaea. Such fantasizing, his explosion into violence, and his hallucinating depression after the crime (*Ann.* 14.10.5) surely suggest a psychotic pattern. In any case, Nero was one living exemplar of the psychology of violence and cruelty that Seneca had much occasion to observe in his public life and features in his melodrama.

Perhaps another manifestation of fantasy was Nero's projection of himself as another person: the entertainer, athlete, and artist. After the murder, Nero felt released from one kind of control and proceeded to indulge what Tacitus calls his "lusts" (*Ann.* 14.13.3). One was to become a charioteer and another to appear publicly and professionally as a dramatic singer to the lyre. Seneca and Burrus still had enough influence to restrict him to charioteering, which he practiced privately in a circus located in the Vatican valley (now part of St. Peter's). The restriction did not last long. Presently the public was invited to attend, young members of indigent noble families were paid to appear on the stage and Roman knights to perform in the arena. The Juvenile Games were established and attracted a clientele of shabby morals that Tacitus castigates. Nero himself appeared on the stage with his instrument before an audience that included Burrus, "applauding sadly" (*Ann.* 14.15.7). Nero also had a group of poetasters, and for entertainment after dinner the fruitless disputes of philosophers were heard. In reporting these activities, the historian shows his own Roman prejudices—a suspicion of philosophical theory and a rigid sense of what was proper for a Roman head of state—and his picture has to be modified by the probability that Nero had some talent for music and poetry.[33] However, Nero's drive for popularity and recognition in ways that were more Hellenizing than Roman reinforces the image of his instability. He was ultimately to have his megalomaniacal tour of Greece as musician, actor, athlete, and liberator, and one almost believes that before his death he really did say, "What an artist dies with me" (Suet. *Ner.* 49.1)!

The role of Seneca and Burrus as advisers of the *princeps* now fades from the historical narrative. The events of the years 60 and 61 seem to show the persistence of their policies—the senate continued its limited functions, the revolt in Britain was dealt with vigorously, Nero performed occasional acts of clemency—but there is no specific mention of them. Early in 62, the team was broken by the death of Burrus from either illness or poison. In Tacitus' eyes, the death was significant as a "loss of resources against daily-worsening public evils" (*Ann.* 14.51.1–4). Burrus was replaced by two prefects, Faenius Rufus and Sofonius Tigellinus, described respectively as a popular administrator who therefore had little influence on Nero and as a vicious rake who therefore was close to him!

Tacitus marks the turning point with uncharacteristic praise. "The death of Burrus broke the power of Seneca because good influence (*bonis artibus*) lost strength when one of its two representatives was lost, and Nero began to listen to worse advisers" (*Ann.* 14.52.1). The bad advisers, no doubt Tigellinus principally, attacked Seneca with charges that echoed those of Suillius against his wealth and that made him out to be a cultural dictator and literary rival of Nero: get rid of this schoolmaster. Seneca learned of the attacks through sources that had some concern for fairness and from Nero's avoidance of him. He requested an interview with the *princeps*. Tacitus writes versions approximating what Seneca said in asking permission to retire and what Nero replied, creating a scene that shows the barrier blocking communication between the two (*Ann.* 14.53.2–56.4). True feelings and motives are masked. Seneca is thankful for all the honors and benefits received, is self-depreciatory and self-critical, and offers to give up his fortune to Nero.[34] Nero is laudatory and evasive but performs the exercise of seeming to reject the request. Despite the subterfuge, apparently the truth was clear, and Seneca began to withdraw from his role as *amicus principis*.

The historian is convinced that the regime rapidly deteriorated to violence and despotism, and records the process briskly. Trials for treason, the bête noire under earlier emperors, had reappeared already in 62. Tigellinus took charge and conspired with Nero to remove possible rivals for the principate. Faustus Sulla was murdered in Marseilles, and his head brought back to Rome. Rubellius Plautus was murdered in Asia Minor, and his head brought back to Rome. Nero divorced (*exturbat*, "threw out") Octavia on the charge of sterility and married Poppaea. A trumped-up charge of adultery (with Anicetus, the naval expert!) was brought against Octavia. She was exiled to the little island of Pandateria and killed by bloodletting and suffocation. Her head was brought back to Rome. Obviously the murders were well certified.

Apparently Seneca completed his withdrawal after the great fire in

64, when funds were gathered ruthlessly for the reconstruction of the city, including the appropriation of temple treasures and in some provinces the confiscation of valuable statues of the gods. Rumor had it that Seneca asked permission to retire far from Rome so as not to be involved in such sacrilege—not a very likely reason for the move. Being turned down, he pleaded illness and stayed home. It was also said that Nero plotted to have him poisoned, but the plot failed, perhaps because his diet of farm fruit and fresh water (a vestige of Sextian vegetarianism?) was difficult to poison (*Ann.* 15.45.6).

Seneca's whole career was so full of varied accomplishments that one marvels at his energy, use of time, and spirit. The last years, 62–65, were no exception. During them, according to our rough chronology of the writings that survive more or less,[35] he completed five works and a treatise on moral philosophy, which is preserved only in fragments but may well have been the most substantial of all. He was freer to move about among his places near Rome and at Nomentum in Sabine country and to visit the bay of Naples and its vicinity.[36] We find him caught in a small boat on rough water between Puteoli and Naples, making fun of his seasickness (having scrambled to shore, he understands now why Ulysses was shipwrecked and cast ashore everywhere: he was *nauseator* [*Ep.* 53.4]) and moralizing about it; tramping the mud and dust of the tunnel through Pausilypum and analyzing his impulsive sense of unreality (*Ep.* 57); on a brief holiday with a friend, traveling light on a fare of dried figs and bread but with notebooks handy, introspectively displeased with himself when he is embarrassed by meeting more presentable and pretentious travelers (*Ep.* 87.4).

In the conditions of electrical violence shown in the pages of Tacitus, political life was a tender topic, and Seneca might be expected to be careful, but without naming names he is remarkably, and perhaps dangerously, frank about his experience. "People often think that I withdrew because I was disgusted with political affairs and disappointed by my ineffectual and thankless position, but now that I have gone into hiding because of fear and weariness, my ambition crops up now and again. For it was not destroyed, but only wearied or even annoyed because it had little influence on affairs" (*Ep.* 56.9). The fragmentary essay *De Otio Sapientis* expresses his attitude quite explicitly. "Zeno says, 'The wise man will enter the service of the state unless something blocks him.' . . . If the state is too corrupt to be amended, if it is filled with evil, the wise man will not struggle uselessly or squander himself to no avail. If he has too little authority or power, and the state will not receive him, if health prevents him, he will not enter the course which he knows to be unmanageable, just as he would not launch a shattered boat or, being a cripple, volunteer for military service" (*Ot. Sap.* 3.2–4). There are, his thinking continues, two commonwealths, the one of an Athens or Carthage, the other "truly public, where gods and men are joined, in which we do not look to this corner or to that, but measure the boundaries of our citizenship by the course of the sun" (*Ot. Sap.* 4.1). It is time to live in the greater commonwealth. That the experience of withdrawal was deeply painful to Seneca may be indicated when he writes: "I think that no one puts a higher value on virtue, no one is more committed to virtue than he who has given up the reputation of being a good man so as not to give up the consciousness of being one" (*Ep.* 81.20).

The bolt of the Pisonian conspiracy fell early in 65. The conspirators were a mixed group: republicans, men taught by Stoicism to hate tyranny, frustrated senatorial aristocrats, those who were affronted by Nero's criminal and un-Roman conduct, his enemies, those who feared him, and hangers-on.[37] Their plan was to kill Nero and replace him with C. Calpurnius Piso or, it was rumored, Seneca (according to rumor, he knew of this [*Ann.* 15.65.1]). Information leaked out. Confessions, denials, accusations, and wholesale executions followed, ultimately taking off the three Annaean brothers.

Here too, information is very inadequate. Did Seneca know of the conspiracy (apparently brewing since late 62 or early 63 [*Ann.* 14.65.2]) and was he directly involved, perhaps in league with the so-called Stoic opposition to the principate? Debate about these matters has been interminable. First, it is doubtful that there truly was a Stoic opposition to the principate. Nero's critics included staunch Stoics like Thrasea Paetus, but republican tendencies and Stoic principles were so fused in men like him that it is impossible to distinguish between the two. As we have seen, the ideas and language of the philosophy were a lingua franca for social and political criticism. They permeated what intellectuals thought, whether they were Stoics or not, and what speakers in declamation said. If the opposition has to be classified, it is more accurate to call it political rather than philosophical.[38] Also, in the political arena Seneca, though a distinguished figure in Stoic letters, was of course closely identified with the regime that he had advised for eight years. Even after his withdrawal from active participation, his loyalty to a conspiracy to overthrow that regime might be considered at least unreliable in a desperate struggle. It was in later years after his death that he became a symbol of Stoic resistance and could be paired with Socrates in a double herm of the second century as a philosopher-victim of oppressive government.[39] As for his knowledge of the plot, he must have known that something was afoot, for the principals were certainly known to him and included his nephew Lucan. Tacitus decides that Nero had no evidence that Seneca was a member of the conspiracy. Rather, he was looking for any way to crush one who was now his enemy (*Ann.* 15.60.3, 15.56.2).

The death scene (*Ann.* 15.62–64) is quite a showpiece, either because Seneca lived it that way or because Tacitus wrote it that way, or perhaps for both reasons. Nero, after receiving a report on an exchange of messages between Piso and Seneca (in the presence of Poppaea and Tigellinus, his kangaroo court on matters of passion), sentences Seneca to death with the customary option for "uncommon criminals" that he take his own life. What then happens according to Tacitus shows obvious parallels to the death of Socrates as reported by Plato. The sentence is received calmly. Seneca has with him a group of friends familiar with Stoicism. When denied access to his will by the centurion in charge, he speaks of his life as his main bequest and a source of moral confidence for his friends. He encourages them in general conversation and with pointed reminders of what Stoicism teaches about adversity.

He embraces his young wife Paulina and tries to calm her. She insists that she will die with him. Seneca respects her wish, fearing also what will happen to her if she survives. They cut their arms with one stroke. Since he bleeds slowly, other arteries are cut. In agony, he persuades her to withdraw to another room but is able to make a long statement to secretaries, which Tacitus does not summarize because it has been released to the public verbatim.

The *princeps* is being kept informed and, to reduce the infamy, orders that Paulina's dying be checked by bandaging. (She is to survive for several years, faithful to Seneca's memory, her pallor showing that she never recovered.) Seneca's death is so slow that a doctor friend gives him the poison of hemlock. It too is slow. He enters a hot bath, sprinkling some of the slaves standing by with drops that he calls a libation to Jupiter the Liberator. He suffocates. He is cremated without rites. "So he had instructed in writing when, at the peak of wealth and power, he looked to his end" (*Ann.* 15.64.6). Several years before he became "friend of the emperor," he had written, "Learning to live takes a lifetime and, perhaps more surprising, it takes a lifetime to learn to die" (*Brev. Vit.* 7.3).

So ends Tacitus' account of Seneca's service under Nero. It has been argued that the historian favors Seneca to the extent that he shields actions that could have been criticized more scathingly, because Seneca was the principal statesman and his "policy was the best available."[40] Seneca belongs to the small company of those with whom Tacitus "appears to identify himself."[41] This appraisal goes beyond what the text of the *Annals* allows. Nero's "press" was obviously bad and deserved to be; and the invidiousness spilled over on Seneca, as the accounts of Suetonius and Cassius Dio show. But Tacitus is a perceptive historian. He singles out the role of Seneca and Burrus as the most important positive and constructive force for stability and decency, which is inevitably compromised and ultimately overwhelmed by wild autocratic indecency. He shows us the decency, the compromise, and the indecency subtly and critically. The picture is clear enough and as unequivocal as·it can be in portraying such a complex phenomenon. That Tacitus is substantially right about Seneca is corroborated in the *Satires* of Juvenal, probably a somewhat younger contemporary. "Had [Seneca's] career as a whole been a discredit to his philosophical profession, we may feel sure that Juvenal would never have overlooked so sensational a contrast."[42] To Juvenal, Seneca is a kind of Anti-Nero. "If the people should have a free vote, who would be so incorrigible as to hesitate to prefer Seneca to Nero" (8.211–12)?

To describe Seneca's public experience psychologically almost defies the imagination. As Tacitus tells it, ambition and aspiration collided with most forms of violence and inhumanity found in the human catalog: adultery alleged and true, dynastic murder, incest, murder by poison, forced suicide, fratricide, alleged homosexual assault, violence on the streets, erotic murder, matricide, decapitation, murder by bloodletting and suffocation—not to mention the more civilized crimes of slander, corruption, and treachery. It is a great wonder that sanity, not to mention steady strength, could be sustained in the thoughts and feelings of those responsible for affairs.

The pages of Tacitus make one feel certain that the nature of Seneca's society is another main root of the drama. However, proof that this feeling is correct is elusive. Some of the interpretative Choruses give evidence of a sort. Five of the eight complete plays contain passages that are dramatic anomalies because they carry the interpretation of dramatic events over into details of contemporary time, not dramatic time. In lines 364–79 of the *Medea*, the violation of natural boundaries by the Argo is extended to a present time (*Nunc*, 364) when the whole world is open to navigation and even the present boundaries will be broken to reveal new lands, a time obviously of the far-extended (373–74) Roman world. The chorus of the *Phaedra* contrasts the order of Nature with the moral chaos (978–88) of a world in which evil men have wealth and Roman political power (*fasces*, 983), crime flourishes in the court, and virtue is unrewarded.

The *Thyestes* contains two such passages. In lines 342–403, true kingship is defined as freedom from desires and fears that are Roman in nature, not mythic: Tyrian purple (345), Spanish gold (353–55), Libyan grain (356–57), the stormy Adriatic (361–62), Parthian weapons (382–84), catapults (385–87), slippery imperial eminence (392); the chorus prefers to be unknown to its fellow (Roman) citizens (*Quiritibus*, 396), obviously an anachronism and probably intentional. The hostility between Atreus and Thyestes is described as if it were Roman warfare (554–57), and the flux of power is illustrated by dominion over Rome's eastern enemies (599–604).

In the *Furens*, the anxious life is the life of Rome: the courting of wealthy patrons, greed, political ambition, and corruption (161–74). Similarly in the *Oetaeus*, royal life is vulnerable to crime, treachery, violence, envy, and greed (604–39); the wife in modest circumstances does not have jewelry and fancy clothes gathered from afar (658–67).

These and similar nonchoral passages scattered through the plays (for example, *Thyest.* 455–67) are very general, like the strictures of a satirist, and do not relate the dramatic material directly and specifically to contemporary society. But they do show that the conditions of the dramatist's own time are consciously in his mind as he writes. Such passages, part of Seneca's own interpretation of the dramatic events, create the presumption that the connection between the drama and the contemporary scene is significant and extensive.

The earlier view was that Senecan drama shows us what could be said in the lecture halls. Therefore the plays are full of political allusions, such as references to the emperor via the portrayal of tyrants. The frequent maxims and general thoughts take on specific contemporary meaning.[43] Recent treatments have been more cautious. The view that the plays are saturated with contemporary politics has been rejected.[44] Parallels between dramatic characters and political figures (Atreus = Nero? In the *Medea*, Creon = Claudius?) are considered possible but undemonstrable because dating is weak.[45] A more sophisticated view includes Seneca among those who express criticism, not opposition, using written code easily penetrated by an audience of like minds. "We hear of enmities between brothers, or between fathers and sons, or wives and husbands; of exiles and mistresses—for which substitute Titus and Domitian, Claudius and Nero, Agrippina and Claudius, Tiberius and Messalina."[46]

It is no wonder that such theories are rife. The homicidal mania of Medea, Creon's tyranny, Phaedra's lust, the impetuous anger of Theseus, Oedipus' psychotic fear, the vicious autocracy of Atreus, Thyestes' weakness, Pyrrhus' abuse of power—all these have their counterparts in Seneca's political experience. It has been well said that "Seneca himself lived through and witnessed, in his own person or in the persons of those near him, almost every evil and horror that is the theme of his writings, prose or verse. Exile, murder, incest, the threat of poverty and a hideous death, and all the savagery of fortune were of the very texture of his career."[47]

If we accept the view that there are specific connections between Seneca's drama and his life, there is virtually no limit to the cryptanalytic ingenuity that can be applied. The relationship between Hercules and Alcmena in the *Oetaeus* is said to mirror the real-life relationship between Seneca and mother Helvia.[48] The self-execution of Jocasta in the *Oedipus*, another argument runs, represents Nero's murder of Agrippina: Oedipus is really the cause of Jocasta's death—she kills herself with his sword—and Jocasta's last words (*hunc pete/uterum capacem, Oedip.* 1038–39) echo Agrippina's according to Tacitus (*ventrem feri, Ann.* 14.8.6).[49] This interpretation is ruined by evidence that the phrase is a rhetorical *topos*. It is used in the *controversia* about the woman tortured by the tyrant in the investigation of her husband (*caede ventrem, Contr.* 2.5.7).

In the *Furens*, Seneca is using the character Lycus as a parallel to the conception of tyrant in the *De Clementia*. The second half of the play shows the similarity between Lycus and his executioner Hercules. Nero is being warned against abuse of his power, although, like Hercules, he has the hope of purification.[50]

The *Oedipus* has been explained as opposition literature calling for the exile of Nero.[51] The motivation of this "decoding" is startling. It seems that this approach is necessary in the absence of any other "deduced reason for Seneca's writing tragedies,"[52] as if all the analysis of the philosophical purposes of the drama had never been done. To demonstrate how Seneca encodes his message that Nero must be banished, the writer argues that Seneca has manipulated details in Chorus II to evoke thoughts of incest and parricide and to create parallels between the lineage of Bacchus and the adoption of Nero by Claudius, Agrippina's machinations, and so forth.[53] Certainly Seneca's hearers and readers were sophisticated, but it is incredible that he expected them to penetrate such riddles.

These one-to-one relationships cannot be disproved conclusively any more than they can be proved, but several factors militate against drawing them. When only two of the plays can be dated approximately, in the early 50s before Nero became *princeps*, speculation about specific history behind the drama has very little foundation. It would be very useful if some of the plays could be dated later, but no specific connection with the Neronian years can be demonstrated. Another realistic consideration has been ignored in the theories about covert opposition to and criticism of the imperial regime: Seneca was politically ambitious, and his success or failure—as it turned out, his success *and* failure—was pinned to the principate as it was. Psychologically, it is unlikely that he would be working within and against the system simultaneously. A final caution involves the very legitimacy of the drama. Conducting political maneuvers in drama clearly devoted to significant philosophical issues is a radical anomaly.

Even so, the drama can be understood fully only if its deeply historical nature is recognized. We have seen that the philosophy is a powerful instrument for identifying and analyzing human vices, weaknesses, and virtues, for conveying strong convictions about human capacities for subhuman and superhuman behavior. We have seen that the intensity of these insights is well served by the intensity of a rhetorical style closely related to declamation. To stop here is to fail to ask the ultimate question, why? Why did Seneca turn to these potent ingredients in writing drama?

Various partial answers are possible: because he was a rhetorically trained Stoic and nothing else would have been natural for him, because he wanted to dramatize Stoic perceptions, and so forth. But the most significant answer is indicated by a quality of his dramaturgy well recognized over a century ago by a historian of drama who was far ahead of his time in sensitivity to Seneca's power and pathos: *the moral passion of his dramaturgy.*[54]

The source of this passion is seen in Seneca's own description of his world. "Nothing is so treacherous as human life, nothing so dangerous" (*Cons. Marc.* 22.3). To look into the soul of a good man is like being transported by an encounter with divinity (*Ep.* 115.3-4). All is chaos, but the struggle for order goes on: fear of another's power, constant wariness, the madness of all men, suicide as ultimate freedom; the vision of Virtue, the unity of gods and men, *humanitas* as the quality of being a human attuned to all other humans, the dream of immortality. Pessimism and theism, despair and aspiration. What is more, the blackness and the brightness are not theoretical states. They are realities seen and felt by a man of keen sensibility whose consciousness of his own frailties and ideals sharpens perception of his world.

The world of his drama and the world of his real life are essentially identical, a battleground of moral extremes. The extravagance of feeling poured into the drama is inseparable from the deep emotions of Seneca's introspection into his society and himself, inseparable from the hope and pain of his personal and political life. So there is a direct relationship between the moral significance of his dramatic *exempla* and the moral conditions of his time. The homeopathy of his drama is a medical specific for contemporary diseases. In these terms, the drama is deeply historical.

If only the evidence for dating the plays allowed us to be more specific! Of course, the dramatic scenes of political content stir speculation. Medea and Creon argue about the qualities of tyranny and kingship. Antigone's *pietas* is set off against the ambitious nihilism of her brothers. Atreus' lust for power and the nature of true kingship are contrasted. Agamemnon's incomplete rationality is pitted against Pyrrhus' mania. All these scenes use conflicts between unprincipled and principled behavior to delineate guilt and responsibility in the political sphere.

The compromise of principles analyzed so brilliantly by Tacitus must have dogged Seneca throughout his public career, for in those days of absolutism a man trying to realize political principles did not have enough power to do so. This imbalance of principle and power, and the resulting complicity in Nero's crimes, was admitted by Seneca himself in the statements written around the time of his retirement about his lack of influence and power. Certainly these conditions would have made Seneca sensitive to the political issues that appear in the plays.

It is more likely that the dramatist was thinking of conditions in the principate of Claudius than of his experience under Nero, but the Neronian episode is the fullest record we have of the strains, hopes, and frustrations in Seneca's real life. The *psychological truth* of the parallelism between the dramatic material and his life is obvious. The stupendous contrasts in reality—the idealism of the *De Clementia*, death in dignity, the moments after the poisoning of Britannicus, the decision to kill Agrippina—belong to the same realm of experience as the horror of Atreus and the glory of Cassandra.

8. MELODRAMA

Classifying Seneca's drama is difficult. When the conventional term "tragedy" is used of both the Greek and the Senecan plays, its meaning is reduced to something like "poetic drama on a traditional, usually catastrophic theme"—close to non-definition. For accuracy and critical discrimination, the dramatic terminology used must distinguish between a drama like the Greek, which characteristically (though not invariably) treats the experience of evil as a condition of life resulting from the nature of the world and the place of humans in it, and the Senecan, where the orientation of thought is much more restricted and evil is always the result of human failure.[1] Conversely, in Seneca nobility is never achieved in confrontation with the natural order but only through harmony with it.

The term "melodrama" has a complicated history in drama and music, and cannot be defined very precisely. But in its usual and general theatrical meaning, it conveys such characteristics as the use of virtuous and villainous stock characters (in the end, virtue wins), sensationalism, spectacle, and the powerful exercise of emotion. Moralism ascendant.

The applicability of "melodrama" to Seneca is a matter of degree. Most serious drama contains some melodramatic elements. There is melodrama in some Greek tragedy, particularly Euripides. Later drama under Senecan influence shows the effects of the moralization of classical tragic drama that took place in Seneca (chapter 1). But Seneca's drama is melodrama to the nth degree.

The principal source of these melodramatic elements in Seneca—the glory of Virtue, the horror of Vice—is Stoicism.

> [Seneca] had to make a decision—whether consciously or subconsciously—about the motivation of the catastrophes in his versions of the traditional themes. From what sources were the catastrophes to come about? From imperfections in the make-up of the world? From chance? From the unfathomable purposes of the gods? From conflicts within human nature?
>
> His Stoicism dictated certain answers to this question. If one

subscribes to the optimistic Stoic view of the universe as an orderly, harmonious, and purposeful structure, it is simply impossible to attribute violence and suffering to the workings of nature or to chance or to mysterious divine purpose. Men may *think* that evil exists in superhuman terms, but this is only because they do not understand the great rational scheme of things. . . . What is more, the great scheme is identical with how things are fated to be and with how divine providence wills things to be. No, in a rational macrocosm the only source of disruption in human life is lack of reason or perversion of reason in man the microcosm. Nor in human nature . . . can there be a continuing conflict or mixed motives, for reason and unreason . . . are mutually exclusive.[2]

The only approach open to the dramatist as a Stoic is to use human character as the cause of all dramatic development. Hercules is brought to catastrophe not by Juno's divine anger as such but by his own moral weakness that Juno enlists against him. Medea must act as she does by reason of her moral nature and the impact of other moral natures upon her: her chronic violence, Creon's tyranny, Jason's weakness. Her womanhood and motherhood are not significantly involved, as they are in Euripides. This total concentration on human causation of evil, excluding external factors—supernatural, metaphysical, social, and circumstantial—leads the dramatist into melodrama.

Also, the moral absolutes Virtue and Vice shape the dramatic conception of character. They mean that a human being is in the one state or the other, or en route to one or the other, a formula that describes all the major characters in the drama. The result is personalities who are intensely committed to good or evil, who die nobly or kill vilely, who are a moral or immoral kingdom within themselves—viciously or virtuously violent, sensational. The extremes of absolute good and absolute evil in collision—this is the stuff of melodrama.

Characters conceived in this moralistic and simplistic way appear on a flat surface. No modulation is allowed by the analysis of human experience exclusively in terms of human responsibility for moral failure or success and in terms of invariable moral absolutes. There is no Sophoclean Oedipus heroic in the face of a hostile world, no Ajax asserting his outmoded code in confrontation with a changing society. Rather, the characters either cause catastrophe or rise completely above it.

Substance of this kind is not necessarily melodramatic, but it has a potential for melodrama. In Seneca this potential is fully activated by the rhetorical form. As we have seen, nothing in the drama is moderate. Emotions and attitudes, destructive and constructive, are pumped up to full capacity. The rhetoric makes the rage, indignation, fear, or courage total. As a result, Seneca's audience is exposed to powerful, contrastive emotions of horror and admiration caused by the moral extremes that are the substance of the drama.

Finally, Seneca's view of his dramatic world in melodramatic terms must have been related to his view of the reality he experienced. We have seen the "self-portrait" of his sensitive, often painful involvement in his tumultuous society. It is obvious that the historical record of his career could be used to make various Senecan "scenarios." When the Neo-Stoicism and the rhetoric are charged with the dramatist's own tortured and passionate life, the result is inevitably melodrama, melodrama of such energy and force that it changed the course of Western drama.

SHORT TITLES

The text used for the drama is Friedrich Leo, *L. Annaei Senecae Tragoediae* (Berlin, 1879), which is widely available through its use in the Loeb Classical Library.

Adam: Traute Adam, *Clementia Principis: der Einfluss hellenistischer Fürstenspiegel auf den Versuch einer rechtlichen Fundierung des Principats durch Seneca* (Stuttgart, 1970).

Arnold: E. Vernon Arnold, *Roman Stoicism* (London, 1911).

Bonner: S. F. Bonner, *Roman Declamation in the Late Republic and Early Empire* (Liverpool, 1949).

CAH: *Cambridge Ancient History*.

Canter: Howard Vernon Canter, *Rhetorical Elements in the Tragedies of Seneca* (*University of Illinois Studies in Language and Literature* 10 [1925] no. 1).

Coffey: Michael Coffey, "Seneca Tragedies including pseudo-Seneca Octavia and Epigrams attributed to Seneca, Report for the years 1922–1955," *Lustrum* 2 (1957) 113–86.

Dudley: D. R. Dudley ed., *Neronians and Flavians: Silver Latin I* (London and Boston, 1972).

Edelstein, *The Meaning*: Ludwig Edelstein, *The Meaning of Stoicism* (Cambridge, Mass., 1966).

Edward: William A. Edward, *The Suasoriae of Seneca the Elder* (Cambridge, 1928).

Henry and Walker, "Phantasmagoria": Denis Henry and B. Walker, "Phantasmagoria and Idyll: An Element of Seneca's *Phaedra*," *G&R* 13 (1966) 223–39.

Herington: C. J. Herington, "Senecan Tragedy," *Arion* 5 (1966) 422–71.

Herrmann: Léon Herrmann, *Le théâtre de Sénèque* (Paris, 1924).

Kennedy, *Art of Rhetoric*: George Kennedy, *The Art of Rhetoric in the Roman World, 300 B.C.–A.D. 300* (Princeton, 1972).

Knoche: Ulrich Knoche, "Senecas Atreus, Ein Beispiel," *Antike* 17 (1941) 60–76.

Lefèvre, "Quid ratio possit?": Eckard Lefèvre, "Quid ratio possit? Seneca's *Phaedra* als stoisches Drama," *WS* 82 (1969) 131–60.

Lefèvre, *Senecas Tragödien*: Eckard Lefèvre ed., *Senecas Tragödien* (Darmstadt, 1972).

Long, *Hellenistic Philosophy*: A. A. Long, *Hellenistic Philosophy: Stoics, Epicureans, Sceptics* (London, 1974).

Long, *Problems*: A. A. Long ed., *Problems in Stoicism* (London, 1971).

Mazzoli: Giancarlo Mazzoli, *Seneca e la Poesia* (Milan, 1970).

— Motto: Anna Lydia Motto, *Seneca Sourcebook: Guide to the Thought of Lucius Annaeus Seneca* (Amsterdam, 1970).

Pohlenz: Max Pohlenz, *Die Stoa: Geschichte einer geistigen Bewegung*, 3d ed. (Göttingen, 1964) vol. 1.

Pratt, *Dramatic Suspense*: Norman T. Pratt, *Dramatic Suspense in Seneca and in His Greek Precursors* (Princeton, 1939).

Pratt, "Major Systems": Norman T. Pratt, "Major Systems of Figurative Language in Senecan Melodrama," *TAPhA* 94 (1963) 199–234.

R-E: *Paulys Real-Encyclopädie der classischen Altertumswissenschaft.*

Regenbogen: Otto Regenbogen, *Schmerz und Tod in den Tragödien Senecas*, originally in *Vort. Bibl. Warburg* 7 (1927–28) 167–218. References are to this version. It was reprinted in *Kleine Schriften* (Munich, 1961) and offprinted.

— Rist: J. M. Rist, *Stoic Philosophy* (Cambridge, 1969).

Sambursky: Samuel Sambursky, *Physics of the Stoics* (London, 1959).

Syme: Sir Ronald Syme, *Tacitus* (Oxford, 1958).

Trillitzsch: Winfried Trillitzsch, *Seneca im literarischen Urteil der Antike* (Amsterdam, 1971).

NOTES

Chapter 1

1. The material of this chapter originally appeared in "From Oedipus to Lear," *CJ* 61 (1965) 49–57, and was later used in Newton P. Stallknecht and Horst Frenz, *Comparative Literature: Method & Perspective*, rev. ed. (Carbondale, Ill., 1971) 218–47. It is reused here in modified form by permission of the Southern Illinois University Press.

2. Bernard M. W. Knox, *Oedipus at Thebes* (New Haven, 1957) 195–96.

3. Knox, 116–38, collects the language expressing the search for truth.

4. E. R. Dodds, *Euripides: Bacchae, Edited with Introduction and Commentary*, 2d ed. (Oxford, 1960) xii.

5. Gerald F. Else, *The Origin and Early Form of Greek Tragedy* (Cambridge, Mass., 1965).

6. Assembled in Sir Arthur W. Pickard-Cambridge, *Dithyramb, Tragedy and Comedy* (Oxford, 1927).

7. Actually, the pieces of evidence are reconciled rather well in Albin Lesky, *A History of Greek Literature*, trans. James Willis and Cornelis de Heer (London, 1966) 223–33.

8. Francis Fergusson, *The Idea of a Theater* (Princeton, 1949) 26, 18.

9. Robert B. Heilman, *This Great Stage: Image and Structure in "King Lear"* (Baton Rouge, La., 1948) 115–16.

10. G. Wilson Knight, *The Wheel of Fire: Interpretations of Shakespearian Tragedy with Three New Essays*, 4th rev. and enl. ed. (London, 1949) 177.

11. Heilman (see n. 9) 10–11, 26, 204; John F. Danby, *Shakespeare's Doctrine of Nature: A Study of "King Lear"* (London, 1949) 124; Hiram Haydn, *The Counter-Renaissance* (New York, 1950) 637, 648.

12. Danby, especially 20–21, 33–34.

13. Danby, 125.

14. Haydn (see n. 11) 648, 651.

15. For example, Harold C. Goddard, *The Meaning of Shakespeare* (Chicago, 1951) 529–30, 533–34.

16. Kenneth Muir, *King Lear* (Arden ed., London, 1952) lvi–lvii.

17. Oscar J. Campbell, "The Salvation of Lear," *ELH* 15 (1948) 93–109; the quotations are from 94, 104.

18. This paragraph is adapted from Pratt, "Major Systems," 224–27.

19. Sen. *Phaedr.* 959–88, in *Seneca: Four Tragedies and Octavia*, trans. E. F. Watling (Penguin Classics, 1966) 136–37.

Chapter 2

1. Karl Münscher (covering the years 1915–21) *JAW* 192 (1922) 185–214 (214). Of other surveys of work on the nine plays and the *Octavia*, the following are most useful: Johannes Tolkiehn (1903–6) *JAW* 134 (1907) 196–206; Tolkiehn (1907–10) *JAW* 158 (1912) 1–20; Tolkiehn (1911–14) *JAW* 171 (1915) 15–31; Friedrich Levy (1913–21) *JPhV* 47 (1921) 103–6, and 48 (1922) 152; Vittorio D'Agostino (1930–52) *RSC* 1 (1952) 47–65; Laidlaw, in Maurice Platnauer, *Fifty Years of Classical Scholarship* (Oxford, 1954) 257–71; Coffey (1922–55); Hans Joachim Mette (1945–64) *Lustrum* 9 (1964) 160–94; D'Agostino (1953–65) *RSC* 14 (1966) 61–81; Giovanni Cupaiuolo (1969–71) *BStudLat* 2 (1972) 290–95.

2. Léon Herrmann, *Le théâtre de Sénèque* (Paris, 1924).

3. Otto Regenbogen, *Schmerz und Tod in den Tragödien Senecas*, originally in *Vort. Bibl. Warburg* 7 (1927–28) 167–218.

4. William A. Oldfather, Arthur Stanley Pease, and Howard Vernon Canter, *Index Verborum Quae In Senecae Fabulis Necnon In Octavia Praetexta Reperiuntur* (*University of Illinois Studies in Language and Literature* 4 [1918] no. 2); Howard Vernon Canter, *Rhetorical Elements in the Tragedies of Seneca* (*University of Illinois Studies in Language and Literature* 10 [1925] no. 1).

5. Good coverage of the earlier period is in Herrmann, 31–77.

6. Herrmann, 78–147.

7. Coffey, 150, on Herzog, "Datierung der Tragödien des Seneca."

8. Developed by Otto Weinreich, *Senecas Apocolocyntosis* (Berlin, 1923) 62–78.

9. André Hurst, "Le char du soleil (Sen. *Med*. 32–36)," *Historia* 20 (1971) 303–8.

10. Conrad Cichorius, *Römische Studien* (Leipzig, 1922) 426–29.

11. Ernst Hansen, *Die Stellung der Affektrede in den Tragödien des Seneca* (Berlin, 1934).

12. See chapter 3, n. 29.

13. Herrmann, 153–232.

14. Otto Zwierlein, *Die Rezitationsdramen Senecas, Mit einem kritisch-exegetischen Anhang* (Meisenheim am Glan, 1966). Zwierlein's work has held up well under criticism; R. J. Tarrant, *Seneca: Agamemnon, Edited with a Commentary* (Cambridge, 1976) 7–8, n. 5, states that "attempts to refute his central positions have been unavailing."

15. Zwierlein, 91.

16. Zwierlein, 110.

17. Zwierlein, 127.

18. Zwierlein, 149.

19. In practice there was not much difference between reading and recitation. See Kennedy, *Art of Rhetoric*, 306 and references there cited for evidence that private reading of literature was often done aloud whether by the person or someone reading to him.

20. Zwierlein (see n. 14) 166.

21. Berthe M. Marti's earlier development of the theory (not even mentioned by Zwierlein), "The Prototypes of Seneca's Tragedies," *CPh* 42 (1947) 1–16,

was received with skepticism; see Coffey, 158–59. I myself withdraw the complete disbelief stated in "The Stoic Base of Senecan Drama," *TAPhA* 79 (1948) 7, n. 17. I should like to accept the theory, weak as it is, since it squares with what I believe about the drama.

22. For Seneca's references to Diogenes and Crates, see Motto, 150 and 149.

23. *The Oxford Classical Dictionary*, 2d ed. (Oxford, 1970) 977a.

24. See Herrmann, 258–66. He himself believes that only Euripides can be considered a source but that Seneca's imitation is "au total assez restreinte" (266).

25. This point is treated in Mazzoli, 171–75.

26. Like Valerius Maximus' *Factorum ac dictorum memorabilium libri*.

27. Herrmann, 280–88.

28. Mazzoli, 231, 240.

29. Herrmann, 284.

30. Friedrich, in Lefèvre, *Senecas Tragödien*, 147.

31. Zintzen, in Lefèvre, *Senecas Tragödien*, 199, n. 125.

32. Wolf Steidle, "Zu Senecas Troerinnen," *Philologus* 94 (1941) 284, n. 62.

33. Lefèvre, "Quid ratio possit?" 134.

34. Herington, 447.

35. A recent example is William M. Calder III, "Originality in Seneca's *Troades*," *CPh* 65 (1970) 75–82. Calder believes that *Troades* 1–66, 165–202, and 814–60 were original with Seneca and that Seneca did not use Euripides' *Hecuba* as a source. He concludes: "His play was a contamination of three Greek sources filled out with occasional original scenes" (82). This kind of theory is very unlikely. If the *Troades* is largely derivative, Seneca probably used a single source containing most features of the play as he wrote it. But this possibility is completely inscrutable.

The same characteristic is found in Pierre Grimal, "L'Originalité de Sénèque dans la tragédie de 'Phèdre,' " *REL* 41 (1963) 297–314: "L'originalité de Sénèque . . . consiste à avoir fondu en un ensemble nouveau deux et sans doute trois pièces antérieures, de façon à faire surgir une situation morale entièrement nouvelle" (314).

36. See W.-H. Friedrich, "Sprache und Stil des *Hercules Oetaeus*," *Hermes* 82 (1954) 51–84, which is evaluated and partially accepted by Coffey, 141–42.

37. This double theme is observed by Coffey, 141. See also Christine M. King, "Seneca's *Hercules Oetaeus*: A Stoic Interpretation of the Greek Myth," *G&R* 18 (1971) 217.

38. Coffey, 141, singles out from Friedrich the excessive use of similes in *Oetaeus* 237–45, but Seneca is emphasizing the confrontation of Iole and Deianira, and does not use similes delicately anyway; Coffey also points to the alleged inferiority in *Oetaeus* of borrowings from the *Medea* and the *Furens*, a dubious kind of argument that could mean only that Seneca used the same material better in one place than in another; *nunc ferar obruta* (757) does not seem exceptional when read in its whole line; the use of *spargere* in various meanings is typical of Seneca's violent and exaggerated language; the reading *trepidus . . . Pindus* (493) is doubtful.

Also, I do not think that Bertil Axelson (*Korruptelenkult, Studien zur Textkritik der unechten Seneca-Tragödie Hercules Oetaeus* [Lund, 1967]) is successful against the arguments for authenticity.

39. Pratt, "Major Systems," 229–31.

40. For example, Arthur Stanley Pease, "Is the *Octavia* a Play of Seneca?" *CJ* 15 (1920) 388–403; S. Pantzerhielm Thomas, "*De Octavia Praetexta*," *SO* 24 (1945) 48–87; Lucile Yow Whitman, *The Octavia: Introduction, Text, and Commentary, Noctes Romanae* 16 (Bern, Stuttgart, 1978) 7–12.

41. Carl Hosius, *Gnomon* 13 (1937) 132–35.

42. Rudolf Helm, "Die *Praetexta Octavia*," *Sitz.-Ber. Berlin* (1934) 283–347; Gertrude Herzog-Hauser, "Reim und Stabreim in der *Praetexta Octavia*," *Glotta* 25 (1936) 109–16; Bertil Axelson, "Unpoetische Wörter," *Skrifter utgivna av Vetenskaps-Societeten i Lund* 29 (1945) 57–58, 67–68; Coffey, 179–80. Particularly interesting are the objective data given by Canter, who assumes that all ten plays are Senecan but finds (176–79) that the *Octavia* is far less rhetorical than the others. The problem is well surveyed in C. J. Herington, "*Octavia Praetexta*: A Survey," *CQ* 55 (1961) 18–30.

43. On Quintilian's view of Seneca, see Quint. 10.1.125–31, 12.10.11; and George Kennedy, *Quintilian* (New York, 1969) 112–13.

44. Eduard Norden, *Die Antike Kunstprosa* (Leipzig, 1898) vol. 1, 277–99.

45. On Seneca's prose style and its implications, see Norden, 306–13; Walter C. Summers, *Select Letters of Seneca* (London, 1910) xv–cxiv; A. D. Leeman, *Orationis Ratio* (Amsterdam, 1963) vol. 1, 260–83; H. MacL. Currie, "The Younger Seneca's Style: Some Observations," *BICS* 13 (1966) 76–87; Kennedy, *Art of Rhetoric*, 465–81.

46. K. Preisendanz, "De L. Annaei Senecae rhetoris apud philosophum filium auctoritate," *Philologus* 67 (1908) 68–112; Canter, 12–13.

47. Ilsetraut Hadot, *Seneca und die Griechisch-Römische Tradition der Seelenleitung* (Berlin, 1969) 179–90.

48. Gustav Landauer, *Shakespeare-Vorträgen* (Frankfurt am Main, 1920) vol. 1, 162.

49. Canter.

50. Canter, 80.

51. Canter, 177–79.

52. Canter, 173–75.

53. Canter, 70–84. For a more complete study of the role of geography in Senecan drama, see Aurèle Cattin, "La géographie dans les tragédies de Sénèque," *Latomus* 22 (1963) 685–703.

54. See the technical studies cited by Coffey, 166–67, 170–73 and Mette, *Lustrum* 9 (1964) 162.

55. Wilhelm Marx (*Funktion und Form der Chorlieder in den Seneca-Tragödien* [Köln, 1932]) and J. David Bishop ("The Meaning of the Choral Meters in Senecan Tragedy," *RhM* 111 [1968] 197–219; includes a critique of Marx) believe that the choral odes use specific meters for specific subjects. The glyconics are used for praise, but the rest of the taxonomy (on which Marx and Bishop do not agree) is not convincing, for subjects overlap by the very nature of the drama. It seems more significant that of Bishop's four main categories

(anapests, sapphics, glyconics, asclepiads), except for the *Agamemnon*, all four appear in four plays and three in the other three, that is, Seneca is achieving a variety of meters in seven of the eight complete plays.

56. Friedrich Leo, "Die Composition der Chorlieder Senecas," *RhM* 52 (1897) 514–18; Clarence W. Mendell, *Our Seneca* (New Haven, 1941) 135–37.

57. See the analyses by Mette, *Lustrum* 9 (1964) 162–71.

58. Canter, 106–22. His categories are: (1) the soul, mind, emotions, etc.; the body, its functions, conditions, etc.; family and daily life; shelter and clothing; farming, horsemanship, hunting; arts and trades; commerce and travel; warfare; law and politics; (2) the animal kingdom; the vegetable kingdom; the elements, weather, night, heavenly bodies, etc.; mountains.

59. Pratt, "Major Systems."

60. Pratt, "Major Systems," 211–12.

61. For example, Pratt, "Major Systems," 203–4.

62. Pratt, "Major Systems," 200–210.

63. Pratt, "Major Systems," 212–14.

64. Pratt, "Major Systems," 214–22.

65. Pratt, "Major Systems," 222–24.

66. Pratt, *Dramatic Suspense*, 1–14.

67. Pratt, *Dramatic Suspense*, 67–68.

68. Pratt, *Dramatic Suspense*, 15–16.

69. Pratt, *Dramatic Suspense*, 93–99.

Chapter 3

1. Syme, 784.

2. Strabo's account of the Turdetani is found in 3.1.6, 3.2.

3. James A. Michener, *Iberia: Spanish Travels and Reflections* (New York, 1968) 156. For an explosive denial of all this, see Américo Castro, *The Spaniards: An Introduction to Their History* (Berkeley and London, 1971) 177–79 ("The Mythical Spanishness of the Romans Born in Hispania"): "Only a hallucination, explicable as a kind of collective psychosis, could make of Seneca and his philosophy a Spanish phenomenon" (177); "The only Spanish element in the belief in Seneca's 'Spanishness' is the state of mind which made the belief possible and the position such a fantasy occupies in the history of Spanish letters" (178).

4. Francis J. Wiseman, *Roman Spain: An Introduction to the Roman Antiquities of Spain and Portugal* (London, 1956) 209. This idea persists in various forms: Bonner, "The love of gruesome detail, in which Seneca is only equalled by his nephew Lucan, may perhaps be partly a Spanish characteristic, but probably owes something to the declaimers" (165).

5. V. S. Pritchett, *The Spanish Temper* (New York, 1955) 63.

6. Havelock Ellis, *The Soul of Spain* (Boston and New York, 1908) 46 and 412.

7. Michener (see n. 3) 96.

8. *CAH*, vol. 11, 501 (Albertini).

9. According to Henri Bornecque, *Les Déclamations et les Déclamateurs d'après Sénèque le Père* (Lille, 1902) 188, Latro was "perhaps" born in Corduba, but Seneca speaks of their friendship as lasting *a prima pueritia usque ad ultimum eius diem* (*Contr.* 1. pref. 13).

10. Michener (see n. 3) 158–61.

11. M. Schanz and C. Hosius, *Geschichte der Römischen Literatur*, pt. 2, 4th ed. (Munich, 1935) 358–61; Eduard Zeller, *Die Philosophie der Griechen in Ihrer Geschichtlichen Entwicklung* (repr. Hildesheim, 1963) 7th ed., vol. 3, pt. 1, 699–706; Pohlenz, 280–81.

12. *Ep.* 64.1–5. All of Seneca's references to Sextius, Sotion, Fabianus, and Attalus are gathered in Motto, 146–58.

13. Pierre Grimal, *Sénèque, Sa Vie, Son Oeuvre avec un Exposé de Sa Philosophie*, 3d ed. rev. (Paris, 1966) 6.

14. The trip to Egypt at this stage of his life is puzzling. The dry climate of Alexandria would be beneficial to his health, and it was an exciting place for a young man who was trained in philosophy and had an appetite for new ideas. However, a mere visit when he was at least in his middle twenties would interrupt seriously his political career on the senatorial track. Right after his return from Egypt in A.D. 31, he campaigned for the quaestorship, presumably (though not necessarily) having already served as a member of the Board of Twenty (*vigintiviri*) and as military tribune. Possibly several of his years in Egypt were spent as tribune. The emperor Tiberius would have to authorize this post since Egypt as an imperial domain was off limits to senators and probably to senatorial aspirants. In fact, Seneca as an equestrian had to have imperial permission for a senatorial career in the first place. However, he was a member of a prominent equestrian family and the nephew-by-marriage of Tiberius' Prefect of Alexandria and Egypt, who had long held this very high post in the empire. These conditions were ideal for getting a special dispensation.

15. Haase, frag. 12. Philae was in the well-garrisoned area of Syne. Could Seneca have been posted there as tribune?

16. Trillitzsch, 122, 124–25, 127, 139, 165–68, 257, 260.

17. Schanz and Hosius (see n. 11) 706; Trillitzsch, 200.

18. For the cults of Isis, Cybele, and the Jews in Alexandria, see P. M. Fraser, *Ptolemaic Alexandria* (Oxford, 1972) vol. 1, 259–65, 272–73, 277–79, 55–56, 284–86.

19. Robert Turcan, *Sénèque et les Religions Orientales* (Bruxelles, 1967) 63–65.

20. Heinrich Dörrie, *Der Kleine Pauly*, 5.290–91.

21. *R-E*, 3.2025–27 (Schwartz).

22. It is an interesting coincidence that in a fourth-century source (Eus. 6.19.8) Chairemon is linked with Cornutus, who must be L. Annaeus Cornutus, a freedman of some member of the Senecan family and teacher of the Stoic poets Lucan and Persius. He explained Greek myths as Stoic allegories and is therefore associated with Chairemon as an allegorizing interpreter. Cornutus was probably born too late to have been involved in the Egyptian visit.

23. For an excellent brief account of "Alexandrian Philosophy: the Main Phases," see Fraser (see n. 18) vol. 1, 480–94.

24. A good introduction to Philo is provided by Herbert Box, *Philonis Alexandrini "in Flaccum"* (London, 1939) xiii–xxxii and Erwin R. Goodenough, *An Introduction to Philo Judaeus*, 2d ed. rev. (New York, 1962).

25. Goodenough, 10, 155.

26. For example, he explicates *Genesis* 2.6, "But there went up a spring from the earth, and watered the whole face of the ground," in terms of the allegorical equations "spring" = "mind" and "face" = "the senses." The hidden meaning found by Philo is that providential Nature for the purpose of sense perception has created a reciprocal relationship between the mind and objects sensed with the result that the mind both receives the "impression" (*phantasia*) of objects through the senses and transmits a reactive "impulse" (*horme*) through the senses to the object sensed (*Leg. All.* 1.28–30). The idea and the terminology are distinctly Stoic.

27. Aug. *Civ. Dei* 6.11, trans. William M. Green (Loeb Classical Library).

28. Philo, *De Somn.* 2.123–28. The governor is thought to be one of the predecessors of A. Avillius Flaccus, prefect from A.D. 32 to 38; see F. H. Colson and G. H. Whitaker, *Philo with an English Translation* (Loeb Classical Library) vol. 5, 609.

29. The chronology in Schanz and Hosius (see n. 11) 682–706, modified from the later material in Trillitzsch, 37–43, follows: *ad Marciam De Consolatione*, A.D. 37–40; *De Ira*, soon after the death of Caligula in 41; *ad Polybium De Consolatione* and *ad Helviam Matrem De Consolatione*, period of exile, 41–49; *De Brevitate Vitae*, 49–50; *De Constantia Sapientis*, near the beginning of Nero's rule; *De Clementia*, 55–56; *De Vita Beata*, 58; *De Tranquillitate Animi*, 59–60; *De Providentia, De Otio, De Beneficiis, Quaestiones Naturales*, and *Epistulae Morales*, after 62. See also Miriam T. Griffin, *Seneca, A Philosopher in Politics* (Oxford, 1976) 395–411 (mainly on the authority of Francesco Giancotti, *Cronologia dei 'Dialoghi' di Seneca* [Turin, 1957]).

30. For example, Margaret E. Reesor, *The Political Theory of the Old and Middle Stoa* (New York, 1951); Sambursky; Benson Mates, *Stoic Logic* (Berkeley, 1961); Johnny Christensen, *An Essay on the Unity of Stoic Philosophy* (Copenhagen, 1962); Pohlenz; Edelstein, *The Meaning*; Rist; Long, *Problems*; Long, *Hellenistic Philosophy*; F. H. Sandbach, *The Stoics* (London, 1975).

31. Arnold, 113.

32. Motto, xiii–xiv, 143–60.

33. See Long, *Problems*, 77–78.

34. Epict. *Fr.* 1.17.6; Mates (see n. 30).

35. Arnold, 128–54; Long, *Hellenistic Philosophy*, 121–47.

36. The following account is derived from Sambursky.

37. For a discussion of this questionable theory, see Long, *Hellenistic Philosophy*, 159–60.

38. Sambursky, 41.

39. Sambursky, 57–58.

40. For a fuller discussion of this intricate point, see Long, *Hellenistic Philosophy*, 167–68.

41. Sambursky, 107.

42. The following section is influenced by Arnold, 175–379 and especially Long, *Hellenistic Philosophy*, 163–209.

43. Samburksy, 106, n. 82: "Ekpyrosis originally denoted that period of the cosmic cycle where the preponderance of the fiery element reaches its maximum."

44. Christensen (see n. 30) 21.

45. Arnold, 228–31.

46. D. L. 7.88, trans. R. D. Hicks (Loeb Classical Library).

47. See Long, *Hellenistic Philosophy*, 170–99.

48. For a brief statement of this concept, see Long, *Problems*, 220 (Watson, "The Natural Law and Stoicism").

49. See the analysis of Cic. *Fin.* 3.20–21 by Long, *Hellenistic Philosophy*, 187–92.

50. Long, *Hellenistic Philosophy*, 204.

51. Arnold, 305.

52. Samburksy, 81.

53. *Const.* 5.3–5. This point is made by Currie, in Dudley, 25.

54. Pohlenz, 306. This view is found in Motto, x–xxiii.

55. Currie, in Dudley, 45–46.

56. More examples: "What is the difference between the nature of God and our nature? In our case the mind is the better part of us, in him there is nothing but mind. He is entirely reason, whereas at times men are so wrong about the universe, which is more beautiful, orderly, and systematic than anything, so wrong that they think it is accidental, chanceful, and wild" (*Q.N.* 1. pref. 14). "Evil and good do not unite and do not co-exist in one man" (*Ep.* 117.29). "Only Virtue possesses moderation, the vices do not admit it" (*Ep.* 85.10). "Both the advantages and disadvantages in life are beyond our control" (*Ep.* 92.16). Disease, pain, poverty, exile, and death are "indifferent, neither good nor bad" (*Ep.* 82.10).

57. For Panaetius and Posidonius, see Pohlenz, 191–247; Edelstein, *The Meaning*, especially 45–70; Rist, especially 173–218; Long, *Problems*; Long, *Hellenistic Philosophy*, especially 210–22; Sandbach (see n. 30) 123–39.

58. The disagreement appears in Rist, 186–200 and Kidd, in Long, *Problems*, 150–72.

59. "Posidonius on Emotions" is carefully treated by Kidd, in Long, *Problems*, 200–215.

60. Medical metaphor in the fragments of Posidonius is common; for example, see the items *therapeuo, iasis, nosos,* and related words in the "Greek Word and Subject Index" of Ludwig Edelstein and I. G. Kidd, *Posidonius I: The Fragments* (Cambridge, 1972) 281, 282, 291.

61. Posidonius, frag. 168 in Edelstein and Kidd.

62. Long, *Hellenistic Philosophy*, 220. So also Edelstein, *The Meaning*, 59.

63. The interpretation here follows Rist, 201–18.

64. So Rist, 214–16.

65. Rist, 216–17. See also Marie Laffranque, *Poseidonios d'Apamée* (Paris, 1964) 519–27 and René Hoven, *Stoïcisme et Stoïciens face au Problème de l'Au-delà*

(Paris, 1971) 57–65.

66. These are collected in Motto, 154–55.

67. The relationship between Posidonius and Seneca is specifically treated by : A. D. Leeman, "Seneca and Posidonius: A Philosophical Commentary on Sen. *Ep.* 102, 3–19," *Mnemosyne* 5 (1952) 57–79; Laffranque (see n. 65) 446, 451–55, 501–5; Pohlenz, 291–324; Edelstein, *The Meaning*, 66–70. The most extensive connection was proposed by I. Heinemann, *Poseidonios' metaphysische Schriften* (Breslau, 1921; repr. Hildesheim, 1968) vol. 1, 159–203. Unfortunately, Heinemann claimed excessively (from a study of twenty-nine letters) that letters 31–124 used Posidonius as a source, that Posidonian texts were the only Stoic books used in the *Letters*, and that the *Letters* are as important for the reconstruction of Posidonian ethic as the *Quaestiones Naturales* are for the reconstruction of his natural science. For the rejection of Heinemann's ideas, see Karl Münscher, *JAW* 192 (1922) 212–13. Heinemann undoubtedly went too far but may have been more right than his critics.

68. *Ep.* 33.4. This point is made by Kidd, in Long, *Problems*, 213.

69. See Wright, in C. D. N. Costa ed., *Seneca* (London, 1974) 44.

70. Kidd, in Long, *Problems*, 150–72.

71. See Ludwig Edelstein, "The Philosophical System of Posidonius," *AJPh* 57 (1936) 305–16; tentatively accepted by Kidd, in Long, *Problems*, 162–63.

72. This language is Edelstein's (see n. 71) 309.

73. See *Ep.* 76.20 and 74.21, 76.25 and 74.14, 76.26 and 74.16.

74. The last two paragraphs summarize the findings of Leeman (see n. 67).

75. Long, *Hellenistic Philosophy*, 221.

76. Rist, 205–6.

77. The moral image of a straight line appears also in the "Posidonian" letter 88 (13).

78. The statement of Sandbach (see n. 30) 138 that Posidonius' "recognition of irrational factors in the *psyche* was simply disregarded" in later Stoicism, is false.

79. Edelstein and Kidd (see n. 60) frag. 155.

80. *Ira* 1.3.4. In 2.15.5 Seneca mentions the influence of climate on character, an idea known to be Posidonian; see Kidd, in Long, *Problems*, 206.

81. The following references are provided in Motto, 43, 84: ambition, *Ep.* 56.10, 75.11; avarice, *Ep.* 56.10, 75.11, 85.10, 106.6; cruelty, *Clem.* 1.25.2, *Ep.* 85.10, 106.6; folly, *Ben.* 7.16.6; intemperance, *Ep.* 85.10.

82. Edelstein (see n. 71) 305.

83. Rist, 217–18.

84. The important passages are cited in H. B. Timothy, *The Tenets of Stoicism, Assembled and Systematized from the Works of L. Annaeus Seneca* (Amsterdam, 1973) 112–15.

85. Eduard Norden, *Die Antike Kunstprosa* (Leipzig, 1898) vol. 1, 309; Kennedy, *Art of Rhetoric*, 469; Wright, in Costa, *Seneca* (see n. 69) 45–46.

86. The following treatments of Seneca's philosophy have been used: Arnold; Pohlenz, 303–27; Arthur Bodson, *La Morale sociale des derniers Stoïciens, Sénèque, Épictète et Marc Aurèle* (Paris, 1967); Ilsetraut Hadot, *Seneca und die*

Griechisch-Römische Tradition der Seelenleitung (Berlin, 1969) especially 79–95, 179–90; Rist, especially 233–55; Hoven (see n. 65) 109–26; Currie, in Dudley, 24–61.

87. See the old, but still very good book, Samuel Dill, *Roman Society from Nero to Marcus Aurelius* (London, 1905).

88. Henry Bardon, *Les Empereurs et les Lettres Latines d'Auguste à Hadrien* (Paris, 1968) 184.

89. Edelstein, *The Meaning*, 59.

90. The usual quick condemnation of his compromise with riches against "Stoic principle" is misinformed; some critics of Seneca should read Stoicism more closely. One of the significant social advances made by Stoicism was to recognize the responsibility of wealth and the value of charity (Edelstein, *The Meaning*, 78–79). Seneca's essay *De Beneficiis* is a very long and involved example of the literature on the proper giving and receiving of benefits, on gratitude and ingratitude, a topic in which he has reason to be particularly interested as a rich man—and one whom the satirist Juvenal considers proverbial for liberality (5.108–10). In terms of philosophical value, wealth is an "indifferent" because it is not needed for Virtue, and the older Stoa seems to have treated it quite strictly as such. Seneca is accused of having departed from this doctrine in placing wealth in the category of the "preferable" (Currie, in Dudley, 47). This criticism is wrong, for "preferables" are simply a subcategory of "indifferents," and the preferability of wealth to poverty is an old idea in Stoicism (Long, *Hellenistic Philosophy*, 192).

Further, the role of "indifferents" seems to change. If, as we have surmised, Posidonius' theory of *psyche* means that the intermediates are potentially good and potentially evil in relation to the rational and irrational faculties respectively, and if Seneca is following him, Seneca's view of wealth as both corruptive and constructive makes sense. On the one hand: "Let us turn to the question of inherited fortunes, the greatest cause of human troubles. For if you compare all the other things which torture us—death, sickness, fear, desire, endurance of pain and trouble—with those evils which our money causes, the latter will far outweigh the former" (*Tranq.* 8.1). On the other: "The wise man does not think that he is unworthy of any gifts which come his way. He does not love riches, but prefers them. He takes them not into his soul, but into his house. He does not throw out his possessions, but keeps them and wants them to provide a greater opportunity for Virtue." "He will give his wealth either to good men or to those whom he can make good" (*Vit. Beat.* 21.4, 23.5). Such contrasting views are not inconsistencies but opposite faces of the problem of wealth, which appear according to the orientation of the argument. The problem that tortures Seneca is how to use wealth for good rather than be used by it for evil.

91. See Edelstein, *The Meaning*, 43–44; Bodson (see n. 86) 90–104; especially Rist, 129–31, 233–55; Currie, in Dudley, 41–43.

92. Edelstein, *The Meaning*, 44.

93. See also *Ira* 2.31.7; *Ep.* 92.30; and Bodson (see n. 86) 57. All these Senecan sources show Posidonian influence. Is this "body" the Posidonian spherical cosmos?

94. Pohlenz, 315–16. Conversely, Seneca uses the new metaphor for the relationship between the emperor and his subjects: for example, *Clem.* 1.3.5.

95. Dill (see n. 87) 328–29; Trillitzsch, 13–14.

96. Hoven (see n. 65) 109–26; Currie, in Dudley, 35–36. Hoven presents the Senecan evidence fully.

97. The latter view is found in *Ep.* 79.12, 93.9–10, 102.21–28.

98. Zeller (see n. 11) 728–31; Pohlenz, 299, 320–21; Rist, 267; Currie, in Dudley, 36–37.

99. Rist, 130. See also Long, *Hellenistic Philosophy*, 115, n. 1.

100. The standard treatment of the correspondence is by Claude W. Barlow, *Epistolae Senecae ad Paulum et Pauli ad Senecam [quae vocantur]* (American Academy in Rome, 1938). See also J. N. Sevenster, *Paul and Seneca* (Leiden, 1961).

101. The references are gathered in Motto, 154–55.

Chapter 4

1. An example of this tendency is Opelt, in Lefèvre, *Senecas Tragödien*, 92–128. Her conception that Senecan drama is tragedy of *nefas* is of course largely correct but inadequate in depth.

2. For a good technical analysis of these theories, see Phillip De Lacy, "Stoic Views of Poetry," *AJPh* 69 (1948) 241–71.

3. De Lacy, 244.

4. De Lacy, 256–63.

5. De Lacy, 266–71. In "Der Mythos im Verständnis der Antike II, Von Euripides bis Seneca," *Gymnasium* 73 (1966) 44–62, Heinrich Dörrie briefly but excellently sketches the history of ancient myth, including philosophical allegorizing. He believes that in Senecan drama mythical heroes "are either examples or counter-examples for the postulates of Stoic ethic" (59).

6. See Knoche, 60–66 and Mazzoli, 19–108.

7. Mazzoli, 134–38.

8. Egermann, in Lefèvre, *Senecas Tragödien*, 37–40.

9. Egermann, in Lefèvre, 37.

10. These references are treated in Mazzoli, 157–264.

11. Mazzoli, 226.

12. Mazzoli, 225–26.

13. Long, *Hellenistic Philosophy*, 220. See also Edelstein, *The Meaning*, 59.

14. Quintilian's language, *ethologia personis continetur*, is basically theatrical.

15. Emil Ackermann, "De Senecae Hercule Oetaeo," *Philologus Suppl.* 10 (1907) 408–22; idem, "Der leidende Hercules des Seneca," *RhM* 67 (1912) 425–71.

16. Otto Edert, *Über Senecas Herakles und den Herakles auf dem Oeta* (Kiel, 1909).

17. Paulus Schaefer, *De Philosophiae Annaeanae in Senecae Tragoediis Vestigiis* (Jena, 1909).

18. For example, C. Brakman, "De Senecae Agamemnone," *Mnemosyne* 42

(1914) 392–98.

19. Otto Regenbogen, *Schmerz und Tod in den Tragödien Senecas.*

20. Laidlaw, in Maurice Platnauer, *Fifty Years of Classical Scholarship* (Oxford, 1954) 261–62.

21. Regenbogen, 193.

22. Regenbogen, 199.

23. Regenbogen, 216.

24. Egermann, in Lefèvre, *Senecas Tragödien*, 33–57.

25. Egermann, in Lefèvre, 43.

26. Egermann, in Lefèvre, 43, following Wilhelm Marx, *Funktion und Form der Chorlieder in den Seneca-Tragödien.*

27. Egermann, in Lefèvre, 47–48, agreeing with Willy Schulze, *Untersuchungen zur Eigenart der Tragödien Senecas.*

28. Egermann, in Lefèvre, 55–57.

29. R. B. Steele, "Some Roman Elements in the Tragedies of Seneca," *AJPh* 43 (1922) 30–31.

30. T. S. Eliot, "Shakespeare and the Stoicism of Seneca," *Selected Essays*, new ed. (New York, 1950) 119.

31. Pohlenz, 325.

32. Berthe M. Marti, "Seneca's Tragedies: A New Interpretation," *TAPhA* 76 (1945) 216–45.

33. Norman T. Pratt, "The Stoic Base of Senecan Drama," *TAPhA* 79 (1948) 1–2, 6–7; Coffey, 158.

34. Pratt, "The Stoic Base," 3.

35. Elizabeth C. Evans, "A Stoic Aspect of Senecan Drama: Portraiture," *TAPhA* 81 (1950) 169–84.

36. Kurt von Fritz, *Antike und Moderne Tragödie: Neun Abhandlungen* (Berlin, 1962) 21–26, 47.

37. F. H. Sandbach, *The Stoics* (London, 1975) 160–61.

38. The objections of Lindskog, Frenzel, and Friedrich are rebutted by Wolf Steidle, "Bemerkungen zu Senecas Tragödien," *Philologus* 96 (1943–44) 259–64.

39. This interpretation is developed more fully in Pratt, *Dramatic Suspense*, 66–69.

40. This point is made by Gregor Maurach, "Jason und Medea bei Seneca," *A&A* 12 (1966) 127.

41. Denis Henry and B. Walker, "Loss of Identity: *Medea Superest?* A Study of Seneca's *Medea*," *CPh* 62 (1967) 169–81, find the theme of the play in Medea's lack "of continuous identity combined with repeated and desperate affirmation of identity existing or to come that makes her role a purely existentialist one" (177). However, the main reason why Medea is not an identifiable individual is that she is a dramatic tradition and a philosophical model.

42. C. D. N. Costa, *Seneca: Medea* (Oxford, 1973) 107.

43. Is he pretending love for the children? Is he deceiving himself? Maurach (see n. 40) 130–34, 139–40, examines several views and comes to conclusions that seem sound and are adopted here.

44. The words *vivat ut tutus mare qui subegit* (596) are ironic after Jason's desire for security shown in the preceding scene.

45. Pratt, "Major Systems," 215–16.

46. Maurach (see n. 40) 134; Costa (see n. 42) 128–29.

47. For example, Henry and Walker, "Phantasmagoria," 224; Donald J. Mastronarde, "Seneca's *Oedipus*: The Drama in the Word," *TAPhA* 101 (1970) 309, n. 30; Wolf-Lüder Liebermann, *Studien zu Senecas Tragödien* (Meisenheim am Glan, 1974) 10–13.

48. Maurach (see n. 40) 125–40 and his supplement in Lefèvre, *Senecas Tragödien*, 318–19.

49. Marti (see n. 32) 233.

50. Pratt, "Major Systems," 232.

51. Pratt, "Major Systems," 231–32.

52. Details are found in Pratt, "Major Systems," 214–18.

53. Lefèvre, "Quid ratio possit?" 151–52. In most respects, this article is excellent.

54. The beginning of this play is problematic both in structure and meaning. My earlier view (*Dramatic Suspense*, 80–82) was that the *Phaedra* has no prologue and that Hippolytus' speech written in anapests (1–84) is a substitute for Chorus I. Now Konrad Heldmann, *Untersuchungen zu den Tragödien Senecas* (Wiesbaden, 1974) 62–89, by careful analysis has shown that it is better to consider Hippolytus' speech a prologue, whose lyric meter rules out a normal Chorus I, even though the *Phaedra* thus (having prologue and five episodes) violates the Senecan norm of five acts.

The first scene is difficult to interpret. Obviously it shows Hippolytus' complete preoccupation with the hunt. Other interpretations try to find deeper implications. Henry and Walker, "Phantasmagoria," believe that the scene "creates a world of dream in keeping with the role of Hippolytus as a seeker for solitude and as the follower of an *unreal* vision of perfection" (232). Herington suggests that the speech conveys "the fresh, cool integrity of Hippolytus" (451). Such ideas are interesting, but there is no textual evidence that Seneca intended such subtleties. Perhaps the best idea, suggested by Heldmann, 85–89, is that Seneca has arranged the structure so as to juxtapose Hippolytus' and Phaedra's monologues and to create a stark contrast between the two characters shown in isolation. Heldmann thinks that Seneca has manipulated the Euripidean prologue, but little resemblance to the Greek prologue remains and no relationship is necessary.

55. Lefèvre, "Quid ratio possit?" 148–50.

56. Henry and Walker, "Phantasmagoria," 224–32, argue that "there is no play of Seneca in which this disparity between philosophic and imaginative content is more marked than in the *Phaedra*" (224). They believe that "the figures of Nurse and Phaedra are almost completely apart from one another; the one isolated in a world of apophthegms and good advice, the other in a nightmare state of fruitless introspection" (230), and that "the dramatic effect of the scene . . . is to create a growing sense of phantasmagoria or nightmare . . . extending outside and beyond the single character and . . . creating a whole

world in its likeness" (231–32). Their findings are correct, but the explanation lies nearer at hand in Neo-Stoic thinking about the disintegrating effect of passion and its cosmic impact.

57. Observed by Lefèvre, "Quid ratio possit?" 136, as a Senecan departure from Euripides.

58. The passage is interesting also because it echoes a possible fragment of the *De Matrimonio* (Haase, frag. 67): "All the violence of tragedy, the destruction of homes, cities, and kingdoms come from the strife of wives and concubines. Parents' hands are armed against children, wicked meals are served, and because of the rape of one girl Europe and Asia clash in a ten years' war." Compare *fumant tot urbes, bella tot gentes gerunt / et versa ab imo regna tot populos premunt* in 561–62 with *domos, urbes regnaque subvertit* in the fragment.

59. Henry and Walker, "Phantasmagoria," 235.

60. Her phrase is *nostrae fata . . . domus* (698). The term *fata* is misleading if taken in the traditional sense of a curse on a house perpetuated supernaturally. Here the word is used Stoically for a human situation that will work its way because it is part of the plan of Nature.

61. The prominence of *ira* in the *Phaedra* is recognized by Lefèvre, "Quid ratio possit?" 137–45.

62. His language (907–8) clearly states that his son's heredity is degenerate, an idea not acceptable to Stoicism.

63. "Anger comes from love as much as from hate" (*Ep.* 18.15).

64. Lefèvre, "Quid ratio possit?" 145–46, argues that the termination of the suicide theme is a defect avoided in the *Phoenissae* and the *Furens* and is evidence of an earlier date for *Phaedra*, but this is not a convincing argument.

65. A similar view is held by Henry and Walker, "Phantasmagoria," 238.

66. Lefèvre, "Quid ratio possit?" 155–60.

67. However, it is hypersophisticated to find with Henry and Walker, "Phantasmagoria," that "they stand for the unreality of the civilized world whose values are elegant and shallow and which is preserved from disintegration only by its single-minded devotion to play and dream" (234).

68. This interpretation seems to resemble the findings of Gerhard Müller, "Senecas Oedipus als Drama," *Hermes* 81 (1953) 447–64, but Müller does not recognize the Stoic implications of fear and Fate. For example, he defines the tragic in Seneca as involving either passionate behavior or innocence victimized by external force (458–59) and holds that the *Oedipus* is of the latter type and does not involve morality (459–60). The point is that, according to the Stoic view of irrationality, until the end of the play Oedipus is just as guilty of it as a Medea or a Phaedra.

69. William H. Owen, "Commonplace and Dramatic Symbol in Seneca's Tragedies," *TAPhA* 99 (1968) 295.

70. Pratt, *Dramatic Suspense*, 91–100.

71. See the rebuttal of such criticisms by Schetter, in Lefèvre, *Senecas Tragödien*, 422–23.

72. Owen (see n. 69) 308–11.

73. Müller (see n. 68) 449–50.

74. Pratt, *Dramatic Suspense*, 92. The foreshadowing is transparent also when Oedipus damns the murderer to the crimes that he himself has "escaped" by leaving Corinth (260–63).

75. Complete analysis in Pratt, *Dramatic Suspense*, 93–99.

76. Wolf-Hartmut Friedrich, *Untersuchungen zu Senecas dramatischer Technik* (Borna-Leipzig, 1933) 62–98.

77. Pratt, *Dramatic Suspense*, 98.

78. Schetter, in Lefèvre, *Senecas Tragödien*, 424.

79. Schetter, in Lefèvre, 426–27.

80. von Fritz (see n. 36) 27–29.

81. For example, Opelt, in Lefèvre, *Senecas Tragödien*, 272–85.

82. Hunter, in C. D. N. Costa ed., *Seneca* (London, 1974), observes that *furor* "is personified by the *Furiae* we meet in the infernal prologues" (174). Knoche, 75–76, believes that this prologue shows the workings of Fate: Fury is an arm of Fate; therefore, the right of the world order must be on her side, that is, she puts into effect the will to evil ingrained in the house of Tantalus. This interpretation can hardly be right. Nothing as ugly as Fury could be aligned with (Stoic) Fate. If the house is chronically evil, it is because its individual members commit their own faults, as Atreus is corrupted by his passion for power (Knoche's own interpretation).

83. Knoche, 70, thinks that the attendant is symbolic in the sense that he, as the subject of a tyrant, represents the rational aspect of Atreus that has been tyrannized by passion; so we are led to see Atreus' passion not from the perspective of the passion but from the perspective of reason enslaved by passion. Obviously, the attendant's arguments against Atreus intensify the picture of the king's irrationality, but this interplay does not make the attendant symbolic. For that matter, the idea of reason tyrannized by passion technically is not Stoic. Reason can be displaced by passion but is never subordinate.

84. This contrast is appreciated by J. L. Klein, *Geschichte des Drama's*, vol. 2 (Leipzig, 1865) 417–18.

85. Knoche, 69–70.

86. Knoche, 71.

87. Knoche, 72.

88. Emidio Pettine, *Studio dei caratteri e poesia nelle Tragedie di Seneca* (Salerno, 1974) 269.

89. René Hoven, *Stoïcisme et Stoïciens face au Problème de l'Au-delà* (Paris, 1971) 78, 124–25.

90. For example, Friedrich (see n. 76) 99–122.

91. This basic feature is completely missed in many criticisms of the play, as when William H. Owen, "Time and Event in Seneca's Troades," *WS* 83 (1970), comments: "The prologue and the First Choral Ode have only a tangential relationship to the action of the drama" (118).

92. Steidle, in Lefèvre, *Senecas Tragödien*, 220–29.

93. Steidle, in Lefèvre, 224–25.

94. Schetter, in Lefèvre, 267–71, believes that the position of the choral passage between two appearances of the dead is not faulty composition, but is

intended to make the spectator uneasy and to create a deep mental reservation. The chorus questions the reality of Achilles' ghost, and their questioning is itself questioned by Andromache's account of Hector's appearance. The result is to suggest that the world is not rationally soluble.

Owen (see n. 91) considers the passage part of a network of intentionally contradictory action sequences and believes that Seneca was far ahead of his time in "a kind of surrealistic production" (137).

95. There is nothing contradictory in the process of her emotions, as is argued by Owen, 119.

96. The parallelism is well analyzed by Schetter, in Lefèvre, *Senecas Tragödien*, 230–66.

97. Perhaps for this reason, Seneca makes Hecuba mute during most of the scene, a feature often criticized.

98. For the use of this imagery, see Pratt, "Major Systems," 213–14.

99. Herrmann, 48–49.

100. Kurt Anliker, *Prologe und Akteinteilung in Senecas Tragödien*, Noctes Romanae 9 (Bern, 1960) 98–101, 122–23.

101. This is essentially the interpretation of Eckard Lefèvre, "Schicksal und Selbstverschuldung in Senecas Agamemnon," *Hermes* 94 (1966) 482–96. See also R. J. Tarrant, *Seneca: Agamemnon, Edited with a Commentary* (Cambridge, 1976) 5. Similarly, William M. Calder III, "Seneca's *Agamemnon*," *CPh* 71 (1976) 26–36, believes that the play "examines the reactions of various people to the fact of death, and condemns an ignorant *vitae durus amor*" (32–33).

102. The system is analyzed by Lefèvre (see n. 101) 485–96.

103. Noticed by Lefèvre (see n. 101) 492.

104. Lefèvre (see n. 101) 495–96. Lefèvre takes the latter view.

105. von Fritz (see n. 36) 25; Zintzen, in Lefèvre, *Senecas Tragödien*, 207–8. Steidle (see n. 38) 250 notes that Seneca is interested in portraying Hercules' overcoming of passion, not the characteristic of imperturbability.

Jo-Ann Shelton (*Seneca's Hercules Furens: Theme, Structure and Style* [Hypomnemata 50; Göttingen, 1978]) identifies this frailty well: "Hercules is indeed strong but he overestimates the value of human strength, which should be an 'indifferent,' and thinks it is equal to *virtus*" (59).

106. In substantial agreement with Zintzen, in Lefèvre, *Senecas Tragödien*, 149–209.

107. Denis Henry and B. Walker, "The Futility of Action: A Study of Seneca's *Hercules Furens*," *CPh* 60 (1965) 11–22, put this matter differently: "The difference between Juno and Hercules is merely this, that Juno is a ridiculous goddess, Hercules a ridiculous demigod with aspirations for full divinity" (18). They suggest that Hercules' decision not to kill himself is more futility because he "has cast away his one chance of asserting his moral freedom" (19) and find that the sense of tragedy in the play has to do not with Hercules, but with "the theme of universal progress toward death" (22). Their interpretation does not recognize that the main feature of the play is the movement of Hercules into and out of madness as defined Stoically.

The question of Hercules' guilt has been much discussed, most recently in

Heldmann (see n. 54) 54–56. The evidence for his guilt is overwhelming once the Neo-Stoic version of the hero is recognized.

Prologues of this type have caused difficulty and led to theories about Seneca's unorthodox use of dramatic time. For example, Jo-Ann Shelton, "Problems of Time in Seneca's *Hercules Furens* and *Thyestes*," *CSCA* 8 (1975) 257–69, believes that "Seneca uses these opening scenes as distinct temporal units in which time moves forward at a much different speed than it does in Acts 1, ff." (258). Thus the prologue figure announces events that will occur (simultaneously) later in the play. This theory of linear time is an overcomplicated way of explaining that Seneca uses his prologues to set up *exempla* that anticipate the dramatic action.

This and other Senecan features (dislocation of space and time, distortion of character, ambiguity, counterpoint movement in the choral odes) have recently been called "Mannerism" (as in the sixteenth century); for example, Jo-Ann Shelton, "Seneca's *Medea* as Mannerist Literature," *Poetica* 11 (1979) 38–82. This term is more important as a description of the nature of Seneca's influence than as an analysis of Senecan drama itself.

108. This characteristic of Hercules in the *Oetaeus* leads Olof Gigon, "Bemerkungen zu Senecas Thyestes," *Philologus* 93 (1938–39) 176–77, to deny that the *Oetaeus* glorifies Hercules as a Stoic hero. He does not recognize that the Neo-Stoic Hercules is different from the traditional figure. The same kind of mistake is made by Pettine (see n. 88); he thinks that Seneca in the *Furens* departs from the theoretical traditional Stoic view of Hercules because he is creating a lifelike dramatic personage (77).

109. See the fragment of the *De Matrimonio* quoted above, n. 58.

110. Berthe M. Marti, "Place de l'*Hercule sur l'Oeta* dans le Corpus des Tragédïes de Sénèque," *REL* 27 (1949) 191–92.

111. Pratt, "Major Systems," 229–31.

112. Marti (see n. 110).

113. Moses Hadas, "The Roman Stamp of Seneca's Tragedies," *AJPh* 60 (1939) 222.

Chapter 5

1. *eius alioqui processus avidus.* I accept the interpretation of O. Rossbach, *R-E*, 1.2238 and Henri Bornecque, *Sénèque le Rhéteur: Controverses et Suasoires*, 2d ed. (Paris, 1932) vol. 1, 179–81. Lewis A. Sussman, "Early Imperial Declamation: A Translation of the Elder Seneca's Prefaces," *SM* 37 (1970) 141, translates, "I am also eager for this advancement in general."

2. The same view is held by Miriam T. Griffin, "The Elder Seneca and Spain," *JRS* 62 (1972) 9.

3. Selected bibliography on Seneca the Elder and Roman rhetoric includes: Hermann Peter, *Die Geschichtliche Litteratur über die Römische Kaiserzeit bis Theodosius I und Ihre Quellen*, vol. 1 (Leipzig, 1897) 3–53; Eduard Norden, *Die Antike Kunstprosa vom VI Jahrhundert V. Chr. bis in die Zeit der Renaissance* (Leipzig,

1898) vol. 1, 240–300; Henri Bornecque, *Les Déclamations et les Déclamateurs d'après Sénèque le Père* (Lille, 1902); Edward; Bornecque (see n. 1); M. L. Clarke, *Rhetoric at Rome: A Historical Survey* (New York, 1963) 85–108; A. D. Leeman, *Orationis Ratio: The Stylistic Theories and Practice of the Roman Orators, Historians and Philosophers* (Amsterdam, 1963) vol. 1, 219–42; Bonner; Kennedy, *Art of Rhetoric*, 301–77.

4. Kennedy, *Art of Rhetoric*, 307.

5. Edward on the *controversia*: The declaimer "does not speak in his own person but as one of the persons engaged in the suit. Hence he is partly an actor and he must speak as his assumed character would speak, that is, he is part dramatist as well" (xxxii).

6. *Suas.* 3, 7. Throughout this section, illustrations are taken from the elder Seneca only, because he is our most important source and his material has an obvious connection with the son.

7. Bornecque (see n. 3) 174–75. Bornecque's judgments are convincing and have been used throughout this section.

8. *Suas.* 2.16, trans. Edward, 52.

9. *Suas.* 2.17, trans. Edward, 52–53.

10. For example, *De Or.* 1.18, 128, 156, 251; 2.193, 242; 3.215–23.

11. *De Or.* 1.124–25, 259; 2.34; 3.214–15.

12. Kennedy, *Art of Rhetoric*, 326.

13. Bornecque (see n. 1) vol. 1, x.

14. See the remarks of Edward quoted in note 5.

15. *Contr.* 2.6.2. The speaker, Fabianus Papirius, is a Stoic.

16. *Contr.* 1.3.8–9. Of the three speakers involved, none is known to be a Stoic.

17. Bornecque (see n. 1) vol. 1, xiv.

18. Peter (see n. 3) vol. 1, 38–40; Clarke (see n. 3) 91–92; Henry Bardon, *Les Empereurs et les Lettres Latines d'Auguste à Hadrien* (Paris, 1968) 164; Bonner, 43.

19. *Suas.* 6.6, trans. Edward, 67.

Chapter 6

1. T. S. Eliot, "Seneca in Elizabethan Translation," *Selected Essays*, new ed. (New York, 1950) 53–54.

2. Ilsetraut Hadot, *Seneca und die Griechisch-Römische Tradition der Seelenleitung* (Berlin, 1969) 189–90.

3. Canter, 55–69; Bonner, 160–67.

4. Canter, 55–69.

5. For a discussion of these, see Charles Garton, "The Background to Character Portrayal in Seneca," *CPh* 54 (1959) 1–9.

6. Garton, 8.

7. Schlegel, in Lefèvre, *Senecas Tragödien*, 14.

8. Friedrich Leo, "De Tragoedia Rhetorica," *Observationes Criticae* (Berlin, 1878) viii.

9. J. L. Klein, *Geschichte des Drama's*, vol. 2 (Leipzig, 1865) 367.

10. Herrmann, 524–25; Mazzoli, 215–32, 238–47.

11. This Latin is a *sententia* echoing Publilius Syrus; see Herrmann, 523–24.

12. Another *sententia*.

13. With extra emphasis from the manipulation of word order.

14. An abba word sequence.

15. With word order manipulated to highlight the oxymoron *Extrema primo*.

16. The theme of "road" again.

17. Brilliant word order in 166–67, *cum stetit ad aras ore sacrifico pater/quam nuptiales!*

18. *amplexu patris*; in the literal sense of "surrounded by their father"?

19. Lines 730–33:

> Idaea cerno nemora: fatalis sedet
> inter potentes arbiter pastor deas.
> timete reges, moneo, furtivum genus:
> agrestis iste alumnus evertet domum.

These lines have been troublesome and are considered spurious by Leo. If *furtivum genus* can describe Paris as "the stealthy son" (abduction of Helen), the whole passage refers to him; *reges* would include Priam as well as Menelaus and Agamemnon. *Agrestis alumnus* refers to the exposure of Paris and his rescue by shepherds.

20. The phrase is Herington's. He treats this quality on 433–43.

21. Herington, 436.

22. Eduard Norden, *Die Antike Kunstprosa* (Leipzig, 1898) vol. 1, 277.

23. J. W. H. Atkins, *Literary Criticism in Antiquity* (Cambridge, 1934) vol. 1, 158 and vol. 2, 206–7, 317.

24. Garton (see n. 5) 4.

25. Kennedy, *Art of Rhetoric*, 3.

Chapter 7

1. The basic data are gathered by Griffin, in C. D. N. Costa ed., *Seneca* (London, 1974) 1–38.

2. Perhaps she influenced Claudius, who secured the remission from the senate according to Seneca, *Cons. Polyb.* 13.2.

3. Arnaldo Momigliano, *CAH*, vol. 10, 702, note.

4. See *CAH*, vol. 10, 871–76.

5. The following account relies mainly on Tacitus, *Annals* 12–15; the commentary of Henry Furneaux, *Cornelii Taciti Annalium ab Excessu Divi Augusti Libri*, vol. 2, 2d ed. rev. H. F. Pelham and C. D. Fisher (Oxford, 1907); *CAH*, vol. 10, 702–42 (Arnaldo Momigliano), 743–80 (J. G. C. Anderson), 781–807 (Ronald Syme and R. G. Collingwood); Syme. Miriam T. Griffin, *Seneca, A Philosopher in Politics* (Oxford, 1976) 67–128, questions the usual assumptions about the role of Seneca in the court and comes out essentially with Tacitus'

conception of this role.

6. Pohlenz, 318.

7. The careers of his two brothers show the abundance of administrative ability and financial acumen in the family. The youngest, M. Annaeus Mela, chose study of oratory as his main interest rather than a political career but became wealthy as a procurator conducting the private business affairs of the emperor; he qualified to wear the broad purple stripe of senatorial rank while remaining an equestrian. The oldest, L. Annaeus Novatus, renamed Junius Gallio after adoption by a friend of his father, was governor of the province of Achaea under Claudius and reached the consulship early in the reign of Nero, being suffect consul in A.D. 55. He is the Gallio of the *Acts of the Apostles* (18.1–17), before whom the Jews of Corinth made a complaint against the teachings of Paul. The governor's decision not to intervene in religious disputes involving no civil wrong—apathetically or correctly according to one's viewpoint—has put him down in history as the Gallio who "cared for none of those things." Lucius admired his older brother for qualities that he himself must have shared and that he certainly considered ideal: "his civility [*comitatem*, the same word used of Seneca by Tacitus] and unaffected agreeableness . . . no man is as pleasant to one person as he is to all" (*Q.N.* 4. pref. 11).

8. Fredericks, in Edwin S. Ramage, David L. Sigsbee, and Sigmund C. Fredericks, *Roman Satirists and Their Satire: The Fine Art of Criticism in Ancient Rome* (Park Ridge, N. J., 1974) 99.

9. Lester K. Born, *The Education of a Christian Prince by Desiderius Erasmus* (New York, 1965) 66.

10. This point is made by Chaim Wirszubski, *Libertas as a Political Idea at Rome during the Late Republic and Early Principate* (Cambridge, 1950) 150–53. See also Adam, 26–27.

11. This section uses the findings of Adam, a thorough study of the phenomenon. A summary of her conclusions is found on 128–31. See also Griffin (see n. 5) 133–71.

12. Adam, 19.

13. Adam, 12–14.

14. The parallel of king to god is expanded to a view of the world with overtones of the Stoic continuum: the king "performs on earth the function of the gods" (1.1.2); even as the mind is the master of the body, so Nero is the soul of the state, his body, and the state will disintegrate if it rejects his mastery (1.3.5, 1.5.1).

15. Adam, 13–14.

16. Adam is correct in emphasizing that Seneca's purpose is Roman and juristic (63, 73, 81), but she underestimates the role of Stoicism in the essay.

17. Wirszubski (see n. 10) 3, 146.

18. Adam, 32.

19. Adam, 128.

20. Edelstein, *The Meaning*, 85–86.

21. Adam, 64–65.

22. Also, the *amicus principis* was not alone in hoping and trusting that moral-

ity would improve "substantially" in the new principate (2.2.1). The senate too took pains to praise Nero's initial acts, "hoping that his young mind would be lifted by the popularity of even small things and go on to greater things" (*Ann.* 13.11.1).

23. Acte was more than a temporary flame; at least Suetonius reports that she was one of three women who put the ashes of the hated *princeps* in his family tomb (*Ner.* 50).

24. Momigliano, *CAH*, vol. 10, 712.

25. These references are collected in Trillitzsch, 357.

26. *Ann.* 14.29–37. See Dio 62.2; his account is discredited by Syme, 762–63 and Donald R. Dudley and Graham Webster, *The Rebellion of Boudicca* (London, 1962) 51.

27. See *Ann.* 13.50–51 and Momigliano, *CAH*, vol. 10, 712–13.

28. See Eugen Cizek, *L'Époque de Néron et ses Controverses Idéologiques* (Leiden, 1972) 119.

29. The reasons given for the long silence of the advisers, "because either they did not want to oppose Nero unsuccessfully or they thought that it had come to the point where Nero must die if Agrippina were not killed first," are more natural as first reactions to learning about the plot than as thoughts merely about Nero's present predicament.

30. For example, Furneaux (see n. 5) [63]–[64].

31. It seems impossible to follow Syme, 551, who cites William Hardy Alexander, "The Communiqué to the Senate on Agrippina's Death," *CPh* 49 (1954) 94–97, and concludes: "It was generally believed that Seneca had lent his talents to the composition of that damaging avowal, and he incurred severe blame. It is not clear, however, that Tacitus shared that belief."

32. Francis Holland, *Seneca* (1920; repr. Books for Libraries Press, Freeport, N.Y., 1969) 93.

33. Henry Bardon, *Les Empereurs et les Lettres Latines d'Auguste à Hadrien* (Paris, 1968) 191–220.

34. Syme, 335, thinks that Tacitus has incorporated Senecan characteristics in his version of the statement—something difficult to prove.

35. See chapter 3, n. 29.

36. The relevant passages from the *Epistulae Morales* are gathered in Trillitzsch, 315–18.

37. Momigliano, *CAH*, vol. 10, 726–27.

38. See Wirszubski (see n. 10) 124–29; Adam, 63–81; Long, *Hellenistic Philosophy*, 233.

39. See Ernst Bickel, "Seneca und Seneca-Mythus," *Altertum* 5 (1959) 90–100; Ramsay MacMullen, *Enemies of the Roman Order* (Cambridge, Mass., 1966) 82.

40. Syme, 551–52.

41. Syme, 546.

42. Arnold, 113.

43. Gaston Boissier, *L'Opposition sous les Césars*, 5th ed. (Paris, 1905) 83–88.

44. Bardon (see n. 33) 235–40.

45. Trillitzsch, 43.

46. MacMullen (see n. 39) 36–37.

47. Herington, 430.

48. Marc Rozelaar, *Seneca, eine Gesamtdarstellung* (Amsterdam, 1976) 595–97.

49. R. S. Pathmanathan, "The Parable in Seneca's Oedipus," *Nigeria and the Classics* 10 (1967–68) 13–20; John Hind, "The Death of Agrippina and the Finale of the 'Oedipus' of Seneca," *AUMLA* 38 (1972) 204–11.

50. Amy Rose, "Seneca's *HF*: A Politico-Didactic Reading," *CJ* 75 (1979–80) 135–42.

51. J. David Bishop, "Seneca's *Oedipus*: Opposition Literature," *CJ* 73 (1978) 289–301.

52. Bishop, 289, n. 1.

53. Bishop, 294–98.

54. J. L. Klein, *Geschichte des Drama's*, vol. 2 (Leipzig, 1865) 363.

Chapter 8

1. See the ideas cited from von Fritz on p. 81.

2. Norman T. Pratt, "From Oedipus to Lear," *CJ* 61 (1965) 49–57 (55).

INDEX

Accius, 26, 27
Ackermann, Emil, 77
Acte, 173–74, 180, 181, 221 (n. 23)
Aeschylus, 21, 26, 112–13
Agamemnon (*Troades*), 56, 108
Agamemnon: presentation of moral
   tension in, 9–10, 77; within chro-
   nology of Seneca's dramas, 13, 15;
   possible sources for, 21; treatment
   of "indifferents" in, 55; elements of
   Neo-Stoicism in, 111–15; de-
   clamatory rhetoric in, 154–57,
   160–61
Agrippina, 175, 176–77, 180; and
   Seneca, 164, 165, 166, 167,
   168–69, 173–74, 177, 181, 182–83
Albucius Silus, 139–40, 142–43
Alcmena (*Hercules Oetaeus*), 125, 127
Alexandria, 40, 41–43, 166, 206 (n.
   14)
Amphitryon (*Hercules Furens*), 120–21
Andromache (*Troades*), 77, 109–10
Anicetus, 181, 182, 185
Antigone (*Phoenissae*), 102–3
Antisthenes, 75, 115
Apocolocyntosis, 14, 168
Archedemus, 45, 63
Ariston of Chios, 79
Aristotelianism, 58, 66
Astyanax (*Troades*), 110–11
Atreus (*Thyestes*), 50, 103–4, 105, 106,
   157–59
Attalus, 39, 135

Britannicus, 165, 169, 174–75, 176
Burrus, Afranius, 165, 166, 173, 174,
   175, 176, 177–78, 184–85; and

Seneca, 167, 168, 169, 173, 177,
   182–83, 184–85, 189

Campbell, Oscar J., 7–8
Canter, Howard Vernon, 30–31, 32
Cassandra (*Agamemnon*), 114, 115,
   160–61
Cassius Dio, 166, 180, 189
Cassius Severus, 138, 141
Catharsis, 73, 76
Chairemon, 41–42, 71, 206 (n. 22)
Chorus: and Senecan recitation-
   drama, 16, 17; meter in speeches of,
   32; general function of in Seneca's
   drama, 79, 87, 130; in *Medea*, 82,
   84, 86, 87, 89, 90; in *Phaedra*,
   95–96; in *Oedipus*, 97, 100; lack of in
   Phoenissae, 101; in *Thyestes*, 103, 104,
   105; in *Troades*, 108–9, 110; in
   Agamemnon, 112, 113; in *Hercules
   Furens*, 118, 120; in *Hercules Oetaeus*,
   123–26, 127; declamatory rhetoric
   in speeches of, 162–63
Christianity, 7–9, 40, 42, 71
Chrysippus, 45, 48–49, 52, 59, 61, 66
Cicero, M. Tullius, 29, 59, 134,
   141–42, 147
Cichorius, Conrad, 14–15
Claudius (emperor), 164–65, 167,
   168, 179
Cleanthes, 45, 52
Clytemnestra (*Agamemnon*), 77, 112,
   154–57
Controversia, 136, 137, 138, 142–47,
   151. See also Declamation (*de-
   clamatio*)
Corduba (Cordoba), 35–36, 37, 134